Contentious Lives

A book in the series

Latin America Otherwise:

Languages, Empires, Nations

Series editors:

Walter D. Mignolo,

Duke University

Irene Silverblatt,

Duke University

Sonia Saldívar-Hull,

University of California

at Los Angeles

Contentious Lives

Two Argentine Women,

Two Protests, and the

Quest for Recognition

JAVIER AUYERO

Duke University Press

Durham & London 2003

© 2003 Duke University Press

All rights reserved

Printed in the United States

of America on acid-free paper ⊗

Designed by Rebecca Giménez

Typeset in Cycles by Tseng

Information Systems, Inc.

Library of Congress Cataloging-

in-Publication Data appear on

the last printed page of this book.

Portions of "The Queen of the

Riot" were originally published

in *Theory and Society* and appear

in revised form in this volume

by permission.

A mi amigo Lucas Rubinich,

with whom I've been

enjoying friendship and

the craft of sociology

for more than a decade.

Contents

About the Series

Latin America Otherwise: Languages, Empires, Nations is a critical series. It aims to explore the emergence and consequences of concepts used to define "Latin America" while at the same time exploring the broad interplay of political, economic, and cultural practices that have shaped Latin American worlds. Latin America, at the crossroads of competing imperial designs and local responses, has been construed as a geocultural and geopolitical entity since the nineteenth century. This series provides a starting point to redefine Latin America as a configuration of political, linguistic, cultural, and economic intersections that demands a continuous reappraisal of the role of the Americas in history, and of the ongoing process of globalization and the relocation of people and cultures that have characterized Latin America's experience. *Latin America Otherwise: Languages, Empires, Nations* is a forum that confronts established geocultural constructions, that rethinks area studies and disciplinary boundaries, that assesses convictions of the academy and of public policy, and that, correspondingly, demands that the practices through which we produce knowledge and understanding about and from Latin America be subject to rigorous and critical scrutiny.

In the 1990s Argentina moved rapidly to a level of economic and political crisis that exploded at the beginning of the twenty-first century. A country that was at the forefront of ideas and progress in Latin America became one of the most visible victims of the neoliberal economy and the IMF's global political designs. The crisis and the shock in which the Argentinean population found itself is generating new forms of social awareness and the emergence of a new political society. In *Contentious*

Lives, Javier Auyero brilliantly captures this moment of crisis and hope, the moment of the brutal intersection of global designs and local histories, narrating the lives of two women (Laura and Nana). Auyero's study is not only revealing of the fact that human life is taking second place in the neoliberal drive toward progress and modernization at all costs, but also indirectly revealing of the profound transformation taking place in Latin America at the beginning of the twenty-first century. Reading this moving and analytical account, one cannot help but think of parallel situations in Bolivia, Ecuador, Venezuela, Brazil, and southern Mexico, where the crisis of neoliberalism is unintentionally generating the beginning of hope.

Walter D. Mignolo, Duke University
Irene Silverblatt, Duke University
Sonia Saldívar-Hull, University of Southern California

Acknowledgments

Truth is elusive, subtle, many-sided. You know, Priscilla, there's an old Hindu story about Truth. It seems a brash young warrior sought the hand of a beautiful princess. Her father, the king, thought he was a bit too cocksure and callow. He decreed that the warrior could only marry the princess after he had found Truth. So the warrior set out into the world on a quest for Truth. He went to temples and monasteries, to mountaintops where sages meditated, to remote forests where ascetics scourged themselves, but nowhere could he find Truth. Despairing one day and seeking shelter from a thunderstorm, he took refuge in a musty cave. There was an old crone there, a hag with matted hair and warts on her face, the skin hanging loose from her bony limbs, her teeth yellow and rotting, her breath malodorous. But as he spoke to her, with each question she answered, he realized he had come to the end of his journey: she was Truth. They spoke all night, and when the storm cleared, the warrior told her he had fulfilled his quest. "Now that I have found Truth," he said, "what shall I tell them at the palace about you?" The wizened old creature smiled. "Tell them," she said, "tell them that I am young and beautiful." —SHASHI THAROOR, *Riot: A Love Story*

As in all things in life, it is a question of time and patience: a word here, another there, an understanding, a glance exchanged, a sudden silence, tiny, dispersed crevices expanding in a wall; the investigator's art resides in knowing how to approach them, in eliminating the borders that separate them, and a moment will always arrive in which we wonder whether or not the dream, the ambition, the secret hope of all secrets will finally be the possibility, however vague, however remote, of failing to be ones. —JOSÉ SARAMAGO, *La caverna*

This book is about the experiences and memories, both individual and collective, of popular contention; it deals with the ways in which protesters live, feel, and remember two recent episodes of collective struggle in Argentina. Much like the truth to which the Hindu story refers, this cultural dimension of protest is subtle and many-sided. The public existence of these experiences and memories, the reader will realize, does not always imply their being easy to reconstruct and interpret. Elusive as they sometimes are, their reconstruction, interpretation, and explanation demand the patience and skill that Saramago reserves for secrets, and also the help of the persons who lived through these contentious episodes and later agreed to share their stories with me. To them, and above all to Laura and Nana, the two women whose lives are the main subject of this book, my first very special thanks.

"That was my history; it is now in your hands. Good luck," Laura told me in a letter after I returned home from my first fieldwork trip to the town of Cutral-co, in the province of Neuquén. During the four weeks I spent in her home, we reconstructed together the history of her life and participation in *la pueblada,* a six-day protest in the Argentine Patagonia, in which she was a central protagonist. "It is part of your job to write about us; I hope you will not betray the trust I have in you," she told me several times. Nana used almost the same words to refer to the book I told her I intended to write about her life and her participation in the Santiagazo, a two-day riot that shook that Argentine northwest city of Santiago del Estero. "You write whatever you want . . . if I am telling you all these things, it's because I trust you." Laura and Nana opened their homes and shared their contentious lives with me. Needless to say, this book, a study of the intersection of their lives with two episodes of popular protest, would not have been possible without their enthusiastic collaboration. I cannot thank them and their families enough. They might disagree with things I say here, but I sincerely hope that the book does not betray *la confianza* they both have shared with me.

I also want to thank Carlos Zurita, Alberto Tasso, and Sonia, Raúl, and Raulín Dargoltz for their hospitality and encouragement while I was in Santiago del Estero, and to thank María Esther and Kelio Fuentes, and Mónica and Christian Palavecino, with whom I stayed while in Cutral-co. In Santiago, Alejandro Auat and Carlos Scrimini, despite their discrepancies, made critical contributions to my understanding of the memories of the riot. Teresa Unzaga, Marcelo Infante, and Carolina

Malanca were very cooperative in guiding me through the archives of *El Liberal* and in putting up with last-minute requests. Gustavo Glombowics was very kind in allowing me access to the electronic photo archive of *Rio Negro*. In Cutral-co, Alejandra Faiazzo and Andrea Vazquez were extremely helpful and encouraging. The rest of my interviewees in both sites deserve my deepest gratitude for their time and patience.

Many friends and colleagues made poignant criticisms and suggestions. I want to give special thanks to Lucas Rubinich, Ethel Brooks, Loïc Wacquant, Michael Kimmel, Naomi Rosenthal, Marc Edelman, James Rule, Elisabeth Wood, John Markoff, Francesca Polletta, Claudio Benzecry, Vera Zolberg, Stacy Goldrick, Roy Licklider, Wayne te Brake, Howard Lune, Carol Lindquist, Caroline Skinner, Elke Zuern, Marina Farinetti, Carmenza Gallo, Joyce Robbins, and Jeffrey Olick. Mark Healey first heard some of my tales from the field and then commented on drafts of parts of this book. I am grateful not only for his critical reading but also for his encouragement along the way. On many occasions, while I was researching and writing, he shared with me his unique knowledge of the Argentine "interior" and his own interpretations of the upsurge of collective action in the provinces. In Rodrigo Hobert and Laura Zambrini I found enthusiastic and resourceful research assistants. I also came to know two smart and passionate young intellectuals and wonderful human beings.

I am greatly indebted to Charles Tilly, who helped me to construct a coherent research object out of the few scattered ideas with which I returned from my first fieldwork trip four years ago. Along the way, his advice, encouragement, and writings were helpful guides and sources of critical insight. More than anyone, he gave me the necessary confidence to pursue the study of the relations between collective struggles and human lives. Thanks again, Chuck.

Ian Roxborough and Tim Moran most likely don't realize that much of the energy for writing this book and many of the ideas that animate it came to me not "while taking a walk on a slowly ascending street," as Max Weber says of how ideas occur to us, but while talking to them over the many dinners that we shared in Port Jefferson, New York. I don't want to hold them responsible for anything I say here, but I do want to acknowledge the support, friendship, and intellectual inspiration of *los compañeros* Ian and Tim.

I presented summaries or sections of this book at the Contentious

Politics Seminar at Columbia University; the sociology departments at UCLA, Northwestern, Brown, Pittsburgh, and SUNY–Stony Brook; the Seminario General at the Casa de Altos Estudios en Ciencias Sociales (Universidad General San Martín); the Centro de Estudios en Cultura y Política (CECYP) at the Fundación del Sur; the Latin American and Caribbean Center at SUNY–Stony Brook; the Facultad de Humanidades, Ciencias Sociales y de la Salud at the Universidad Nacional de Santiago del Estero; the David Rockefeller Center for Latin American Studies at Harvard University; the conference "Out of the Shadows: Political Action and the Informal Economy," at Princeton University; the So-cial Sciences School at the University of Buenos Aires; the Facultad Latinoamericana de Ciencias Sociales (FLACSO-Ecuador); and the Latin American Studies Association Annual Conference. I wish to thank all participants in these forums for lively and helpful discussions, espe-cially Germán Lodola, Gianpaolo Baiocchi, Lisa Brush, Eric Klinenberg, and José Itzigsohn. Earlier versions of some chapters were published in *Theory and Society, International Sociology, Apuntes de Investigación,* and *Revista Venezolana de Economía y Ciencias Sociales.*

I also extend grateful acknowledgment to the John Simon Guggen-heim Memorial Foundation and to the American Sociological Associa-tion's Fund for the Advancement of the Discipline Award supported by the American Sociological Association and the National Science Foun-dation for their financial support, and SUNY–Stony Brook for a gener-ous leave of absence and for an individual development award. For their editorial assistance I am thankful to Carol Lindquist and April Marshall.

My colleagues and friends at the Centro de Estudios en Cultura y Polí-tica (CECYP) are also worthy of my deepest gratitude. For the past four years, we have been struggling against all odds to meet, have produc-tive discussions, and publish our *Apuntes de Investigación* in Argentina. Maybe it's time we acknowledge what a wonderful intellectual atmo-sphere we have at the Fundación del Sur, and at the virtual space of our apuntes-cecyp@yahoogroups.com. To a great extent, this book was conceived and nurtured in this both real and virtual place. Our mentor there, Lucas Rubinich, ought to have a special mention. He guides us, inspires us, and sometimes gives us rides in his 1975 Dodge. It was in *la máquina,* talking to Lucas, where the idea of writing this book was first entertained. Although it was he who first heard the outline of this book and thought it was a good idea, Lucas should not be blamed for any of its shortcomings. It has been a real pleasure to work again with Valerie Millholland and Miriam Angress at Duke University Press. Many thanks also to Pam Morrison and Bill Henry for their detailed final editing. No words are needed to thank our family in New York, Graciela and Victor Penchaszadeh; *los titulares* will do it: *Gracias Penchas!*

A long conversation on the N train and innumerable discussions at home with my *compañera* Gabriela Polit made this book what it is. I can't imagine what it would have been had her support, insight, and critical reading been absent. She first heard the stories of Laura and Nana, advised me on ways of interpreting them, and finally read, criticized, and reread the entire manuscript. It was that subway conversation that made all the difference in my way of approaching their life stories as, to a great extent, gendered quests for recognition and respect.

Nelly and Carlos Jácome, and their sons and daughter, David, Martín, and Andrea, also deserve a special place in these acknowledgments. I cannot think of a better place to finish this book other than their home in Los Chillos, Ecuador. Our son Camilo, Gabriela, and I cannot thank them enough.

Introduction

On the Intersection of

Individual and Collective

Biographies and Protest

"This is for you," Nana, a thirty-six-year-old employee at the state court-house, mother of six, says as she hands me a crystal from a chandelier in the Government House. "I took it as a souvenir, when we occupied and burned down that corrupt house . . . keep it as a memento of my Santiago." Caught by surprise, I ask her, "What does it mean to you?" "It's a keepsake," she answers, "and I'm really happy because you're interested in it. That means that it is a valuable keepsake. At least it's useful, because you are interested in it. It's a souvenir. I said to myself, 'I will go there [into the burning Government House] again, because I want a souvenir.' What does it mean to you?"

This is our last conversation about her participation in the Santiagazo, an uprising that shook the northwest Argentine city of Santiago del Estero, and the whole country, on December 16, 1993. That day, the city of Santiago witnessed what the *New York Times*, 18 December 1993, called "the worst social upheaval in years." Three public buildings—the Government House, the courthouse, and the legislature—and nearly a dozen local officials' and politicians' private residences were invaded, looted, and burned down by thousands of public workers and city residents who demanded their unpaid salaries and pensions with arrears of three months and voiced their discontent with the widespread governmental corruption.

"You can have it, take it with you . . ." Laura, a forty-four-year-old mother of three, currently unemployed, tells me as she hands me her notebook, and then adds, "Part of what we, the picketers, did is in this notebook." Laura carried this notebook with her during la pueblada, a protest in which thousands of residents of Cutral-co and Plaza Huincul, two oil towns in the southern province of Neuquén, barricaded the national and provincial roads, effectively isolating both towns, in June 1996. *Los piqueteros*, as protesters in the barricades called themselves, demanded "genuine sources of employment" and the physical presence of the governor to discuss their claims. After six nights and seven days in the road, Governor Sapag acceded to most of their demands in a written agreement he signed with Laura, the picketers' representative.

The notebook, she tells me in our last conversation, "is now part of your life. You are the one working on this, not me. I feel proud about what we did. Now it's your turn. You prepared yourself to write about us. How you do that is your problem, not mine. It is part of my past; it's now part of your present." During the several weeks we have spent together, Laura has shared with me not only the notebook in which she recorded the many discussions picketers had during the road blockade but also the letters she wrote to her friends about the episode, and her personal diary.

Laura and Nana took the uprisings to their hearts. "After the sixteenth," Nana tells me, "I don't wear makeup. I can let my gray hair grow. I don't wear miniskirts anymore. I became a commando woman, a battle woman. I took all this very seriously, ever since the sixteenth . . . To me, the sixteenth was the battle that I won." Laura also speaks about the pueblada in personal terms. In reference to the agreement she signed with the governor, Laura says: "I was signing against all the injustices, the humiliations, that I suffered throughout my life." Nana and Laura are not members of a political party, union, or other kind of organization. They have different histories. They live miles apart, in different provinces, and had not heard about each other before I ventured into their lives. Yet they both think of these contentious episodes in personal terms. For both, the popular revolts meant something special: they both admit that the fervent days in the streets and roads "marked" their lives, that since then, their lives have radically changed.

C. Wright Mills would say that when episodes of collective contention happen, a public employee like Nana becomes a rioter, and a private tutor like Laura becomes a picketer. Wright Mills would then add that neither the protesters' lives nor the history of the uprisings can be understood without understanding them both. "Understanding them both" is the task of the sociological imagination. This book examines the intersection of these episodes of popular protest with the life histories of Nana and Laura, two women living in neglected regions of Argentina, paying particular attention to the ways in which Nana's and Laura's biographies shape their actions and words during the uprisings and the different effects that both episodes have had on their lives. Throughout this text I also seek to answer the question Nana posed to me more than two years ago: what are the meanings of that "souvenir"? I intend to explore whether Laura's notebook (and by implication her picketing) is, as she says, part of her past or, as I suspect, part of her present self-identity. Nana's keepsake, Laura's notebook, and the stories they told me are extremely significant because they are carriers of what interests me most about the intersection of biography and history: the links between the meanings that protest takes on during and after the fact (i.e., the "lived experiences" of collective action) and the individual biographies of protesters.

Contentious Lives is not solely about Nana and the Santiagazo, and Laura and the pueblada. It is about a way of looking at the intersection of contentious events with human lives. Previous works have indeed examined the intersection of biography and protest, focusing mainly on the militant past of social movement participants, their migration from one social movement organization to the next and the subsequent transmission of mobilization tactics, and the impression that social movement participation might or might not make on the individual lives of activists.[1] By and large, the works that scrutinize the meeting point between biography and contention concentrate on the case of *activists*, a focus that leaves the participation of people like Laura and Nana underproblematized. The roots of their contentious actions and words, their lived experiences of popular struggle, are sunk in a complex layer of biographical themes that go well beyond their activism; in point of fact, neither Nana nor Laura nor many of the protesters in Santiago and Cutral-co have a history of militancy. The ways in which they live the protest (what they do, what they think, how they feel during the episode) are deeply informed by their biographies; that is, their experiences of the uprisings stem, in part, from schemes of action, perception, and evaluation that, forged in their lives *prior* to these contentious episodes, are enacted in the streets of Santiago and the roads of Cutral-co. This book explores the ways in which Laura and Nana recast their actions, thoughts, and feelings in the roads of Cutral-co and in the streets of Santiago in terms painfully familiar to them, thereby illuminating the continuity between their life stories (i.e., their trajectories not merely as activists but as women, wives, lovers, mothers, workers, etc.) and their experiences of these contentious episodes.

Nana and Laura act out a set of subjective dispositions during the uprisings, but they do not experience their road and street actions alone. Their "lived protest" is rooted not only in their biographies but also, and just as importantly, in an array of relations and meanings created during the contentious episodes, particularly in the shared self-understandings of protesters. In other words, Laura's and Nana's experiences of la pueblada and of the Santiagazo are embedded in their own histories and in demonstrators' activated collective identities; identities that are in turn rooted in the collective history and current plight of both places. This book looks at the way in which protesters' life stories meet and mesh with the collective understandings of the actors who voice their discontent during those days.

In protesters' accounts, we will be able to recognize the relevance of the mobilization of resources, of the opening of political opportunities, of the crucial role played by framing processes in the origins of these two uprisings. These processes and other mechanisms (brokerage among different protesting parties, for example) that observers deemed central in the emergence and course of contention are indeed present in these episodes and might certainly help to explain them.[2] This book, however, does not center on the causal mechanisms leading to these protests but focuses on the ways in which protesters collectively (and contentiously) construct, think, and feel their joint actions. Thus this book focuses on meaning making and its explanation at the individual and collective levels. With concepts such as insurgent identities (Gould 1995), narrative identities (Somers and Gibson 1994; Polletta 1998a, 1998b), disjoined/embedded identities (Tilly 1998a), collective memories (Lee 2000), oppositional consciousness (Mansbridge and Morris 2001), framing (Benford and Snow 2000), and discursive repertoires (Steinberg 1999) (just to name a few of the many analytical tools now in use), current approaches to collective mobilization draw attention to the structuring of particular kinds of subjectivities in the emergence of contention.[3] The stories presented in this book build on some of these concepts to understand the meanings that these two episodes have for two protesters and, more generally, the collective self-understandings of the actors involved. *Contentious Lives* is thus an interpretation of the ways in which popular collective struggle is lived and felt, individually and collectively, by protesters. In its focus on the ways in which picketers and rioters make sense of popular revolt, the book brings together two classic concerns of the anthropology of practice and of the sociology of protest, namely, the examination of social phenomena "from the actors' points of view" (Geertz 1973; Wacquant 1995; Prieur 1998) and the analysis of contention focusing on insurgents' self-understandings (Gould 1995; Ginsburg 1989).

Why is the intersection of collective experiences and individual biographies important? What do they add to our understanding of the meanings of contentious episodes? The Santiagazo and the pueblada were highly singular events at the time of their occurrence. The Santiagazo was the most violent protest in contemporary democratic Argentina, and a unique event in modern Latin America.[4] It is not common to see hundreds of people parading around town, burning and sacking public buildings and private residences. It was an uprising that converged on the residences of wrongdoers *and* the symbols of public power; a protest by "hungry and angry people," as the main Argentine newspapers called it, in which (almost) no stores were looted and that had no human fatalities; a "riot," finally, that was remarkably different from the episodes that authorities and elites alike usually classify under that name in that the burning and looting are located at the temporal and geographic center of the event.

For a week, thousands of residents of Cutral-co and Plaza Huincul blockaded the access to both oil towns, effectively halting the movement of goods and persons. They demanded jobs, asked for the presence of the governor, and rejected the intervention of their democratically elected representatives. The sheer number of protesters (twenty thousand, according to most sources) made the troops of the Gendarmería Nacional back off. The next day, Laura, a picketer popularly elected as the protesters' representative, signed an agreement with the governor in which most of their demands were met. La pueblada is another extraordinary event in contemporary democratic Argentina: these days we don't usually see troops retreating in defeat and authorities acceding to popular demands.

Unique, yes, but hardly isolated. With Argentine regional economies in complete disarray and the slashes in public spending required by "structural adjustment" policies (Rofman 2000; Rubins and Cao 2000; Sawers 1996), the last decade witnessed the generalization of collective struggle in the interior provinces; road blockades and sieges of (and attacks on) public buildings became widespread in the South (the provinces of Neuquén, Río Negro, Santa Cruz, Tierra del Fuego) and North (Jujuy, Salta, Tucumán, Corrientes, Chaco, to name just a few) of the country.[5] Scholars agree that new and unconventional forms of protest are transforming the Argentine interior into a veritable landscape of protest (Tenti 2000; Entel 1996). Some characterize this collective practice as part of an emerging repertoire of collective action (Schuster 1999; Farinetti 1999, 2000).[6] Others attempt to come to terms with the novelty of this form of contention in terms of the changing dynamics of collective identity (Scribano 1999); still others see in it an indicator of an insurgent oppositional front, a "grand movement" against global neoliberal capitalism of sorts (Iñigo Carrera 1999; Klachko 1999). Although important disagreements plague these disparate attempts, most, if not all, see structural adjustment policies at the root of the upsurge of protest.

John Walton and David Seddon (1994; see also Walton and Ragin 1990) describe and explain the wave of popular protest that followed the implementation of structural adjustment policies and government austerity measures in the developing world from the 1970s to the 1990s. The authors contend that the specific origin of "austerity protests" (i.e., "large-scale collective actions including political demonstrations, general strikes, and riots" [1994, 39]) lies in the period of global adjustment that followed the international debt crisis. Walton and Shefner (1994) apply this same global approach to the analysis of the generalization of protest in Latin America. During the last decade, a decade that witnessed a global leaning toward neoliberal economic reorganization, "the broad implementation of austerity measures as a condition of structural adjustment and debt restructuring represented an attack on the very means that made urban life sustainable. Austerity led to popular protest in the times and places that combined economic hardship, external adjustment demands, hyperurbanization, and local traditions of political mobilization" (99).

True, at the end of the day, the international debt crisis and the impact of neoliberal recipes for the structural problems affecting economies in the global South are surely to be blamed for the wave of popular protest in Argentina and in most of Latin America and, in turn, for these particular episodes. Servicing the foreign debt has become the single largest budget item in Argentina and in most countries of the subcontinent. To avoid outright default, the conditions of the IMF and World Bank on loans they make have tightened and come under the name of austerity schemes or "structural adjustment" programs. Among other things, these programs have forced the nations in the South to slash social spending and privatize state property (Laurell 2000; Korzeniewicz and Smith 2000). Recently, the IMF and the World Bank began to put pressure on the Argentine national government to extend the adjustment to the provinces so much so that in January 2000, the fiscal deficit in the provinces became one of the main obstacles in the negotiations between the IMF and the Argentine finance minister.[7]

It would be impossible, if not ridiculous, to try to understand la pueblada and the Santiagazo without a grasp of the effects of the privatization of the state oil company in Neuquén, Yacimientos Petrolíferos Fiscales (YPF), and the attempts to reduce public employment in Santiago del Estero. But the structural factors at the root of these contentious episodes only begin to tell us how protesters *live* the events; structural adjustment hardly exhausts the answer to the crucial question: what are the protests about? Rather than seeking to inscribe both episodes in a larger cycle of contention (new or not), in a grand wave of protest against the dire consequences of structural adjustment (inevitable or not), or in an incipient movement of resistance (more or less radical), I examine the biographical and relational ways in which their protagonists make sense of them. What difference does this focus on protesters' interpretations of the episodes make in our understanding of contentious episodes in general, and of la pueblada and the Santiagazo in particular? A big one, because once we take protesters' self-understandings seriously, we will see that these uprisings are indeed about structural adjustment, but they are also about other "local" issues such as government corruption and residents' dissatisfaction with their elected representatives—the uprisings are as much about politics as about the economy. Furthermore, once we focus analytic attention on protesters' experiences and biographies, we will also see that the protests are as much about an individual and collective quest for recognition and respect as about the material living conditions. In other words, to assign demonstrators in both sites agency only as genuine antiadjustment protesters is to write misleadingly; it is to be obdurate about local political dynamics and to be ignorant of the indigenous meanings with which participants imbue the protest. In this book I argue that protesters in Santiago del Estero and Neuquén are indeed in search of their jobs and salaries, but they are also in search of dignity.

Why Laura and Nana?

"No social study that does not come back to the problem of biography, of history and of their intersections within a society has completed its intellectual journey," writes C. Wright Mills in the first chapter of *The Sociological Imagination.* This book is as much about the meanings of the uprisings as it is about the lives of two of the participants—lives that, to a certain extent, are defined ("marked," as both Laura and Nana say) by the episodes.[8] The reasons why I chose to tell the stories of Laura and Nana, and through them the lived experiences of both episodes, are different. I contacted Laura because she was the visible face of the picketers' organization. Listening to her, I was surprised to realize how deeply linked her participation in (and understanding of) the protest is with the story of her life. She first got involved with the picketers' actions out of a "gender offense" that would be incomprehensible without a grasp of her story of domestic abuse and violence. During those seven days in the road, Laura had two obsessions: to protect the protest from politicians, and to protect protesters from repression. This anxiety over protection and caring did not stem from a purportedly universal female condition but came from a particular social trajectory, a gendered biography that bred a particular set of dispositions. Her story is interesting because it illuminates the continuity (or even circularity) between routine daily life and contention.

The Santiagazo has no visible leaders or protagonists to be contacted. I chose Nana for other reasons. The fact that before becoming, in her words, "an activist of the Santiagazo" she had been, for many years, "the queen of the Carnaval Santiagueño" makes her a sort of living ideal type of one crucial (though neglected) dimension of the protest: its carnivalesque aspects. Her words and actions before, during, and after the uprising encapsulate, better than anybody's, the revenge, parody, and hierarchy inversion that, being defining aspects in carnival, are at the center of the Santiagazo. But Nana's story also condenses another set of meanings that the protest has for most of its protagonists. Listening to "the queen," I was often struck by the analogy between her individual life, a story of suffering and overcoming, and the form and fate of the 1993 protest: both she and the riot speak about a frustrated, but never-ending, search for respect.

However, Laura's and Nana's stories are interesting not only because of what they tell us about the uprisings and the ways in which active participants live them. In talking about themselves, Nana and Laura taught me a lot about the reality—the misfortune, I should say—of women living in a world that (still) has clearly determined boundaries for men and women, about the perennial rigidity of an androcentric sexual order, about life in towns that are suffering the combined effects of the withering away of the welfare component of the state and the rise of mass unemployment, and in general about the fate of regions that have no place for many of their residents. And much like Rosine Christin in "A Silent Witness," I realized that people like Nana and Laura have to be listened to in a different way because they "can talk about a life saturated with collective history only through a personal language, 'little things'" (1999, 360), things that, as Nana told me many times, "you are probably not interested in." They, more than any other interviewee, allowed me to understand the life of women (and men) of my age living in ignored (both by policy makers and by social scientists) regions, the way in which they make sense of both the lack of future and the reasons to react (sometimes individually, others collectively) against hopelessness with indignation or revolt. In the language of the "little things," of the everyday-life anecdotes to which I devote special attention throughout the book, they also allowed me to understand in very concrete terms what the "struggle for recognition" is about.

In *Pascalian Meditations,* Pierre Bourdieu argues that the "search for recognition" is the ultimate spring of human action. The need for justification, legitimation, and recognition is, according to Bourdieu, a basic anthropological fact. This thirst for recognition can only be quenched by the specific social worlds that human beings inhabit. This quest, in other words, can only be satisfied by the "judgment of others," which—as uncertain and insecure as it is—then becomes the major principle "certainty, assurance, [and] consecration" (Bourdieu 2000, 313); or, as Axel Honneth (1995, 132) puts it, human beings' normative self-image depends "on the possibility of being continually backed up by others." Both Bourdieu and Honneth acknowledge that the avenues through which

persons can satisfy this all-too-human need for recognition are histori-
cally variable. On the one hand, the stories of Nana and Laura are interesting because they illuminate the ways in which this search for being
acknowledged and valued stumbles along class and gender lines. Nana's
and Laura's recounting of their lives reflects the way in which working-
class women experience class inequalities and gender hierarchies in a
particular place and at a particular time as they attempt to realize the
basic human need to be recognized and respected.

On the other hand, the stories of the Santiagazo and la pueblada, of
the ways in which protesters live and remember them, are interesting
because they demonstrate how this quest for recognition can be pursued
jointly. In collective action, much as in other social games offered by the
social world, there is a thrill, a joy of sorts, that goes well beyond the anticipated profits—in these cases, wages and jobs. In recent years, scholars of collective action have increasingly been paying due attention to
what I would call, borrowing from Philippe Bourgois (1995), the "search
for respect" involved in contentious politics (McAdam 1988; Calhoun
1994; Jasper 1997; Saint-Upéry 2001). In her study of Salvadoran peasant
guerrillas, for example, Elisabeth Wood (2001a, 2001b) asserts that participation in guerrilla actions per se carried what she calls "emotional
in-process benefits," giving grounds for pride, and allowing militants to
express moral outrage and to assert a claim to dignity. As she puts it
(2001a, 268): "Moral outrage, pride, pleasure, along with more conventional reasons such as access to land, impelled the insurgency despite
the high risk and uncertainty." By now hardly anyone would deny the
existence of this crucial dimension of insurgency. Few, however, have
explored the sources and shape, the trajectory, of this quest for dignity.
Where does it come from? What form does it take?[9] True, protesters
seek respect and assert pride because this is what social existence is all
about—the "basic anthropological fact" about which Bourdieu so per-
ceptively talks. But as we will see, protesters in specific times and places
feel the need to emphasize this aspect of their struggle because they
sense they have been disrespected, insulted, or cast out by specific others
or by particular circumstances. From the protesters' points of view, both
uprisings have the power of rescuing them from oblivion, a neglect that
has definite names and faces. In the streets of Santiago, in the roads of
Cutral-co, Nana, Laura, and many fellow rioters and picketers emerge
from official indifference and search for something that far exceeds the

bread and butter. The protest is, for them, a time when they feel justified, accepted, and appreciated. It is only by listening closely to the stories they have to tell that we can learn about this (other) set of meanings.

On Fieldwork, Stories, and Experiences

My fieldwork (see appendix) consisted mainly in collecting stories that participants, authorities, and bystanders had to tell about both contentious episodes. Laura, Nana, and many others shared many stories with me not only about the uprisings but also about their past and present lives. *Contentious Lives* draws on these narratives to build an argument about the biographical and relational roots of the experiences of popular protest.

Social scientists have taken good advantage of storytelling (D. James 2000; Passerini 1987), mainly emphasizing its potential as a window into (but not a mirror of) the meanings of extremely diverse collective and individual practices, from killing cats (Darnton 1991) to reading the Bible (Ginzburg 1980), from cockfighting (Geertz 1973) to prizefighting (Wacquant 1995). Scholars of collective action are also increasingly paying attention to narrative. Stories are crucial not only in creating the possibilities for collective action (in plotting, for example, the political opportunities to act, in framing "objects, situations, events, experiences, and sequences of action")[10] but also in constructing the experiential meanings of events during and after the fact and thus the self-understandings of those who, on either side, participate in them.

We now know that oral narratives do not reveal behavioral patterns or consciousness in a straight or unmediated way (Passerini 1987). As Daniel James (1997, 36) puts it in his superb analysis of Doña María's life story: "If oral testimony is indeed a window onto the subjective in history, the cultural, social, and ideological universe of historical actors, then it must be said that the view it affords is not a transparent one that simply reflects thoughts and feelings as they really were/are. At the very least the image is refracted, the glass of the window is unclear."

In all their uncertain character, the stories that actors tell after the event not only speak about the ongoing political construction of the uprising (the "social construction of protest") but also speak to the protesters' hopes, expectations, emotions, and beliefs at the time. As unclear as these voices are (even more so, especially since, as we will see, they have been obscured by the official discourse), they are one of the few keys that—as rusty, bent, and unpredictable as they are—can help us to understand the ways in which people make sense of collective struggle. There are, fortunately in these cases, other sources into the shared understandings of participants and into the collective meanings of protest. In this book I do not rely solely on oral recollections but also draw on video footage, journalistic accounts, and—in the case of Cutral-co—the notebook kept by one key actor.

Those accounts will, I hope, help us to get as close as possible to the diverse experiences of the uprisings, to the ways in which picketers and rioters make sense of their actions and of themselves, knowing, however, that there is a perpetual tension between the experiences at the time and the memories told to the analyst years after the events. As Roy (1994, 24) lucidly writes:

> To understand an event, not to mention a phenomenon, we must encompass the varying experiences of that event, even though we must understand that what we understand is only an approximation. That the approximation departs from the experience of the actor is not a problem; it is the point. How experience is experienced is one topic of importance. But how that experience is formulated, remembered, and retold tells the hearer something beyond "what happened," which we cannot in any case know and which did not in any case happen, since what happened happened to many different people differently.

The book is divided into two parts, one devoted to Laura and la pueblada, the other one devoted to Nana and the Santiagazo. The first chapter in each part seeks to answer the following—admittedly broad—question: what events, both in the large frame of their lives as residents of a city experiencing the combined impacts of structural adjustment policies and state neglect and in the small frame of their everyday lives, coalesced to inspire their contentious actions? The general answer that I dissect in both chapters is that grievances deriving from everyday routines, the local perceptions of politicians' wrongful conduct, and general understandings of structural adjustment processes came together in the making of the uprising. The bulk of both parts focuses on the lived experiences of the uprisings, paying particular attention to both Nana's and Laura's accounts. I then move to a reconstruction of their life stories, key to understanding their experiences. The last chapter of each part concentrates on the memories of the events after their occurrence. In the conclusions, I tackle some important methodological issues I faced during my fieldwork, in particular the role of the social analyst in the interactive reconstruction of the meanings and identities of collective protest, a role that despite comprehensive treatments of the scope and workings of "qualitative methods" has been rather underexplored.[11]

At a time when a concern with the form and impact of globalization seems to pervade almost every corner of social analysis, to undertake a narrow investigation of two protests in two small towns in the South might seem utterly parochial, and my interest in two individuals dangerously anecdotal. Cats in eighteenth-century France (Darnton 1991), cocks in twentieth-century Bali (Geertz 1973), a stubborn miller in sixteenth-century Italy (Ginzburg 1980), a sham husband in sixteenth-century France (Davis 1983), and, more recently, a bewitched man in contemporary South Africa (Ashforth 2000), a Saab repairman and mechanic in upper New York (Harper 1992), and a hustler in Chicago's black ghetto (Wacquant 1999) convinced me that we can still learn a lot by embarking in "merely local" studies, that the risks of succumbing to anecdote and parochialism are not inevitable. We do not study villages, Clifford Geertz reminds us; we study *in* villages larger social processes, in this case the making of the meanings and memories of popular contention. During the years I spent traveling around the Argentine interior, talking to people and studying local newspaper archives in search of contentious stories, I became more and more convinced that, at least for the study of protest in contemporary Latin America, C. Wright Mills's "promise" remains unfulfilled. The walls separating the grand, "serious" narratives of protest and the minor, seemingly unimportant "private" spheres of people's lives still need to be broken down. The intersection of contentious biographies and histories remains an uncharted terrain. It is to this task that the pages that follow are devoted.

Part One

The Picketer

FIGURE 1.

Laura Padilla and Governor Sapag signing
agreement. Cutral-co, June 26, 1996. © *Río Negro*.

On June 26, 1996, in the city of Cutral-co, province of Neuquén, Argentina, Governor Sapag and Laura Padilla sign an agreement (see figure 1). The whole country watches this moment on TV, reads about it in newspapers, or hears about the details on the radio. The agreement puts an end to a protest of thousands of residents of Cutral-co and Plaza Huincul, who blocked all the local, provincial, and national roads in the area surrounding both towns, effectively halting the movement of people and goods for seven days and six nights.

The day before the agreement, Laura Padilla writes in a letter to a friend, "other picketers take me home, I can't even walk. I didn't eat or sleep well for days. . . ." Five main barricades—Torre Uno (east), Aeropuerto (west), Picún (south), Añelo (north), Parque Este-Oeste (northwest)—and tens of smaller pickets, with varying numbers of women, men, and children in each, isolate this oil and gas region from the rest of the province and the country (figure 2). During days and nights, one slogan unites the hundreds of picketers: "Nobody comes in, nobody gets out. We want Governor Sapag to come here. We want jobs" [No entra ni sale nadie; Sapag en casa. Queremos trabajo].

It all begins with the news of the cancellation of a deal between the provincial government and a Canadian firm to build a fertilizer plant in the region of Cutral-co and Plaza Huincul, a plant that will provide hundreds of jobs during the time of construction and then fifty permanent positions. Some local radio stations spread the bad news, presenting it as a "final blow to the future of the region," and encourage residents to express their anger in the road, at the site that memorializes the discovery of petroleum in the region, the Torre Uno (an oil derrick). In a few hours, hundreds of residents mobilize on the Torre to manifest their discontent at what they perceive as an arbitrary decision by the governor. As the day comes to an end, some protesters decide to stay in the road and, coordinating their actions through local radio, blockade all access to both towns with burning tires, barbed-wire fences, old machines and cars, stones, and their own bodies. Some of the leaders during this initial stage of the protest belong to the oppositional faction within the governing party, the Movimiento Popular Neuquino (MPN). This fac-

FIGURE 2.
National Route 22, Cutral-co,
Neuquén. June 1996, © *Río Negro.*

tion (the "blancos") have been promoting the project of the fertilizer plant for Cutral-co for years, and they now perceive that the governor is wrongly calling the project off. The "blancos" (the faction of the former governor Sosbich, and the former mayor Grittini) and the "amarillos" (the faction of the current governor Sapag, and the current mayor Martinasso) seem to be taking their infighting to the roads of Cutral-co and Plaza Huincul.

Both towns form the second-largest area in the province in terms of population and provide natural gas and gasoline to other areas of the province and the country. One-third of the petroleum extracted in the country comes from Neuquén, a huge part of it from this area. Until the year it was privatized (1992), the government petroleum company, Yacimientos Petrolíferos Fiscales (YPF) provided jobs for a large percentage of the residents of Cutral-co and Plaza Huincul and was the center of economic, social, and cultural life of both towns. Since 1992, with the rapid increase in joblessness (close to 30 percent of the population is unemployed) and poverty (more than half of the population lives below the official poverty line), the specter of the "ghost town" has haunted residents old and young.

After a day on the barricades, a meeting is called at the Torre Uno. Some of the local notables express their disgust with the governor's de-

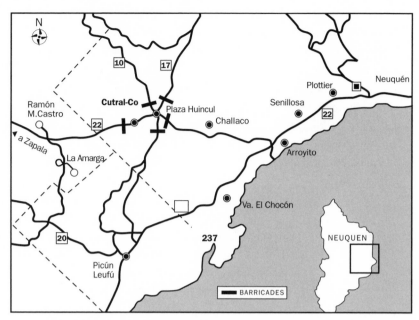

Map showing the five main barricades on routes 17 and 22. Torre Uno (East), Aeropuerto (West), Picún (South), Añelo (North), Parque Este-Oeste (Northwest).

cision and call for his resignation. Others, mainly those with little or no political experience, who have stayed on the picket lines during the previous night, are strangely left out of the public discussion. That first meeting looks much like a well-attended political rally during an electoral campaign. The only difference is that instead of returning home, participants go back to the barricades. There, partly out of disgust with local politicians, some picketers give birth to their own organization, the "Committee of Pickets' Representatives." Laura Padilla is one of its spokespersons, and the presence of the governor "to give us solutions [i.e., jobs]" emerges as the committee's main claim.

After two days of protest, the control of the blockades seems to have passed from the hands of the initial organizers to the hands of self-assembled picketers. By now, residents are massively participating day and night in what is called a pueblada. On Sunday, in a mass offered by the archbishop at the Torre Uno, a group of picketers asks for his mediation in the conflict. With the spread of rumors concerning the coming of the troops from the Gendarmería Nacional and of news related to the stubborn refusal of the governor to come to town, two positions begin to crystallize among the protesting crowd. On the one hand, there are those who want to form a commission of representatives and go to Neuquén to talk to the governor. On the other hand, the picketers' position is to "resist and wait for him to come here." A meeting at the building of the Red Cross is called on the afternoon of June 24 to elect representatives to negotiate with the governor in the capital. Angry picketers tell those attending that nobody will be allowed to leave town: negotiations will occur only when the governor comes to town. The Red Cross is stoned, and one vehicle is set on fire in demonstration of the picketers' determination.

It is below 30 degrees at eight o'clock in the morning on June 25 when the federal judge Margarita Gudiño de Argüelles, in command of the four hundred troops of the Gendarmería, comes to Cutral-co with the intention of clearing the National Road 22. With the help of tear gas and rubber bullets, the gendarmes clear the first picket, less than a mile from the Torre, but as they attempt to move forward, they find that approximately twenty thousand people (close to half of the total population of both towns) are awaiting them. The judge asks a group of picketers if she can talk to some representatives. Among them is Jote, who tells the judge, "There are no representatives here; come and talk to the people." From the roof of a van, her arm held by a masked picketer, the judge addresses the crowd with a megaphone and recuses herself from the case, telling the crowd that the crime they are committing far exceeds her competency: "This is not a simple road blockade; this is a popular rebellion against the established authorities." As the judge informs the crowd that she and the gendarmes at her command are leaving, the crowd cheers her, sings the national anthem, and shouts, "The people won, the people won! The people united will never be defeated!"

In the afternoon, Governor Sapag finally decides to come to Cutral-co. In front of thousands of residents who are standing at the Torre Uno, during a freezing winter night, the governor gives a brief speech praising the residents for this popular manifestation. He says, "With the same emotion that we just sang the national anthem, I salute you, and I congratulate you for this patriotic demonstration. You showed the whole country what's the situation in Cutral-co and Plaza Huincul, how it is in the province of Neuquén, and in the whole neglected Patagonia. You have done a very good service so that we in the government can make claims [to the federal government]. I am here because you asked for it.

I will stay here the whole week so that people can talk to me. Stay calm and trust me." As he finishes his speech, some protesters insult him, and others shout, "We want jobs." The governor matter-of-factly replies, "You lost those jobs when YPF left."

The next morning a meeting with the representatives of the picketers is called. The night before, Laura, weakened after six cold days and nights on the road, is taken to the local hospital and prescribed some strong tranquilizers so that she can sleep. In the morning, a fellow picketer shows up at Laura's house and tells her that Governor Sapag awaits the representatives in the municipal building. "In the meeting," she writes in a letter to a friend and later repeats to me, "the old man [the governor] was talking and talking. I don't think I was listening. I was just looking through the window, seeing that it was raining and snowing. He was describing his plans to distribute the aid. In my mind I had the command given to me on the picket line: there has to be a written agreement. I simply remember that I stood up and told him: Everything you are saying, you have to write it down and sign it . . . It is snowing outside, there are people on the roads. Do something . . . Write down an agreement."

The handwritten agreement states that the protest was a "clear demonstration of the hunger suffered by the population" of both cities. To put an end to the seven days that shook the province and the nation, the agreement promises public works that will provide locals with jobs, delivery of food, and the reconnection of gas and electricity to approximately 2,500 families whose service was cut off owing to lack of payment. The agreement also states that the governor will declare both communities in "occupational and social emergency," specifies some of the projects that the provincial government will begin or support to create jobs, promises that the provincial bank will assist local businesses with new credit lines, assures the people that no punitive measures will be taken against those who took active part in the protest, and finally guarantees that new investors will be sought to build the fertilizer plant. The text of the agreement is quite vague, contains promises that were already made (the week before the governor himself announced that the plant will be *licitada* [bidding for a contract] as soon as possible) or that were beyond the capacity of the signer; however, it summarizes the claims and hopes of picketers and residents: jobs for Cutral-co and Plaza Huincul, "genuine sources of employment," as it is repeatedly claimed by picketers and residents during these days. Although many know that the fertilizer plant will provide, at best, fifty full-time jobs (for an unemployed population of more than five thousand), it represents in the minds of many the "last hope" that both cities will not disappear after the privatization of YPF; the plant is taken to be a sign of the government's real concern for the uncertain future of both communities.

Laura Padilla and Felipe Sapag shake hands, and right after the governor touches Laura's face in a very paternal way, she tells him that she now has to go and ask "the people to see if they agree on these terms." "This is a joke, we just agreed on something," Governor Sapag replies. Very calm, seemingly in control, Laura, with cameras and microphones surrounding her, says in her low voice, "Give me two hours, and I'll ask the picketers . . . I think they will be in agreement." "I was just a representative," she insists in many of our several conversations. In a letter to a friend, she puts it this way: "During those days, my voice and face represented them [the pickets]. I was just a symbol. It was not my opinion. It was not my decision. It was the pickets' opinions and decisions that were expressed through me." That's why she "needs" to "ask the people about the agreement." Laura and some other fellow picketers stop by the seventeen pickets and, in popular assemblies, approve the agreement. Hours later, after cleaning up the roads of burning tires, bricks, old cars, and other elements placed there to block traffic and the advance of the federal troops, picketers celebrate in the streets of Cutral-co the end of the protest and return home. Five years later, in the living room of her modest house in General Roca, over the many mates I prepare and the cigarettes she frantically smokes, she tells me that when she signed the agreement with the governor, "I was signing against all the injustices, the humiliations, that I suffered throughout my life."

The day I first meet Laura, she receives me with a borrowed VCR and two tapes ready to be watched. One of the tapes features the program that the local channel of Cutral-co made about *la pueblada del '96* with images of those seven days on the road, interviews with politicians, picketers, and residents of both communities. "The tape," she tells me, "doesn't exactly reflect what happened because it was done by one of the associates of the former mayor." The other tape shows Laura, with her three children, in *Hora Clave*, by then the most popular political program in the country. In that program, recorded in Buenos Aires just a week after the protest, Laura talks with conductor Mariano Grondona about her contentious experience:

> We had to ask for peace, we had to say no to violence . . . we had to yell out what we were going through. We were shouting, "Mr. Governor, come here and see us." In the same way he came to look for votes, he had to come and see that he hadn't done anything. As days went by, the suffering united us. I think that all of a sudden, we learned to love each other. We didn't know each other, we didn't recognize each other's faces, but the love we felt for each other was great. I think that the (federal) judge noticed that when she recused herself from the case . . . if you ask me how do I see unemployment, I see egoism. There is egoism in the people who are in charge, in the people who say, "I will do this and that if you vote for me." What happens afterwards? There is no afterwards. [With the absence of employment] we begin to feel sick . . . when you don't have a job, you don't want to leave the house, you begin to shut yourself up, and there are politicians who take advantage of that. We didn't want to talk with the proper authorities, we do respect them; I think that we clearly demonstrated that we are very respectful of the authorities. But at that time, we wanted the authorities to listen to the people, and that is what ultimately succeeded.

Asked about her days on the road and her children, Laura, in a very sweet and calm voice, replies, "I returned home and we cried . . . there was a lot of fear and uncertainty. It was the first time that we were shouting that we were bad . . . When the judge came and recused herself, we lost our fear. When the governor came, we demonstrated that we were a people without fear." Visibly moved, the conductor asks Laura about her thoughts concerning the solutions to the seemingly intractable problems affecting both communities. Laura, a week after the agreement promising even more things than those pledged during a tight electoral campaign, vents her doubts and hopes about life in a town that many think is destined to vanish after the privatization of YPF: "We don't foresee the solutions in a clear way. We had the word of a governor. I believe that in just a week Cutral-co changed . . . [we now have] a little bit of hope. We are waiting for solutions at the level of the national government. We are delighted with the reconnection of gas and electricity, with the bags of food that the government is sending us because we need them. But, what else? Because that's not all. In this [mobilization] we were twenty thousand people, and we were not asking [just] for a bag of food. We want long-term solutions. We want to have a future. I want to look at her [daughter's] face and tell her, 'You are going to [be able to] study.' And the same thing goes for these other two [sons]. Because a week ago, you would feel ashamed when looking at their faces, because we had nothing to tell them, nothing to promise to them, we knew that there was nothing [to expect]."

As we watch this video, Laura begins to cry. I myself feel strangely moved by the testimony of someone I just met but with whom I will become friends and learn to understand in the several weeks we spend together. Days later, I ask her about her emotions when first watching the program with me (it is the first time she has watched the video in more than four years): "I felt shocked, because I felt . . . how can I explain this? I felt it was my commitment . . . I agreed to be the means through which the picketers could express themselves. I was the vehicle, but someone else could have been in my place. Cutral-co needed a person through which it could express itself. And that was me." A month later, she returns to the meaning that her appearance in *Hora Clave* has for her: "In that program, I represented the people, saying that the town was in bad shape, that we needed solutions for the long term, solutions that allow us to plan a better future for my sons and my grandsons." In 2001 Laura thinks and feels pretty much the same way she felt that night on TV and the nights and days she spent sleepless in the road: "Cutral-co struggled for its dignity, for the dignity that comes with a job. I wouldn't change a word of what I said that night (on TV). . . . I am very happy with what I said that night, I feel good. I wouldn't change. If they interview me today, I would speak about the anger I have, because I kept waiting for the solutions, I thought they [the politicians] would react. I would speak about the cynicism of the politicians and the ignorance of the people. The people don't know about their rights and duties. In part, the failure of la pueblada has to do with the ignorance of the people. Because the politicians used the mobilization for their own purposes."

"In August, right after la pueblada, we received police information that a group of foreigners was coming to Cutral-co from Bahia Blanca [Buenos Aires], through Neuquén," the local public prosecutor, Santiago Terán, tells me in an interview in March 2001. "They were coming to the area with three tasks: first, to set 'Piturro' Aranda free. 'El Piturro' was in jail condemned for homicide. They were planning to break into the prison and set him free. He was the right hand of the local drug czar, 'El Chofa' Guzmán. The second task was to bring drugs into the city. And the third task was '*to kill Laura.*' At the time we didn't know who this Laura was, but after a little while, through intelligence reports, we learned that this Laura was Laura Padilla. Apparently she was upsetting the people with whom 'El Chofa' was working, and thus his task was to get rid of her. I immediately told her about this. Her reaction was: 'Why me?' We never knew why, but the truth is that she, Laura, was a very public figure at that time, and she was hitting hard with her words, with the things she said on radio and TV." Seeing my surprised and puzzled face, Santiago adds: " 'El Chofa' always worked for local politicians, he was raised by them and became their armed hand." Through a loyal thug, local politicians were, according to the public prosecutor, planning to get rid of the outspoken picketer.

"Laura is living large in a new house . . . working in a private school and making a lot of money," a local journalist tells me, "or at least that's what people say." This is hardly an isolated or idiosyncratic belief. Many residents with whom I talked in Cutral-co and Plaza Huincul (some of them former picketers) do believe that Laura is a sellout, that politicians gave her money and a well-paid job in exchange for her departure and silence. Laura herself is aware of this widespread belief: "People say that I took a lot of money and I disappeared." In a farewell letter she wrote me in March 2001, she states, "I don't mind being stained by politicians. From that rubbish, only rubbish can grow . . . I didn't do it for money. My dignity was at stake. And nobody fools around with my dignity. If someone else took some money, that's their problem, not mine."

The six nights in the road are, by all measures, an intense collective experience for Laura and her fellow picketers. They are doing something utterly new in the history of both towns and of their own lives. How do they make sense of it? The brief opening narrative condenses the main themes, or better, the questions I want to explore about the contentious episode as lived experience. How does Laura, a divorced mother of three, an underemployed private tutor with no history of previous activism (in fact, with a visceral disdain for anything political) become the "representative" of hundreds of picketers and, by extension, of the two towns? What impells her to the road in the first place? Who is this woman who speaks about unemployment as a matter of egoism and protest as an act of love and ends up presumably being a target of local thugs? Laura thinks of herself as a representative, a medium, a symbol of the picketers' concerns and demands. Why does she think about that agreement in such personal terms? How does Laura come to share with her fellow picketers a common definition of their predicament, and most important, of themselves? Who are these people who demand being seen and heard by the governor himself, who think of the protest in terms of a search for dignity? What is the nature of their claims? What events in the larger framework of these threatened towns and in the small worlds of protesters' everyday lives push people like Laura to stay on the road?

In the course of these seven days, protesters put forward a definition of themselves and of what the protest is about. But they are not alone in this process of boundary and meaning making. Authorities also seek to classify demonstrators and their actions—as it is manifested in the governor's speech at the Torre Uno. This war of words outlasts the protest and becomes one of its most important contentious legacies. "Who *were* the protesters?" "What *were* they shouting about?" Those are questions that begin to take shape as soon as picketers return home. What happened to Laura *after* this "historic day"? Why do residents in Cutralco think that she and most picketers are sellouts? How does the community remember the episode? Answering these questions implies not only exploring the background conditions of the protest but also tackling issues concerning the relational and dialogical making of a collective self-understanding, the biographical makeup of protest, and the impact that involvement in insurgency has on individual lives. It also entails an exploration of the process of memory making that begins with protest itself. As we will see, in this process, the spread of rumors about the picketers' postprotest actions plays a decisive role.

The following chapters ask how protesters make sense of protest, how they understand themselves and others, how one single protester (not a marginal one but the picketers' main spokesperson) gets involved and experiences this massive contentious event, and what the collective memories are of it. Chapter 1 reconstructs the day before the protest, paying particular attention to the immediate origins of the uprising. Here I focus on Laura's everyday life during the weeks before the protest and on the crucial role played by a prominent local radio station and by some local politicians in encouraging and facilitating the mobilization.

This chapter also looks at the larger background in which la pueblada occurred. Here I will focus on the ruinous effects that the privatization of the government oil company had on both towns. Particular attention will be given to the rise of joblessness and poverty. To understand Laura's involvement in the protest and the way in which she makes sense of it, chapter 2 examines her history of suffering, only in part linked to the rapid process of inmiseration. Her life story works as a sort of introduction to chapter 3, "Being-in-the-Road," the main chapter of this first part, devoted to a reconstruction of the experiences and self-understandings of protesters: What are they shouting about and against? How do they define themselves? Chapter 4 explores the aftermath of protest, with an eye on the spread of rumors about protesters and on the effects that the protest has on Laura's life.

In the reconstruction of the meanings that la pueblada has for its protagonists, I will use Laura's history (as expressed in her diary, her letters to friends and acquaintances, the notebook she carries during the seven days of the protest, the several conversations I have with her, and the life story we jointly record) as a narrative guide. In a sense, her story is emblematic of some of the ways in which the people of Cutral-co and Plaza Huincul experience the protest. However, her story has some particularities that I don't want to miss. They impinge on the way she lives the protest and, in particular, on the process through which she becomes first involved in a barricade and, later, the representative, "the symbol," of the picketers. Special attention will be paid to the themes that, present in her life as a mother of three children with a history of victimization by domestic abuse, and humiliation and stigmatization by the court system, reappear in her actions as a picketer. We will witness Laura's (not necessarily conscious) use of the elements learned in her everyday life to navigate (and make sense of) the protest. It would be impossible, I argue, to understand the reasons why Laura stayed in her picket and became one of its leaders without understanding Laura's history of domestic violence, the process by which, with the help of others, she breaks out of the circle of violence in which she was trapped, becoming deeply aware of women's subordination and marginalization. This sense of awareness is at the root of her decision to stay in the picket. In fact, it was out of a gender offense that she decides to stay to show "to that macho [in reference to a fellow picketer] that we women are not stupid." Her participation in the enterprise as a whole, I argue, can only be understood if we look at her history and at the interactions she has with a small group of people during the first days of the protest. This *continuity* between her life as a woman and wife and her life as a picketer is worth exploring at length because it is a window into the lived experience of the protest.

It is important to remark, however, that Laura's story does not exhaust the history of the lived protest. There are many aspects about which she is partially aware or that transcend the level of a single protester, no matter how important. Her story will thus be the guide, but not the only source, for my reconstruction and analysis. Along the way, I will open up her narrative to other voices and stories that, together with hers, coalesce in a collective lived experience of the protest. This will necessarily entail going deep into some aspects of Laura's life, as well as making some excursions into the lives of other key protagonists of this collective experience. The narrative follows pretty much the course of my fieldwork: armed with Laura's notes and insights, I follow some of the paths hinted at in those pages and interviews. They take me to her neighborhood, the Barrio 176 Viviendas; to interviews with her friends and neighbors; to conversations with two former mayors (Grittini and Martinasso), fellow picketers ("El Jote," Rubén, Daniel, Mary, Cecilia, and others), teachers, journalists, municipal officials, the public prosecutor (Santiago Terán); and finally, but not the least important in the history of the protest, to Justo Angel Guzman, "El Chofa," the man who presumably was on a mission to kill Laura, a man whom some called the local drug czar and others a native Robin Hood. As expected from this list of names, in the course of my investigation, the lines between the ethnographer, the friend, and the detective blurred in ways that could not have been predicted as I made my first trip to Cutral-co.

Chapter One

The Day before the

Pueblada: A Town

on the Edge

What follows is an edited version of Laura's diary covering the first day of the protest; the original version mixes past and present tenses (see figure 3):

Thursday, June 20, 1996. It was a normal day. I woke up early. My same duties were awaiting me. No work was forthcoming, but I had to go and wait for it. Everything was as usual. I had to go to court to check the paperwork for the child allowance I was claiming from my husband; that was tedious, tiring, humiliating. The only difference was that I had to get the boots so that my son could dance as a gaucho at school. Those were small details that, in some other economic condition, would make me feel proud. But I have to face all this wonderful stuff with a heavy weight on my shoulders. I don't have any money to enjoy it; and even the piece of cloth with the colors of the Argentine flag that my son has to wear on his arm is a problem. But there are so many things that I have to do during that day that I just don't want to think about them, I just do them.

That Thursday, I came back home earlier than usual from the house where I teach nobody (because people just show up to ask how much do I charge; since last year we lowered our fees so much that I feel ashamed; we cannot even buy a half a kilo of bread and two liters of milk). In the (rented) house where we teach, we don't have radio, and we cannot buy the newspaper, so I have no idea of what is going on in our town. Around 12:15 P.M., my neighbor Claudia knocks on my door and asks me, "Do you know about the whole mess?" "No," I

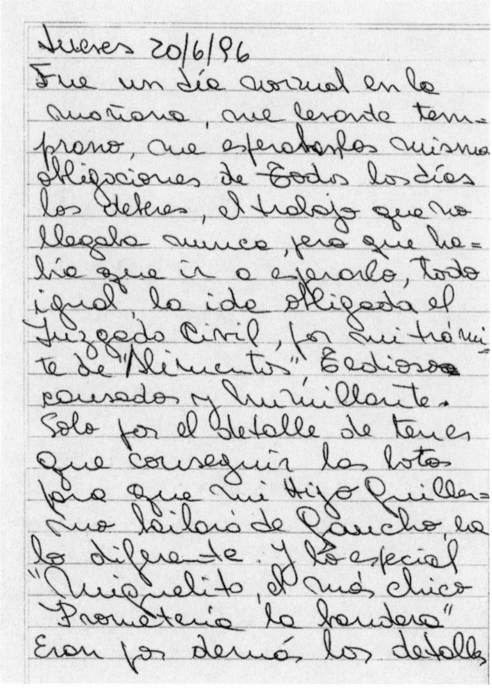

FIGURE 3.
Laura's diary.

reply, "What's going on?" "Turn on Radio Victoria and listen. They are going to block the (national) route."

"What? Why?"

"Because they won't build the fertilizer plant. The governor canceled the deal with Agrium."

"Bah! That's just another game of those on top," I told her, and tuned the radio.

I listened to the radio, but I didn't understand what was going on: "They will block the route, stores will close for the day." There were phone calls in which people vented all their anger, anger, a lot of anger.

I took care of my kids before they left for the school celebration [June 20 is "Flag Day"]. They were beautiful. Miguel was using his new school uniform. A neighbor procures the uniform from the store where she works; maybe I won't be able to pay for it, but I am happy, my kids are not suffering the misery that is tormenting me.

The party was terrific. I cried when I saw Guillermo dancing, and when Miguelito said the pledge to the flag. I took a lot of pictures. I was feeling fine; my kids were the prettiest. We had hot chocolate and went back home.

At 4 P.M., I went back to work, and there I met Jorge. He teaches math, and during the afternoons, we spend a lot of time drinking mate. With Jorge, his wife Susana, their two sons, I found a family. Jorge's parents [Maria Esther and Kelio] are marvelous friends . . . Jorge is my ally in good and bad times; he makes me feel I am not alone; I always need his words and his smiles . . . He works with me, and he is studying to become a math professor. That afternoon, we were talking about what was going on. He told me the history of Agrium, the fertilizer plant, the different factions within the governing party MPN, and all the things I had to know. He knows about these things because he was born and raised here.

As we were chatting, we began to doubt: should we open or close? The radio was clearly saying that what was going on was no joke. It was 6 P.M. when my daughter Paula came in saying that the mess was

Se entera del M.P.N: amarillos
y blancos.
"La movilización la organizaron
los blancos"; esa era la conclu-
sión o lo que había llegado.
Era por la planta de fertilizante
o por la banca, de haber perdido
es que en la provincia del Nqn
o sos blanco o sos amarillo.
no hay otra.
El gobernador es amarillo y la
novia es blanca.
En fin, hablaban de pobreza y yo
soy pobre. —
Amaneció el día 21/6; 9 hs salí
a buscar leche por mi barrio
después de varias horas de dor-
mir y no escuchar la radio,
soy pobre; pero jamás partici-
pé de algo así, mis padres me

for real, and that her classmates had gone to the road. "Everything is closed," she added before going back home to take care of her two brothers. "I will be there early," I told her.

When I went back home, I turned on the radio, and I listened to all the angry comments that the people were making, anger, a lot of anger: "Another political promise was vanishing." Unemployment, "Father YPF" was gone, hunger, nothing to do.

I went to bed with the radio at my side; by then I had begun to identify with that poverty that, although it has been part of my life for quite a long time now, I never thought about it, less so analyzed it. And I cried for the three years of solitude, the three years of efforts, of struggles for my three kids that are the only reason why I keep going, and going, and going; three years of fights against a humiliating court system, a system that humiliates those who have nothing . . .

That night I cried a lot . . . I am not well, that's the truth. And I cried and I identified with the comments that people were making on the radio. I didn't have a phone, and I fell asleep . . . This is the last

pataron; pero que haces, esto todo
cerrado,
Con una vecina charlamos y decidí
ir a la ruta, se publicitaban
grandes asados y medios para
ir gratis.
En fin, un día de campo, y
con esa mentalidad, marché
a la ruta, a comer un asado
con mis vecinos, todo gratis; qué
iba a pasar, si no iba dónde esto,
son los políticos.
"La radio" "Los mensajes y
la desesperación de un pueblo"
"todos a la ruta"
La realidad: Desocupación y pobreza. - Justicia - injusta -
¡¡"Pero, contamos rutas"!!
Mi realidad: Desocupación -
pobreza - injusticias - esa era mi
vida.

thing I thought: "If everything is closed, where will I buy the milk for my kids?" Maybe I thought that because the milk for my children is my only concern since I got divorced [July 12, 1993]. I don't recall at what time I fell asleep or what was the last message on the radio. I only knew that there were a lot of people in the route, that people were bringing food and clothing. And I also knew that I was not well, and that I was poor. I wanted to go to the road, but I couldn't leave my kids alone. I cried, I cried, I should be there in the road.

I am poor, with no possibilities, with no hope, thirty-six years old, alone, hoping that someone feels compassion for me.

The only things I have are those kids, my students. They taught me to love, trust, with their innocence, their simplicity, and their trust in me. All my income comes from the two students I have. I don't receive child support. That's why I cried and I said to myself: I am poor, I live in the poverty that other people have decided for me and my children. Unjust justice: they receive very big salaries, and they don't do anything for me. They steal under my name.

The radio was my only connection to the world surrounding me. Those messages, those angry cries, and the conversation I had with Jorge. The factionalism within the MPN: yellows and whites. "The mobilization was organized by the whites," I concluded that. The mobilization was because of the fertilizer plant . . . The morning of the twenty-first, I looked for some milk in my neighborhood stores, but everything was closed. I am poor, but I never participated in something like this, my parents would kill me [if I join in]. What shall I do? Everything is closed.

I talked to my neighbor, and we decided to go to the road. The radio was announcing big barbecues, and they were saying that the cabs were free if you wanted to go. In other words, it was like a day in the country, and with that mentality, I went to the road, to have a barbecue with my neighbors. Everything was free. What can go wrong? I was not going to the place full of politicians. The radio was saying: "Everybody to the road." The reality: unemployment and poverty, injustice. My reality: unemployment, poverty, injustice. That was my life.

On the Radio

There are many themes in Laura's pages that merit close attention and that I will explore later—the description of her daily concerns, her references to her humiliating dealings with the court system, et cetera. For the time being, let us concentrate on the key role played by one of the local radio stations, Radio Victoria, during that first day. Laura is certainly not the sole recipient of those radio messages. Early on June 20, Radio Victoria airs the cancellation of the deal between the provincial government and Agrium and "opens its microphones to listen to the people's reaction,"—as Mario Fernández, director and owner of the radio station, says. "In a way, the radio station called on people. We said: What should the people do? Stay at home or demonstrate? . . . We began receiving phone calls from people who said that what was going on was terrible . . . and saying that the people should participate . . . A neighbor called saying that the people should show their discontent. We got a lot of phone calls, and we aired them. We talked to the people, and the people told us what to do. They were talking about getting together and jointly expressing [their opinions] . . . Someone said that we should get together in the road" (quoted in Sanchez 1997, 9).

All my interviewees mention those radio messages as central in their recollections, not only in terms of the ways in which the radio calls on people but also in terms of the way in which Radio Victoria portrays the cancellation of the fertilizer plant project. On Radio Victoria, former mayor Grittini (who for years has been insisting that the plant would be the solution to the main problems affecting both communities since the privatization of YPF, providing hundreds of jobs, and marking the beginning of a new destiny for the community) and his political ally, the radio station owner and director, depict the cancellation of the deal with Agrium as a "final blow to both communities," as the "last hope gone," as an "utterly arbitrary decision of the provincial government."[1]

Daniel remembers that "there was a lot of anger . . . the radio said that we should go out and demonstrate, they were saying that it was the time to be courageous. I had a future to struggle for, even though I had nothing, I had my daughter. We have no skills, no studies, no nothing . . . I don't know whose decision it was to block the road. The only thing I know is that someone said that we had to blockade it . . . and people went out because there was need and hunger." "I learned about the blockade on the radio . . . they were talking about the social situation," Zulma says. Laura, Daniel, Zulma, and the rest point toward both the same framing articulator and its similar functions: the radio both makes sense of the "social situation" and persuades people to go to the road. Zulma and Laura also indicate another central actor in this framing process: friends and peers. In Laura's case, it is her beloved friend and coworker, Jorge; in Zulma's, her friends from the community center where she is working and the acquaintances she meets in the road: "When I went there with my friends, people began to tell us what was going on, why we were fighting, and saying that we could not afford to lose more jobs as we did when YPF was privatized. My girlfriends from the community center and I agreed that we were not going to go back to work until this thing was solved."

As the radio broadcasts "the ire that we felt," as Daniel explains to me, calling people to the Torre Uno on Route 22, cabs bring people there free of charge. Is this a sudden eruption of indignation? Are radio reporters and taxi drivers merely the first to spontaneously react? Hardly

so. Although the story of the spontaneous uprising has some accep-
tance among residents of both towns, many others privately acknowledge that a massive mobilization of resources was crucial during the
initial steps of the protest; the roots of this mobilization lie in the factionalism within the governing party, the MPN, and particularly in the
actions of the former mayor Adolfo Grittini. It is indeed a thorny topic
to raise, because it puts in question the story of spontaneity that residents proudly tell to each other and to me about the protest.[2] But even
those who deeply believe that the pueblada is an unprompted reaction
("because of the needs and the hunger") mention the word "politics"
when asked about their thoughts concerning the presence of possible
organizers during the first days of protest:

DANIEL: In the first picket, the one on the curve before the Torre Uno, we
were around thirty persons. Mattresses, food, coffee, and milk were
brought to us . . .
JAVIER: And who brought you all these things?
DANIEL: Well, maybe . . . politics . . .

JAVIER: Tell me a little bit about the first organization? Who decided
where to place a barricade?
MARY: I think that everything was coming from the top, it was all prepared. Because it was a big coincidence that everything took place
around the Torre Uno. But I have no idea who organized it or who
spread the first warning. But we saw (especially the first couple of
days) a lot of politicians . . . even so, I stayed there out of curiosity.

JAVIER: How was it all organized?
CECILIA: I really don't recall, but . . . I might be wrong, but I think politicians began. I went to the Torre Uno because my brother invited me,
that's all. But I know that politicians were the first to begin. At that
time, I didn't care because it was a just cause, it was for the people
who were in need. I didn't care whether politicians were or were not
around.

JAVIER: So, you, the picketers, were not the ones who decided to blockade the road . . .
JOTE: No, no, no . . . This was encouraged by one of the factions of the
MPN. There was a radio that promoted the whole thing. It was like
calling for a rally . . .

Many in Cutral-co agree that the impressive amount of resources mo-bilized during the first days of the pueblada can be traced back to the figure of Adolfo Grittini, who was waging a personal fight against his former ally and declared enemy Mayor Martinasso—a factionalism that, after the protest, escalated into a "festival of (mutual) bombings," as the public prosecutor explains to me, referring to the bomb attacks that politicians launch against each other from January to March 1997. In an interview that he prefers not to tape, "because the truth cannot be told to a tape recorder," Daniel Martinasso tells me: "Grittini backed the protest during the first couple of days. How? Well, in the first place, buying a couple of local radio stations so that they call people to the route." "Is it that easy to buy a radio station?" I ask him. "I myself paid Radio Vic-toria so that they broadcast nice things about my administration. The radio's reception area was built with the money I paid to the owner . . . that's how politics work in Cutral-co."

The efforts of Grittini and his associates (Radio Victoria's owner Fer-nandez being a key figure at this stage) do not stop there. Apparently he also sends the trucks that bring hundreds of tires to the different pickets and some of the bulldozers to block the traffic. He is also be-hind the distribution of food, alcohol, and cigarettes that circulate in the pickets. Although there is not firm evidence, many sources (not only Mayor Martinasso, who has obvious reasons to point the accusing fin-ger at him—after all, the protest is at the root of his later impeach-ment and destitution—but journalists, politicians, and picketers) indi-cate that, especially during the first two days, the major resources come from Grittini's faction. Some even say that Grittini pays fifty dollars per night to hundreds of young picketers and that his associates pro-vide them with wine and drugs. In a conversation I have with him in his shop, "El Chofa" Guzmán (if anything, an expert in local politi-cal dirty dealings) admits that this version is not far-fetched. After five years in jail for drug possession charges, he is on probation, and for obvious reasons, he doesn't want to give names. But during our two-hour talk, he tells me that the distribution of drugs and alcohol among young picketers is one, and not the most vicious, of the local ways of doing politics. The public prosecutor agrees with Martinasso and, curi-ously, given his personal animosity toward the man whom he publicly accused of being the "local drug czar," with "El Chofa." According to Santiago Terán, "Police information and the voice of the people, which is usually the wisest opinion, told me that Adolfo Grittini was encouraging people to protest against the social situation . . . there were political interests behind the mobilization, these interests told local merchants to support the protest with food, meat sausages, wine, milk, bread. . . ." Or as Laura explains to me: "Grittini is the owner of three of the four gas stations in Cutral-co and Plaza Huincul. That's why during the first days there was free gasoline, for everybody, but especially for cabs and buses. . . . Everything was free, gasoline, meat, milk, cigarettes, wine, firewood, everything . . . and everything in the route, in the pickets."

Videos and newspapers record Adolfo Grittini's presence among the protesters, mainly during the first two days of the protest. In a long interview, I ask him about his actions during those days in as many ways as I can possibly imagine. What I get is a firm vindication of la pueblada as a "spontaneous action in defense of what the town and the people deserve," but no admission whatsoever concerning the material support given to the protest. Furthermore, as opposed to his archrival at the time, Mayor Martinasso, Grittini does not acknowledge any connection between the factionalism within the MPN and the emergence of the popular mobilization. Much like his associate, radio station owner Fernandez, the former mayor insists on the spontaneous, sudden, and natural character of the revolt, (probably) to cover up what many informants told me are his (and Fernandez's) own significant organizational efforts, mainly during the first two days:

JAVIER: During my first days here, many journalists told me that I would not be able to understand this mass mobilization without figuring out what was going on within the governing party.

GRITTINI: No, no, no . . . that had nothing to do. The truth is that it had nothing to do with it, absolutely not. . . . When we saw that the government was not going to go ahead with the fertilizer plant, the people spontaneously took to the streets. It was a defense, it was a natural thing to do. It was something spontaneous that just happened.

JAVIER: So no one organized, no one was the first to mobilize . . .

GRITTINI: We might have had something to do with the mobilization, in the sense that we told what was going on to one radio. The media asked my opinions . . . Maybe we did mobilize, but just by saying: We have to defend our things. . . . I am not the father of the creature. I believe it was spontaneous; people just went to the road by themselves.

Later in the interview, I come back to the same theme, asking, "So did you call people to the streets during the first day?" His response is still ambiguous:

GRITTINI: No, no . . . I believe that I called the people, saying, "Let's go out and express our anger, let's go to the radio and tell the people what's going on."

JAVIER: Who started the first day?

GRITTINI: We began. People heard me on the radio. And I told them that the plant was not going to be built.

Whether or not Grittini's faction is behind it, the mobilization of resources and the framing process do indeed take place: the radio station airs its angry messages, telling people that "something has to be done" and calling them to go to the Torre Uno. Cabs drive people there and to the other barricades for free; tires are brought to the pickets; food, cigarettes, and other essentials are distributed free of charge ("We even get diapers for the babies!" Laura and other women recall). This mobilization of resources and this framing process (which I believe to be preconditions of the protest), however, operate not a vacuum but under background conditions that are ripe for a large-scale protest.

Inmiseration

But it is so cold in Cutral-co. They tell me once this land was in bloom, springs of childhood, fertility, oil and bread, oil and peace. Where have those yesterdays gone? An old lawless Mapuche said, watching the people go by, the neighborhoods fighting to survive, the children of those who will never leave . . . Happy days are coming back, a paper boy cries, he looks fifteen. He leaves me thinking, he asks me to believe, I look at the old Mapuche and I don't know what to do. And if I give it a try, and I stay . . . maybe I'll help. —SERGIO GARCÍA, "Mensajes de Invierno"

[E]mployment is the support, if not the source, of most interests, expectations, demands, hopes and investments in the present, and also in the future or the past that it implies, in short one of the major foundations of illusio in the sense of

involvement in the game of life, in the present, the primordial investment which
—as traditional wisdom has always taught, in identifying detachment from
time with detachment from the world—creates time and indeed is time itself.
—PIERRE BOURDIEU, *Pascalian Meditations*

Laura and I arrive at Mónica's house. They haven't seen each other for
about a year, and the reunion makes both of them cry and laugh at the
same time. As I make my way to the bakery at the corner, I suspect that
Laura explains to Mónica the purpose of my visit. When I come back,
Mónica plays a tape for me. "But it is so cold in Cutral-co . . . ," the song
says. As we listen to it, Mónica tells me:

> Sergio [the author of the lyrics] reflects the impotence I feel; it is a
> symbol of what's going on in the town. La pueblada happened be-
> cause of the needs, the misery, and because politicians were making
> fun of us. The whole town was there. Everybody went out to say, "We
> are fed up, we cannot take it anymore, we are dying of hunger, we
> want someone to listen to us, for God's sake." People said, let's die
> in the road, what difference does it make? Dying of hunger at home
> or dying in the road, shot by the military? That's enough, let's block
> the road!

Mónica is not alone in linking the uprising to the rapid impoverishment
of both towns. Laura, in her diary and in innumerable conversations,
and all of the people I talked to in Cutral-co and Plaza Huincul refer to
the generalization of unemployment and the related impoverishment in
the years prior to the protest. They also refer to the life *before* this rapid
process of decay begins, to the times when, as the song goes, "this land
was in bloom," that is, to the years before the government petroleum
company, YPF, around which both towns lived, is privatized, shedding
thousands of employees.

El Sol

Kelio and María Esther, the parents of Jorge (Laura's closest friend),
opened a bakery named "El Sol" in 1961. A registered nurse from Salta,
María Esther came to Cutral-co in the 1950s to work in the hospital
run by the Exxon oil company, by then the only hospital in the area,
where she met Kelio, who was working in the oil fields. Kelio quit his

job and, with the help of a friend, opened the bakery. For thirty years, El Sol was the town's main bakery, employing fourteen people (three at the counter, five bakers, five pastry makers, and one delivery boy), and using approximately 500 kilograms of flour per day to prepare the many rounds of bread. Nowadays the bakery is run by Kelio, at the counter, and Ricardo, one of his sons, working the oven and doing the delivery. They now use less than 150 kilos of flour, and the former site of the bakery is now a storage space for old and useless machinery and for the empty glass showcases that held "the cakes, the sandwiches, and the pastries" that used to be the talk of the town. "See how desolate this place looks?" María Esther asks me. Most of the bakery's production is now bought by the local state to supply its soup kitchens. "That helps us quite a bit," Kelio admits.

"Everything turned bad the year after YPF closed," María Esther asserts — and it is useless to insist on the fact that YPF did not, in fact, close down and leave town but simply, though significantly, changed hands. "We began to shrink, and see where we are now, a store this small. It used to be a store of eighty square meters. And now, you see, it's about sixteen square feet. We grew smaller . . . we didn't want to get rid of it because this is my husband's life . . . he used to go to the club, to hang out with his friends, but now he doesn't go because he needs money for that. You need to buy a drink, put some money down for the food, or sometimes invite everybody for a round. It's better to stay at home if you're going to be ashamed."

In their seventies, María Esther and Kelio have their house — the house where they lived for more than forty years, where they raised their sons and grandchildren, and where they generously put me up for more than a week — up for public auction because of an outstanding debt to the provincial bank: "I think we are going to lose it," María Esther tells me in frustration. She then sadly explains how she shut herself off from the rest of society, never venturing beyond her doorstep: "I don't go out because I feel ashamed; I became a hermit." It was to people like her and thousands of others that Laura was referring on the TV program *Hora Clave* when she said: "When you don't have a job, you feel bad, you feel sick . . . you don't want to leave your house."

State Retrenchment and Its Effects

Privatization generates efficiency and jobs . . . more investment, more wealth, and more jobs. —ROBERT UTT, Heritage Foundation

The lack of a future, previously reserved for the "wretched of the earth," is an increasingly widespread, even modal experience. —PIERRE BOURDIEU, *Pascalian Meditations*

In March 1941, in a letter to his parents, Juan Carlos Dominguez, a YPF oil worker, writes: "One sees YPF everywhere, even the car plates have the logo of YPF." His letters describe the harshness of life and work in Plaza Huincul, but also the economic well-being of workers and the attractions of life in the desert. In a letter sent in May 1941, he tells his parents: "This month's salary was not that great because I only earned $197.50." His total expenses, he describes, were around $121.33, "and without other news I enclosed a money order for $70." Even in a bad month, a worker could send more than one-third of his salary to his family (Saade 1986, 294).

Both Plaza Huincul and Cutral-co were born of, and developed through, oil activity. Since their inception in 1918 and 1933 respectively, both towns grew with the rhythm of (and became highly dependent on) the benefits provided by oil production and by the activities of the state oil company, YPF (the first government company, founded in 1922). With the discovery of petroleum in the area came its territorial occupation, and with it, settlement, everything carried out under the aegis of state action. The rapid population growth of both towns reflects the expansion of YPF's activities. From 1947 to 1990, the total population increased from 6,452 to 44,711, an impressive demographic growth by all accounts (Favaro and Bucciarelli 1994).

The state company provided not only jobs for its workers. True, the cradle-to-grave enterprise welfare of YPF benefited its workers with higher-than-average salaries, extremely good housing serviced by company personnel ("Anything that was broken in the house was fixed by YPF," I was repeatedly told by former YPF workers), access to a good hospital and health plan, and paid vacations ("Once a year, we had free plane tickets and two weeks in a hotel in Buenos Aires or anywhere in the country"). But it was the whole social and economic life of the region that was boosted by the presence of the state company. YPF did not merely develop productive and extractive tasks. The state company built entire neighborhoods and provided others with sewage and lighting. YPF also erected a local high-quality hospital, a movie theater, and a sports center and provided school buses that everybody could use. In other words, YPF "was everything for both towns: work, health, education, sports, and leisure" (Costallat 1999, 6). Even those who did not benefit directly from the company's welfare could somehow profit from its presence: the commerce and service sectors enjoyed the high purchasing power of state workers.

In less than two years, an economic system and a form of life that lasted more than four decades was literally destroyed. The privatization of YPF was passed as law by the National Congress on September 24, 1992, and soon enough the devastating effects were felt in the region. As of 1991, YPF had 52,000 employees. Toward the end of the following year, it reduced its personnel to 13,500. In the Administración Plaza Huincul, the cutback was even harsher: it went from 4,200 employees to 600 in less than a year (Favaro et al. 1997). Since privatization, YPF not only cut back its personnel. It ceased to be the welfare enterprise around which the life of both towns evolved (the company even moved its headquarters out of Plaza Huincul) and became an enclave industry run under strict capitalist guidelines: its emphasis on the extraction of mineral resources rather than on the exploration of new areas guaranteed record levels of oil production and profits in the years following privatization.

A new collectivity was born under the name of "ex-ypefianos," former employees of YPF who were laid off under the policy euphemistically called "voluntary retirements," financed by a loan from the World Bank. A group of those fired were close to the retirement age, and with their high pensions, they are the ones who now energize the local economy. It is said that close to half of the income generated in both towns now comes from the retired (Costallat 1999; La Mañana del Sur, 10 August 1996, 8). Although they are not part of the economically active population, their higher-than-average pensions support entire families in both towns. A second group of ex-ypefianos received their indemnifications and created small companies that serviced the now private YPF. As part of the oil deregulation program, these newly created companies managed by ex-ypefianos enjoyed a privileged relationship with YPF for a limited period of time, selling services and performing tasks that used to be carried out by its workers. After this period of time, usually one to two years, these new companies began to "compete" in the open market for the YPF contracts. With no expert advice and no training in the organizational, technical, administrative, and managerial aspects inherent in running a company, almost all of these newly founded enterprises failed. A few of them are still struggling to pay their employees a minimum wage.

A third group of ex-ypefianos took the money from their indemnifications and ventured into new terrain: self-employment. Suddenly, in a period of less than a year, both towns witnessed kiosks, bakeries, groceries, car-service stations, and video stores popping up on every corner in town. "Dozens of bakeries opened up in the course of 1992," María Esther recalls. This heightened competition together with the general impoverishment of the working classes of both towns sealed the fate of El Sol. The high salaries paid by the company to thousands of its workers (from fieldworkers to highly skilled personnel) were not there anymore, and as soon as the money from the indemnifications ran out, both towns began to feel the real consequences of the "modernization of the state," as national authorities called the privatizing frenzy. Approximately US$1 million ceased to flow within the commercial circuit annually, reducing by more than half the number of workers employed in the commerce sector. Although no demographic data are available for the year 2000, the dramatic decrease in the prices of housing stock (40 percent in 1997) should be an indication of the slow but sustained process of out-migration (Favaro et al. 1997).

"When YPF left, it was the end of the world," Saadia tells me over a round of mates, and her blunt opinion is shared by many in both towns. Headlines of the major regional newspaper captured this general mood as the first effects of privatization (not those anticipated by pundits such as Robert Utt, certainly) began to be felt in Cutral-co and Plaza Huincul: "Uncertain Future Awaits Cutral-co and Plaza Huincul" (*Río Negro*, 21 January 1992), "Alarming Unemployment in the Oil Region" (*Río Negro*, 6 May 1992). As massive layoffs were taking place, the articles described a "general feeling of uncertainty" about the beginnings of the process that is now in its mature form: hyperunemployment. In 1997 the economically active population of Cutral-co was 25,340. Of those, 30 percent were unemployed. More than half of the population of both towns lives below the official poverty line (Favaro et al. 1997, 17). Nowadays only 35 percent of those 7,408 are subsidized by federal or provincial "work plans," receiving an average of $150 per month. "There was," says Zulma, one of the coordinators of the local Employment Network (Red de Empleo), "a real increase in subsidies after the protest of 1996." However, in the last two years, she asserts, "both the total amounts of subsidies and the stipends have decreased." Most of the "work plans," as they are called, have to be renewed every three to six months. "And every time one plan is canceled, we have to bring two cops to the office because people get really mad, really violent . . ." As someone who herself has been a beneficiary of one of these plans, her comments should not be understood as a criticism of those subsidized. She understands better than anybody the terrible effects of unemployment: "Poor people fight against each other to get a subsidy . . . People come to ask for a subsidy in very bad shape . . . more so those who used to work at YPF."

"The struggle against Becoming a Ghost Town," the regional newspaper *Río Negro* headlined an article devoted to portraying the plight of Cutral-co on March 26, 1994. Among other things, the article describes the 30 to 40 percent decrease in the local commercial activity. "Now that YPF is gone, I don't think this town will disappear." This phrase was repeated time and again in my interviews and informal conversations. So much so that I began to think of it as something other than a hopeful diagnosis. It expresses the widespread concern of the residents of both towns about their bleak prospects.

YPF is, in fact, not gone (on the contrary, it extracts more oil than ever), but gone is the company that "gave life" to both towns ("oil and bread," as the song goes) and thus the idea of a future life in the area. For some, unemployment becomes indeed a modal experience; for those with no education and no skills (according to a report produced by UNQUI-based researchers, the local unemployed population is in a "highly critical condition" given the lower-than-average levels of education and the higher-than-average age), the future holds the hope of occasional employment for a limited period of time or access to a subsidy and a bag of food sent by the government through a food assistance program. As Daniel, who in his thirties has never experienced stable employment, tells me: "Cada tanto pinta algo [Every now and then, something comes up]. Fortunately we have the subsidy and the bag of food; without that, I don't know what I will do." Others, like Mary and her husband, oscillate between full employment and state assistance. She takes care of an elderly couple in exchange for a $150 subsidy; her husband is working under contract in a local transportation company. "But nobody knows what will happen with the company," Mary tells me, describing how her life has lately become a game of chance, "nothing is for sure." She shows me the box in which the provincial government sends her food once a month and sadly adds: "It is hard to get used to it. I was not used to receiving things. I worked all my life, this hurts your pride . . . but you have to leave your pride aside, and look for your son, he needs the milk, every day."

Others, who have stable jobs working in the educational system or in the municipality, fear not so much for themselves but for their offspring and for the future (or lack thereof) that the town has in store for them. As we listen to "Mensajes de invierno," Mónica describes with clarity and confidence what she wants for herself and her son—to finish high school and to go to college. Closely read, Mónica's words communicate the uncertainties that she, as well as many a resident, has:

> I don't think that the town will vanish, I am an optimist. . . . Listen to the song, it says: "And if I give it a try, and I stay . . . maybe I'll help." I want my son to stay here, I don't want him to leave. Where am I going to go? Why shall I leave? No! I formed a family here. This land gave me possibilities. The square witnessed my first encounters with my son's father. Cutral-co is the place where he was born. No, I stay. And you know that with my salary [$400 a month] you can hardly make it. But I stay here.

Leo, a high school teacher, summarizes this sense of a vanishing future deeply linked to the disappearance of work. He also illustrates the general feeling, present in almost every resident I talk to, of being the plaything of external constraints—a feeling, needless to say, that is rooted in the rapid process of inmiseration produced, almost a decade ago, by the retrenchment of the state, and now by official indifference: "I don't think that Cutral-co will disappear, but it will be a town of children and old people. Those who are old enough to work will have to leave, and they will come back to enjoy their retirement. I am sort of resigned to the fact that my sons won't stay here. As soon as they finish high school, they'll leave. It is a real shame when you have to leave because there is no other way."

In her diary, Laura speaks in very general terms about this poverty and hopelessness, about the widespread joblessness and misery. It would not be possible to understand the meanings that la pueblada has for residents and picketers without a grasp of the larger historical picture, that is, on the structural adjustment process and its local translation, the privatization of YPF. Although rapidly eroded by market forces, residents' historical experiences with decades of YPF welfare informed not only shared definitions of their present predicament but also their will to resist individually and collectively—as Mónica puts it when, with the song "Mensaje de Invierno" sounding in the background, she talks about her memories of a lost time, her determination to stay, and her understanding of la pueblada: "People used to live well here . . . I love each and every thing here. I have my roots here. I love this wind, this soil, because it is wind from the Patagonia. Cutral-co is my refuge, and I won't leave. The pueblada was all about this, about staying here. We won't move from the road because we are here to stay." Or as Rubén, a picketer, puts it less than a month after the June events: "I was there because I wanted jobs, that's all. I wanted to have a future, a certainty so that I could stay here, so that I don't have to leave Cutral-co" (*Tribuna Abierta,* 15 July 1996, 4).

Laura's diary also describes the deprivations of her life since the time of her divorce and the humiliations suffered at the hands of a callous court system. As crucial as the background structural conditions are to understanding the lived protest, they are not the sole source of the meanings that protesters ascribe to this massive mobilization. The emergence of the protest finds Laura at a very difficult moment in her life. It would be equally difficult to understand her participation in the protest without delving into her biography. It is now time to excavate and unearth the themes that I deem crucial in comprehending her contentious experience.

Chapter Two

Laura's Life: "How

Did I Fall So Far?"

After days of talking about the episode, I ask Laura about her previous experiences of collective action or of road blockades. She denies any prior activism and links her involvement to her own life "in jail."

LAURA: I had no knowledge whatsoever, no prior experience. I was living on another planet. I read about protests by public employees or unions in the newspaper, but that was something that was very far away from my own life. Don't forget that you are speaking with a woman that . . . I always say that I was living in a jail. Domestic violence doesn't allow you to think. Being at home was like being in jail; I couldn't even go to the grocery. I changed my life when I got divorced. The person with whom you are speaking lived two lives, one in complete darkness, the other one was a very white light. When I began to teach private lessons, I became surrounded with kids; they were the light of my life, the happiness . . . There are many things that marked my life.

The pages of Laura's diary speak about the general conditions of unemployment and poverty but also talk about her own suffering, her own poverty since the time she divorced in July 1993. Those were three years "of solitude, efforts, and struggles," years of a lopsided fight "against a humiliating court system." Her participation in la pueblada is directly linked to these three preceding years, to the things she learned during that "awful time," and indirectly to her whole life. Her decision to stay on the road and her actions, thoughts, and feelings during those days (even her decision to quit the struggle months after the episode) are deeply informed by some crucial moments and issues in her life, "marks," as she puts it. Therefore, before delving into the process through which she becomes first a picketer and then a "representative and symbol," we need to explore these elements of her life.

The following reconstruction of her life story is based on more than twenty hours of taped interviews, and innumerable conversations and letters. To guide the reader toward the several sociologically relevant features present in Laura's story, I have added headings taken from phrases in the interview. I do not believe that her story "speaks for itself"; the reason why I decided to keep the story in "her own voice" stems not from the "spontaneistic illusion" (Bourdieu 1999, 621) that supposes that actors' voices convey their own truth but from the conviction that the way of telling the story is part of the story itself. The criteria used for the reconstruction of Laura's life combined those provided by the story itself (those to which Laura dedicates more thought and time) and those that I deemed central to understanding her plight. A childhood dominated by strict parents, a violent marriage, a tortuous divorce, and unending dealings with the court system are the main themes that unfold in her life.

"I Left the Jail of My home for That of a Husband"

Laura Padilla was born in General Roca, Río Negro, forty-four years ago.

> I grew up almost without a father. I was one year old when my dad started to work at YPF, and I was nineteen when he quit and my daughter Paula was already a year old. I lived all of my childhood and my adolescence without a father because mine went to work at the seismography work site, and he came home only on weekends. My father never joined the MPN, nor the union, and for this reason he suffered a lot with [Governor] Sapag. They kept moving him around, never giving him a permanent post. I grew up in a family where politics was a prohibited topic. The politician, in my house, was [considered] a dirty fellow. I don't like politicians. . . . My mother raised us with all the love in the world, but she wouldn't let us live [our lives], she wouldn't let me go out, she didn't permit me to have friends. She locked us up in the house, she took and brought me home from school, she didn't like my friends, she didn't like that I would go out,

she didn't let me go to the disco because it was for whores . . . I left the jail of my home for that of a husband. . . . To be married was to be in jail . . . I got legally married to Juan at age twenty-four. But prior to that I had had the baby girl at eighteen with a boyfriend with whom I refused to marry; my family never forgave me for it. I was with my mother and father until I got married, but it was like the stain remained on the family. Since I was a little girl I understood I had to have a husband and a home, this was the command. And Juan had gotten that same message. I believe that we loved each other; what we didn't realize was the sort of relationship we were going to have. I had never lived anything like the life of a beaten woman or an abusive man. Never. My father, never . . . It also had a lot to do with him never being at home. The little that I saw of my parents' relationship was all love and peace. For me matrimony was those weekends. I idealized marriage a lot. With my husband we had differences from the first day. During the engagement I had fought a lot to have a house, to have comforts. We both had good jobs. I worked at the Caja de Subsidios Familiares. I had a good salary as a public employee. My husband worked at a construction company, and apart from that, he was studying to be an accountant at the university in Neuquén. From the first moment the relationship was very bad; the first day we entered our house, after getting married, my husband told me, "Pick in what 50 percent you are going to live, because 50 percent is yours . . ." That day I found out that for the two years we had been building the house, it had bothered him, because in his family the tradition is that the house is always in the man's name, the woman's name doesn't appear in writing. These are trifles (stupidities), but . . . And later the violence, the violence was almost immediate. When I got married he gave his name to my daughter Paula. It was like I had to say thank you every day. Those were the messages from the first months of being married. It was as if he had committed an act of great heroism by giving his last name to a child that was a bastard. My first separation was due to my father calling me because he was out of sorts. I asked for permission to leave, and Juan ordered that I return in a taxi, and that my father not bring me home. When my father brought me back, he threw the freezer over there in the street. I remember that it was snowing, and I was in my nightgown with the baby. It was nighttime. I separated from him. Since I was working, I filed for divorce. I was already five months pregnant. In the first months Juan was very interested in the pregnancy; since that day he kicked me and threw me out of the house, with more than fifty centimeters of snow, he disappeared. I had to start a court proceeding; right away the judge decided about the house. They gave me the chance to return home, when I returned, a girl I worked with went with me, the house was completely empty, he had taken everything, only the walls remained. I organized the house as much as I could, Guillermo was born, my husband didn't appear. The first meeting with the divorce judge was for the twentieth of March, 1985. I had lots of witnesses, although I didn't know much about the laws. We had many witnesses who'd seen him when he was ready to fight, when he was threatening me and the baby. At one point, a neighbor saw him with a pistol to my head. All of this because I didn't obey, things like going to my mother's house without his permission. Or because she had come to visit me and had taken Paula to visit with her. Since he had put his last name, neither the baby nor I could have relations with the Padilla family. I had to visit my mother-in-law every day, one ate lunch at home but every day one had to eat at the home of my mother-in-law. I hated that. Before the first divorce proceeding, Juan comes to ask forgiveness, he hugs the baby, and I super in love tell him yes. So I went to court and said I didn't want to separate from him. The witnesses all went back home, all of them believing that I'd made the worst mistake of my life; but he was there, who was my husband, the father of my children. We had a more or less good relationship for a year, until he decided to have another child . . . well, I mean to say, it was a relation without blows, full of trips to the beach, to the mountains, we went out almost every weekend. Until he wants another child, he plans it, he selected dates, figured calculations, looked over doctors because he wanted a son on the sixth of June, which was his birthday. And the calculations gave him August as the time he had to plant the seeds. Thus we went four months without having sex because he was saving himself in order to make a male. Already in September of 1986 I was pregnant. In December he resorted to the blow once again, for whatever thing bothered him. On top of all of this, during that good period with him, I did not see my parents, or my friends from work. I worked, but I was prohibited from talking with my coworkers, a thing with which I complied. They never understood what was happening to me. When they would come up to talk to me I would tell them that I couldn't because I was going to have problems. I went around isolated. As the pregnancy went on, I resigned because my husband said that with three children I would not be able to work, that it was going to become bothersome, that my job wasn't necessary because we were fine. Therefore I resigned in November; when I cashed my salary I bought myself a sewing machine and a washer—that one I have there. And he got mad because of that, because I didn't want a regular washer, but a good one that did everything . . . he got mad and we went almost a week without him buying food, he wouldn't buy milk, nothing for the children. I protested one night, it was very hard, it was an act of courage. He turned around and left. I was alone again, with the pregnancy, and I wasn't working anymore. No one would pay attention to me. It was terrible, until in May Miguel Angel was born. I had to go back to my mother, my mother lived reproaching me, saying I was a *tarada*, an idiot, that the one to blame was me . . . My father never existed, he was like a mute. This is how Miguel Angel was born. I had started a proceeding for food quotas . . . these were my first fights, they treated me extremely bad, little more than calling me a *boluda*, a stupid, that how could I fight with someone who had that income. I complained about visitations too, because he started coming at night, he would throw stones on the metal sheets of the roof, and he wanted to come in the house. One day he broke all of the windows. The children and I were in the hallway very frightened. At the first meeting about visitation they treated me like shit, like someone immature, like everything you can imagine. I even have a report from a psychologist that says that at first I would have a good disposition, but at the end of the conversations it was always me that caused problems because I didn't want him to enter the house to visit the baby. The judge resolved that Sundays the father had an hour to come to the house, whether I liked it or not, because the house was in both of our names, because we didn't have a separation of goods, and furthermore because I could not break the relationship between father and son. The first Sunday that came, I prepared the bottle for Miguelito and left him alone in the dining room. My neighbors didn't want to stay with me anymore, I didn't have a single person who wanted to keep me company. I couldn't leave the house by itself either because I was afraid he would set himself up and I wouldn't be able to get him out again. Nothing happened the first Sunday; the second Sunday, I did the same thing. I prepared a bottle for the baby and left him alone in the dining room. I went out to the bedroom, and he came behind me, and he was carrying the gun in his belt, and he put the gun to my head and said he was going to kill me because this wasn't a life for either of us, he would kill me and himself. And I vowed and swore an eternal love. And that I wanted him, and that I loved him, and I convinced him that I loved him. That is how we came to have sex that night, and he put the gun on the nightstand, I am never going to forget because I didn't sleep all night, looking at the gun. He wouldn't let me leave even to check on the baby who was in the cradle. It was horrible. The baby fell asleep in the cradle in the kitchen and Guillermo fell asleep in the bedroom, alone, without us checking on them. The next day he brought his clothes and started to live with me. . . . I was terrified, I was terrified, for myself, for the children. I believed he would kill us all that night. And besides it surprised me because he came calmly. I generally could recognize him because he would blush a lot, and he wasn't blushing. When he returned, I changed into a well-dressed and silent married woman. We had two cars; I never learned how to drive. I was a housewife. He was happy because I was the one who would cook, attend to the children, be at home all day; he went out to work all day, and I was there to prepare mate when he got up. He, in this way, started to be happy.

"Mine Was a Very Violent Story"

Juan got work at a business in Cutral-co . . . he did well at the company, and we decided to move. He said that in General Roca we had problems with his parents and mine. He decided; I didn't decide anything, as if I didn't exist. During those days there were always beatings. In order to give you an idea: we had eaten ice cream that I had prepared, and two spoonfuls were left over. I, cleaning the kitchen, decided to make more ice cream, and what was left from the other the kids ate. When he came back at four in the afternoon, the ice cream I had prepared wasn't ready, so he asked me for what was left from the night before. I told him that the children had eaten it. You don't know the beating he gave me. And he grabbed all the ice cream containers, there were around thirty, and he scattered them all over the house, in the living room, armchairs, beds, all over the house. And afterward he left. And I was cleaning. The only thing I did was to cry and clean. Until one day he struck me and I fell into the freezer and passed out. Paula and Guillermo went out, believing I was dead, to look for the neighbors. But my children didn't say that "Dad had hit Mom," rather that Mom had fallen. So he went along with a neighbor who was driving, because he said that neither of the two vehicles was running. He takes me to the hospital, and he says to the doctor that I was hysterical, nervous, and that I always fell. And the doctor came close to my bed, caressed my forehead, and said to me, "I believe you, *gorda.*" That was all. I didn't speak. Later I found out that the doctor told Juan that if he didn't bring me back at 3 P.M. the next day he would file a domestic violence complaint. I didn't even know what domestic violence was. The doctor put me in contact with social services at the hospital. It was the first time in my life that I trusted someone. At hospital services, a social worker told me not to lie anymore, that they already knew that my husband had hit me, that I had not fallen, and that they were offering me the chance to change my life, but it was going to take me many years, that I would have to have psychological therapy. And I argued with her, because I had been to psychologists, and besides don't forget that we went to mass every Sunday and I confessed to the priest that my husband beat me. The priest told me to pardon him and pray for him. Even more, he gave me penance; it was me that ended up praying two Our Fathers and three Ave Marias. And there I started to go to the groups, but I didn't tell the truth to Juan. Because he came at 4 P.M. from the business, and I had groups Wednesdays from two to four. . . . When I started to go to the groups, one of the things I tried to do was to begin to drive, that was my greatest freedom. I told him that I wanted to learn to drive because we already had two cars, I wanted to take the children to school. My husband controlled everything, I didn't have friends, they were his friends. A jail. To avoid my learning to drive, he decided that we'd move within a half block of the school . . . I wanted to learn to drive; for me it was ridiculous to have two cars and me having to walk on foot. In reality there was no need, I didn't even do the shopping. I was inside the house, unless we all went out together, the perfect family. We all went shopping together, radiating happiness. Here I got sick, I couldn't walk, my legs gave out on me. I started with treatments for anemia, it was already 1991, and little by little I stayed in bed, to stay more in bed, my legs gave out on me, it was fatigue, exhaustion . . . Juan treated me like a vagrant, an invalid, as if I wasn't good for shit. I began to stay in bed, sometimes losing consciousness, hours would pass without me knowing what happened . . . In this way two years of my life passed. The last year I couldn't even get up to go to the bathroom. I was unbelievably fat. . . . What I had was a thyroid problem, but I had been diagnosed with anemia. When I had one foot in the coffin, a female doctor at the hospital who was replacing the doctor who always attended to me saw the problem and gave me some hope . . . I started treatment for the thyroid June 12, and by July 12 I was already separated from Juan. . . . I knew from the women's groups that the serious illness that I had was domestic violence. Ideas from these talks had stayed with me. Mine was a very violent story, I decided to live . . . And I began to have talks with my husband, and to tell him that things were going to change. And he said to me, "Yes, because you are going to be able to get up, cook, be with the children." And he didn't pay any attention to me, he didn't understand what I was saying to him. What I wanted to change was the way he treated me. It was the dealings we had as a couple. I was realizing that for him I was going to continue with my life of humiliations, of washing dishes, washing floors, having food on schedule, to live cooking. That was my change for him. And for me it was something different.

"If I Have to Look for a Bruise, I Go"

One night, Laura escaped with Paula from the house, looked for her other two sons, who were staying with Juan's mother, and left the three of them in General Roca with her own mother and father, *los Padilla*, with whom she had not had contact for years "because Juan forbade us to visit them." Laura then returned to Cutral-co, and another ordeal began, this time with the irrationalities and humiliations of the court system.

> I returned to Cutral-co, and I went directly to the courts. A secretary of the judge told me, "Laura, you don't have a bruise. You abandoned your home. You are not going to have a right to anything, and forget the custody of your children." And I asked her, "What is it that I have

to do? Look for a bruise for myself?" "At the least," she told me, "a bruise." I thought, "I have had millions of bruises, today I need one and don't have any." I remained taken with the fact that the first thing I would lose would be the custody of my children and that the one to blame for that happening was me. Therefore I said, "If I have to look for a bruise, I go." I went to look for a taxi, I called Juan, I told him that I needed some of the children's things. . . . I went into my house and said to Juan, "Get me three glasses, three plates, three cups, three sets of silverware, three chairs, three beds, I'm taking a television with me." He started to get mad, each time more flushed, more furious . . . At one moment, I went to the bedroom, and he grabbed me around the neck and pressed on my throat, very typical of the beater. He lifted me in the air. And I said to him, "Let me go, now." And when he let go of me, I started asking him again, "Three sets of sheets, three blankets, three . . ." When I was in the baby's bedroom he threw me a punch, if it had hit me I wouldn't be telling this to you. I still felt the air (from it) that passed by my face. In the groups I had learned that one of the ways to defend oneself is to scream, that provokes shock and they stop hitting you. I left screaming in the middle of the street, I was screaming, "He hit me, he hit me." The neighbors called the police. I screamed so much. It was not the first time he had hit me, but it was the first time I was reacting in this way, and that the neighbors called the police for me, yes, it was the first time. They had the image of a perfect marriage, we went out as a family, everyone together. The loving father taking the children to school, watering the little plants, the loving wife brewing mate, that was the image they had. The neighbors called the police, but they never thought it was because he beat me. And something like five police cars came. For this, I continued taking things because I didn't have the bruise yet. I had it recorded that I had to have the bruise; but I didn't have it. I came in looking for him to hit me, with all of the fear that he would really hurt me. When the police arrived, there were like twenty of them, they came in, I crouched and crawled through their legs, and left Juan inside the house. I returned to an aunt's house with whom I was staying, I got in bed and went to sleep. I got up at 4 A.M., without knowing what to do. I went to make a complaint, but I didn't have the bruise. And I said to myself, "I am going to make an accusation . . ." Juan was an important person in the community. Fifteen minutes after I announced that I was going to make a complaint about beating, he appeared at the station. The same police had advised him. And Juan said to me, "Quit fucking around, let's go home." And me, "No." I wanted to make the complaint in front of an official. And he was telling me to stop being ridiculous. When the official got to me, the only thing I had was a grazing that one of the boots of the police left on my forehead [when I crawled through their legs]. I wanted them to have a doctor examine me so that the official didn't examine me . . . in reality I wanted to delay everything because I didn't have the bruise. I had to wait, this made it like eleven in the morning. When the forensic doctor comes, the thing became ugly to me because he wanted to examine me. It was the first theatrical performance of my life. The doctor came closer, and I yes remember what it is to have a blow to the head. The pain that it provokes in you when they scrape your hair. That I knew. "It hurts," I was telling him. It was three hours until he signed a certificate of slight lesions for me. Already tired. With the certificate, I returned, and later with enough insisting I made the legal complaint . . . I knew from the groups that the complaint is the limit that they put on the beater . . . it is so that they investigate his behavior.

"What Happened to Me in My Life? How Did I Fall So Far?"

Laura wanted to get her husband out of the house so that she could live there with her three children. But the court secretary told her that having reported domestic violence was not enough. "They informed me that a whole investigation was required. I got really mad. After everything I went through. . . ." During a week, she spent whole days going from the court building, to the real estate office who had the lease on their house, and then to her own house where, in front of everybody, she rang the bell and shouted to Juan, "Leave the house now, go away!" A week later, she received a call from Juan's lawyer with the news: her husband was leaving the house. When she went back, her husband had taken every single valuable object from the house and broken the things he couldn't take with him. As soon as she got her house back, she went to General Roca in search of her children.

My children's clothes had all remained with my mother-in-law, but I had boxes with their baby clothes. Thus I went to Caritas [Catholic Church Charity Organization] and traded the baby clothes for clothes in more or less their sizes, with that I started to manage. Juan called me on the phone saying that we had to talk. My neighbor was helping me financially. Her son was my first individual student; she paid me fifty pesos. This same neighbor took charge of bringing me another student. And Juan who was calling me every night . . . When it was past seven or eight at night, and Juan wasn't calling me, I was scared because he could come. I had big armchairs, with a table, we would put the table and armchairs, fastening the doors, and with the chairs fasten other doors, because the experiences of other separations when he would try to enter the house at night had stayed with me . . . It was terror. When Juan would call it was that I had gone to sleep calmly because I knew he was in General Roca. . . . Juan would threaten me over the phone, "When I leave I will kill you, be careful when you cross the street because I kill you."

Laura had no income with which she could afford the $500 rent. The owner's lawyer sent an eviction letter. She thought she could find refuge with the local ombudsman. "He paid no attention to my problem, saying that they were overwhelmed with other cases. But the fact is that the ombudsman knew Juan personally. A month and a half went by and nothing happened. I was so mad that, following the advice given to me in the women's group, I made a formal accusation against him." Meanwhile the eviction process advanced, and Laura went to see the owner's lawyer in person. She remembers her first meeting with him: "The first day the lawyer told me that he was tired of women carrying all their children around, that the only thing these women know is how to screw up other people's lives, that these women are trouble, much like the one who cut that guy's penis [referring to Lorena Bobbit]." Laura knew that this was her chance to obtain a house from one of the public housing plans. Nasty as he had just been to her, this lawyer was, she had been told, a very well connected figure. In a town where most public goods (a house in the projects, a subsidy for the unemployed, a bag of food) are obtained faster through personal relations, it took him one phone call to solve both his client's and Laura's problem. A month later, Laura moved to the newly inaugurated housing project Barrio 176 Viviendas.

"When I first saw the house I was going to live in, I cried for three nights in a row. For me, that neighborhood was a slum. The house didn't have floors, no appliances, no heating, no nothing . . ."

She began to teach private lessons to high school children in her house until, with the help of the father of one of her students, she was able to rent a place in the center of the town where, together with her friend Jorge, they opened a private institute.

> In all of the separation process, going to the domestic violence groups, I learned about the cycle of violence, I learned about the honeymoon period which is when the beater repents and the woman has hope again, believes again that the story will change, that everything is going to be different, I learned how the beater goes along accumulating tension that ends with an explosion . . . I also realized what happened in one of the reconciliations, the time he put the gun on the nightstand, that was rape. I took a long time to overcome it, it gave me a shock, it was like taking on being a single mother, with all the violence that signifies, abused woman, with all the humiliations, and on top of all that a rape. It took me a long time to process that; I cooked and would cry, I went to take a bath and would cry, or I went to go to sleep and would cry. I had to go to psychologists all over again, because it was something that, after being in groups for a long time, I asked again: What happened to me in my life? How did I fall so far? How did I fail to defend myself? I wouldn't forgive myself for it. Until, little by little, through conversations, the groups . . . I discovered that there were others who had been through the same.

By June 1996 Laura was barely making ends meet, as she describes in her diary. She was suing her husband to obtain child support, but without a private lawyer, the lawsuit was making little, if any, progress. She was also trying to recover the house that they had in General Roca. Her plans were to obtain the house that her husband was renting to a third person, and move back to the middle-class neighborhood in General Roca with her three children. These were her worries on the morning of June 21 when she listened to Radio Victoria broadcasting the angry comments of the residents of Cutral-co; they were speaking in terms painfully familiar to her: poverty, unemployment, hopelessness, injustice.

Chapter Three

Being-in-the-Road:

Insurgent Identities

There's a kid out in the open, out on route 22, looking innocently at what he cannot understand, a rock like a toy, that smoke's not from his train, today he's not playing on the corner by the garage. There's a kid carrying hopes, out on route 22. He won't say a thing, pain will speak for him, today he won't be writing his name on the blackboard, today he won't have a snack in the cafeteria, today he won't hear his father head out early to work, today a kid went out on the road, and sat down in the middle, to wait.—SERGIO GARCÍA, *Bajo el cielo un niño*

We, the kids, on the road, we had no education, no skills, but we saw the hardship with our own eyes.—DANIEL

The subject is not in the world in the way in which an intrinsically-describable object is contained in another, like water in a glass, for instance; rather the subject is in a world which is a field of meanings for him, and thus inseparably so, because these meanings are what make him the subject he is.—CHARLES TAYLOR, "Embodied Agency"

"*Che*, this is no joke. There are very well dressed people in the crowd," an old gendarme comments as the approximately two hundred soldiers from the Gendarmería Nacional approach the twenty thousand residents standing at the Torre Uno. Without knowing it, the gendarme is making an important sociological observation about the composition of the crowd. The twenty thousand protesters include "well-dressed people," that is, middle-class residents, together with the poor and unemployed. And so it is "no joke": a protest that goes beyond the repressive capacity of those two hundred soldiers, not only because of the sheer numbers but also because of the target's diversity. The available evidence proves the gendarme right. More than half of both towns' populations are awaiting the soldiers on the morning of June 25, among them poor people from the infamous 500 Viviendas and well-to-do residents from the city center.

Laura recalls that "in the pickets, you had a poor mother with her kids, workers who had been laid off from YPF, the unemployed, the subemployed, but you could also find teachers, professors, doctors, lawyers, accountants, salespersons, housewives. In each picket, it was all mixed." Cecilia agrees with Laura's description: "The whole town was at the Torre Uno . . . people with jobs, shop owners, workers . . ." This heterogeneous crowd awaits the gendarmes passionately singing the national anthem ("I never sang the anthem with so much emotion and pride," Cecilia remembers) and chanting, "If this is not the people, where's the people" and "The people united will never be defeated." They are also cheering, "Cutral-co and Plaza Huincul!" and shouting, "Sapag, come here!" As the troops of the Gendarmería move closer, the federal judge who is in command tells a couple of picketers who are in the first barricade that she wants to talk to some representatives: "There are no representatives here," they tell her. "The people are here . . . come and talk to the people." Jote, a picketer, tells her, "There are not thirty crazy demonstrators out there, there are not forty subversives, it's the people." "The judge and the gendarmes," he tells me, "were really scared."

Four years later Laura, implicitly referring to many popular interpretations of the pueblada, tells me, "To say that this was a protest carried out by the unemployed or the excluded is to make a wrong reading of what was going on. All the *pueblo* was there."[1] Laura's reading of the protest was (and still is) shared by the residents of both towns. During the seven days in the road, protesters tell reporters, "We want jobs. We provide the gasoline, the oil, the electricity, and . . . is this the pay we get? We want Felipe [Sapag] to come here. The whole pueblo is here. There are no politicians here. The people are here!" Years later, participants in la pueblada tell me: "We wanted Sapag to come here, to see us, to see the people. Everybody was there, the whole town."

This crowd defined itself as united ("The whole pueblo is here"), numerous ("We are thirty thousand, not five thousand"), committed to one goal ("We want jobs. We want Sapag to come here and give us a solution"), worthy ("We provide the gasoline, the oil, the electricity, and . . . is this the pay we get?"), and lacking leaders ("There are no politicians here"). Both in their ways of referring to themselves and in the crowd's social composition, that is, in its discourse and in its social relations, the protesters put forward a participatory identity that goes beyond that of "the excluded, the unemployed, or the poor."[2] They are, for themselves and for those who are in charge of their repression, "the whole people."

This insurgent identity does not just happen; it is a collective and contentious construction.[3] During their six nights and seven days in the road, protesters make incessant efforts to define themselves, voicing who they are and, just as important, who they are not. Exploring how this collective self-understanding comes about is crucial to getting closer to the protest as lived experience, to understanding the experiences of their ways of being-in-the-road, the modes in which protesters make sense of la pueblada. I will approach the road as a field of meanings following mainly Laura's path but also exploring the actions and sayings of some of the most prominent picketers and some other residents. How does Laura get involved in the protest? How does she become a representative? How does she come to share a collective identity with the rest of the fellow picketers? How does this sense of we-ness inform her and the others' actions on the road? Last, but hardly least, how are her actions and experiences linked with her story of suffering and victimization? And how is this collective experience rooted in the towns' history and current plight?

A Day in the Country

It came as a surprise to me that Laura, the "symbol of la pueblada," "the (nationally known) picketer," at first did not attend the road blockade as a way of manifesting her discontent. After she gets the milk for her three children, she tunes to Radio Victoria to follow the news. "In the pickets, they were asking for grill broilers. They didn't have enough of them to cook the incredible amount of meat, chickens, and *chorizos* they had. Someone later told me that everything was sent by Grittini. And so there I was, at home, and I told my neighbor: 'What a boring day! What if we go to the road to have a barbecue? With the grill I have, we will be able to get into one of the groups.' " "Life was so tedious in Cutral-co," Laura says, "going to the road blockade was like an excursion." By now Laura is aware of the political character of the protest. Yesterday her friend Jorge told her that the factionalism within the MPN was behind the demonstration. "I had needs, that's true. But that was my story. My story would never become associated with anything political. Politicians were in the road blockade at the Torre Uno. I would never go there. I went to a less important barricade, with fewer people, and lots of food."[4] Laura's distrust of politicians is deeply informed by her biography. As we saw, her father was "screwed up by politics; they kept sending him all over the province, to different places, because he was not a party or union member"; and she grew up in a family where everything political was considered dirty. More recently, in her job as a private teacher, she learned more about the dark side of local political life: "Most of my students were the sons of local politicians and officials. Their families were breaking apart; parents didn't pay any attention to their kids, they were on drugs; their parents would buy them expensive stuff but not listen to them . . ."

Although she knows where she doesn't want to go, except for the radio, Laura has no way to know about the other four main barricades that are rapidly isolating both towns from the rest of the province. "Through the radio, I find out that in Añelo they are in need of grill broilers. That's nineteen kilometers from home. Taxis take you there for free. And so I go there, to have a barbecue, to spend a day in the countryside with my children."

Rubén, who will later become one of Laura's fellow picketers, also avoids the Torre Uno and goes to the blockade in Picún. "Because I live nearby, and I said to myself, 'The Torre is full of politicians, *todos los rosqueros.*' There were people I didn't trust, union leaders, politicians, activists. . . ." Mary shares with Laura her initial lack of awareness concerning what the protest is about: "I didn't go to the Torre Uno because it didn't call my attention . . . I don't know, when we were in the cab, the driver said that Añelo needed people. I didn't know the place, but the driver told me that it was close. And so we went there . . . I went there to drink some mates in the countryside."

"We arrive at Añelo around 10:30 A.M. with my neighbor. There are close to two hundred people," Laura explains to me. There she sees that the barricades are not just one but two, one blocking State Route 17, the other blocking the entrance to the YPF distillery. In the course of the next few hours, three more barricades will be placed in the dirt roads

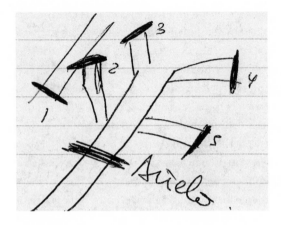

FIGURE 4.
Laura's drawing of the
five pickets in Añelo.

(*picadas*) so that the whole area is blocked to traffic coming from the
north. Añelo is the main picket, with four other "subpickets" adjacent
to it (figure 4).

Some people in the main picket are familiar with Laura; they know
she teaches adolescents, and so they ask her to go to one of the subpickets
where a group of youngsters are "hanging out, they have been drinking
all night." The fifty youngsters, some of them drunk, receive Laura with
a mocking "Hey, watch out, mother-in-law is here." Laura recalls that "I
know some of them, they are acquaintances of my daughter. The kids
are angry because they have nothing to eat. So I tell them to stop drinking if they want some food. With some other women, we organize the
distribution of firewood, meat sausages, grill broilers, bread, chicken,
so that the kids can eat . . . under the promise of not drinking. And so
the kids come to the main picket to eat, and the fun begins. They bring
music, radios, guitars."

In the picket, Laura explains to me, "The motto is 'Nobody comes in,
nobody goes out.'" No vehicle is allowed to go through Añelo; unless
you can certify that you live in one of the two towns, picketers will not
move the burning tires, rocks, old cars, and themselves from the road;
nobody ("absolutely no one") is allowed to leave town through Añelo
(and, from the available evidence, through the rest of the four main barricades; "We were besieged," the public prosecutor remembers). Around
noon, the radio informs the people in Añelo and in the rest of the pickets
that there will be a meeting at the Torre Uno, and delegates from each
picket should attend. "People in my picket ask me to be a delegate. Raúl,

a guy who has been there since early morning, organizing the blockade, tells me, 'Laura, you go, you did a great job with the kids, you should go.' And I reply, 'I'm not going, no way, what am I going to say?' 'Go there and tell them that we are in need. None of us know how to speak,' Raúl tells me." Laura is the teacher, the one who, for the rest of the picketers, "knows how to speak." The picket of Añelo also chooses Raúl to attend the meeting, but he refuses to go: "He says he doesn't know how to speak in public," Laura remembers.

The meeting at the Torre Uno is an impressive gathering of more than five thousand people. Laura is amazed by the number of people and astonished at the lack of attention paid to the pickets' delegates. She describes what happens in the meeting:

> When we get there, surprise! Those holding the microphone are reading their speeches, they are not improvising, they are using foul language, they are asking for the resignation of the governor. The people in my picket are not like that, they are there because they are hungry; they are mothers with their kids who can get diapers and milk for free. They are in the picket not because they want the governor to resign. Those holding the microphone never call upon us, the representatives of the pickets. They don't even say that we are there, they ignore us.

Those "holding the microphone" are, in Laura's mind, the local politicians. "I just can't stand this. It's too much, it's all politics. I am angry because they are playing with the needs of the people, they are not taking into consideration the hunger of those mothers who show up in the pickets to have some food," Laura remembers, phrasing in third person what is, in fact, her own condition: she is the mother who goes to the picket to have food and some distraction from the dullness of everyday life in her poor barrio. "I ask myself: what the hell am I doing in this meeting? I better go back to Añelo." Her suspicions are shared by other would-be picketers. Less than a month after la pueblada, Rubén recalls, "When I went to the Torre, I realized that it was as like a political rally, there were as always three or four politicians making promises. . . ."

As Laura arrives at her picket, "people from the Torre Uno are telling the other picketers that the trucks carrying oil and gasoline are to be allowed to go through our barricade, saying that we shouldn't be blocking the oil traffic. And the people from my picket are mad, indignant, our motto is 'Nobody comes in, nobody goes out,' not even the trucks carrying gasoline. *Se armó un quilombo!*" Here is where the trouble begins.

Gender Trouble in the Road

Laura spoke about la pueblada many times before. She told the story of those seven days on TV once, to newspaper reporters twice, and to several friends—the most articulate expression being the letter I use to reconstruct part of her contentious experience. However, there is one incident that remains obscure in these narratives, an incident that I come across by chance, after hours of conversation. For reasons that will become clear shortly, this episode is crucial to understand Laura's involvement and determination. The following is Laura's reconstruction of the dialogue that takes place in the middle of the chaos when picketers are angrily telling the envoys from Torre Uno that nobody, "not even the oil trucks," will pass through Añelo:

RAÚL (talking to Laura): Didn't you go to the meeting at the Torre Uno and tell them that nobody will pass through the picket?

LAURA: Listen to me. They didn't pay us any attention. That meeting was a farce. They didn't call us, they didn't care for our opinions . . . they didn't even want to know what's going on in the pickets.

RAÚL (talking to the people around): *See, this shit happened because we sent a woman . . .*

LAURA (angry): Stop there, hang on there, *negro de mierda*. You were supposed to come with me. And you convinced me to go. And now you say that a woman is good for nothing. You are the one who's useless because you didn't want to come with me . . .

RAÚL (dismissive): *See, she is like all women, she loudly bitches inside her home, but outside . . .*

LAURA (now very angry, on the verge of tears): Look, *negro sorete*, we are now going to the radio. I will get all the pickets' delegates together, and I will show you that I am telling the truth. After that, I hope I don't see you in my fucking life again!

Laura is now joined by Omar, who comes from another picket. Omar, who was present at the meeting at the Torre Uno, tries to persuade Raúl: "Laura is telling the truth," but Raúl keeps saying that Laura is useless.

And so Laura asks Omar to take her to Radio Victoria. The microphones of the radio are opened to each and every resident to express his or her anger and frustration. But Laura uses that outlet to call for a meeting of the picketers, in the Aeropuerto, "at the other end of the city, at the extreme opposite of the Torre Uno, without politicians. On the radio, I say: 'This meeting is for the representatives of the pickets. No politicians should come.' "

Laura has no history of prior activism, and a deep distrust of anything political. When did she decide to stay in the road, with all the risks and suffering implied and no benefits for her self in sight? After days of talking with her, of driving her around the main pickets and listening to her stories, of watching videos and reading newspapers, I realized that the question is misleading. Pace rational action theorists, so fond of instances of calculation and decision making, there is no moment in which Laura made a plain make-or-break choice to stay on the road, no occasion in which she ran the costs and benefits of possible action plans through a (to borrow Nina Eliasoph's felicitous expression) "psychic adding machine" to decide on a plan that will maximize her investment of energy, both physical and emotional (1998, 251). She was actually *sucked into* the role of picketer by the interactions she had in the road, interactions deeply shaped by elements of her own biography. To be blunt, she stayed on the road because she felt disrespected. True, her last three years were years of poverty and inmiseration, years that would give her or anybody else enough reasons to protest. But she wasn't there for that; "That was my story, never to be associated with anything political." Those three years, "three years of efforts, of struggles," as she writes in her diary, were also years of "breathing airs of liberty"—as she puts it when referring to the absence of her husband. They were years of learning about the respect that women deserve from men—something that, given her history of domestic abuse and violence, was not at all clear in her mind. They were, in other words, *years of material decay but also of moral empowerment.* That day in the road, Raúl—a man, it is important to remark, who was clearly from a lower socioeconomic status than the one Laura used to belong to (note her remarks about him being a "negro de mierda")—touched a nerve, giving Laura the looked-for chance to obtain the respect and recognition she had learned about during those three years: "I was mad with Raúl . . . it really bothered me; he treated me badly, as if I was stupid because I was a woman. I was offended, as if we women are useless. No way." And so she became a picketer, in part, out of a gender trouble.

Laura's biography informs her first interactions on the barricade (she is "the teacher, the one who knows how to talk" and "how to deal with kids"), the precipitating event in her becoming a picketer, that is, the gender affront, and many of her actions during those seven days. In the next sections we will see how her stubborn opposition to violent actions, and her obsessive concern about the well-being of mothers, children, and youngsters on the road, are also—as expected—related to her own story. For the time being, all we need to know is that she voiced all these worries not in front of popular assemblies at the Torre Uno (where most analysts would look to unearth the meanings of this protest) but in the small meetings in Añelo, and more specifically in front of her two closest fellow picketers, Omar and Raúl, with whom after the offense she became inseparable. The three of them were, Laura recalls, "the Three Musketeers."

We are still on the second day of the protest, a long way from the signing of the agreement and from Laura becoming the "symbol of la pueblada." However, one thing is by now clear. Her involvement with the picketers' actions greatly depends on her commitment to a small group of people: "the kids" that still make her cry when recalling their determination to stay on the road day and night, the women and children that had to be "protected," and Raúl and Omar, "the true picketers." As Laura puts it: "I could have said, 'I'll go back home.' That's in fact what I told Raúl: 'I'll show you that I'm telling the truth, and I'll leave.' I don't know why I did stay; we had to protect people. You began to think about the other, who is defenseless. As you began to talk to others, to have a conversation about protecting the people who were on the road, you became involved. My intention was to leave, but I stayed. Once it all started, you had a commitment." In other words, at the basis of Laura's participation in this large-scale collective action is a commitment to "her" picket, *el piquete de Añelo*. And this relational commitment has deep roots in her history.

The Picketers' Own Protest

And so begins Laura's six-day career as a picketer. Although the way in which she becomes involved in the protest is highly singular, the way in which she begins to understand the collectivity of those protesting, the way in which she defines who she and her fellow picketers are, is hardly unique: it begins to take shape at that meeting in the picket of Aeropuerto, where the first picketers' organization is born.

Four years after the episode, Jote, the picketer seen on TV shouting, "The people won, the people won" as the gendarmes turn around and leave town following the orders of the judge, tells me: "The first day, they, the politicians, secretly organized the whole thing. But on the second day, talking among ourselves, in the picket, we realized the protest was a political maneuver. And so we began to organize, saying that politicians should stay outside, and stressing that we only wanted to talk to one politician: the governor himself." In the meeting at the airport, far (both physically and symbolically) from the Torre Uno, the picketers agree that politicians are trying to use the protest for their own purposes (the general suspicion is, as I described, that Grittini is using the excuse of the fertilizer plant to wage his personal war against his former ally Mayor Martinasso and, by extension, against his former competitor in the internal elections of the MPN, Governor Sapag). "At the meeting," Laura tells me, "I was able to share my thoughts with the rest of the picketers. We all had a common feeling: they, the politicians, were using us, they ignored us at the Torre Uno. We knew that blockading the road was a crime, but we also knew that people would not leave the road: people had food there. At the meeting we agreed on the following things: protect the women and children in the pickets, take care of the food, demand jobs, protect youngsters and drunkards, and have another meeting the following day. We first organized around those simple things, because plain people with no political or economic interests among them can easily agree on simple things." I will come back to her concern — anxiety, I should call it — about safety; for the time being let's follow the rise of the first picketers' organization. In the process, Laura's, Jote's, and others' private disgust for local politicians became the basis for a protest within the protest, and a common (though fleeting) identity.

The next day, the local channel broadcasts Laura's first TV appearance, reading a communiqué from the recently formed "Committee of Pickets' Representatives." She looks tired and sounds hoarse: "Yesterday, when they called us to the assembly, we felt disappointed because we couldn't speak up. That's why we called a meeting. We had another meeting in which we gave a petition to the archbishop. We agreed on the following: 'We, *self-convened neighbors,* demand the governor . . .' " It was a long list of demands including jobs; support for the unemployed; moratoriums on local taxes, electricity, and gas bills; cheap credit for local businesses; and the "reactivation of the fertilizer plant project."

As I said, the postponement of the construction of the fertilizer plant is the protest's precipitating event. However, in the following days, the very dynamic of the event pushes that claim to the background, so much so that during the next days, picketers hardly mention the plant (it will reappear as the last item in the agreement signed with the governor, almost as an afterthought). Although protesters never cease to demand "genuine sources of employment," after the third day in the road, the claims lose specificity ("We want the fertilizer plant") and become more general ("We need jobs") but, at the same time, more urgent ("We want Governor Sapag to come here, now"). As this happens, the roar of the crowd begins to concentrate in the demarcation of boundaries between "us," the picketers and the people, and "them," the politicians. The first communiqué puts forward an initial collective characterization, that of "self-convened neighbors." In the course of the next few days, this self-definition will change its terms ("the people," "citizens") but not its main meaning: those protesting in the roads and staying day and night in the pickets *are not* politicians. In other words, much of what goes on during the protest begins to revolve around the very self-understanding of protesters: "We are the people. No politicians are among us"; so much so that in the collective experience of la pueblada, the definition of who the picketers are and what the protest is about takes precedence over their actual claims. As Omar puts it less than a month after the protest: "[After the first meeting at the Torre] I convinced myself that we didn't have to struggle for the fertilizer plant but for something else. The plant is important for Cutral-co, but not for the people, because it is not a source of employment . . . In the meetings an idea grew stronger and stronger: Mr. Sapag has to be here, explaining what's going on to us. We went around the pickets . . . and the only thing picketers said was that the governor had to come here . . . I think that we wanted him to see how (badly) we were doing."

A series of events trigger this shift. The governor's public speeches dismissing the protest and accusing picketers of committing a crime (i.e., the road blockade), of being manipulated by a group of "politicians with no reputation" (in reference to Grittini), enrage picketers and foster a veritable "war of words" between picketers and authorities. This war of words is, for the most part, a battle around the definition of the main actors in conflict.[5] The second episode that fuels the demarcation of "us" versus "them" is the attempt by local politicians to keep the protest under their control during the meeting at the Red Cross. I will analyze these events with an eye on the effect they have on the ways in which the protest is lived by Laura and her fellow picketers.

Ruben recollects that in the pickets, "We didn't want any politicians. If they came, we kicked them out. We wanted to resist, to force Sapag to come here." Every chance they get to speak to a local radio or TV channel, residents of Cutral-co and Plaza Huincul voice the same determination: "Sapag should come here and listen to us," "What we need here is the governor's presence. We need him to come and talk with us. After that we'll see if we cease the protest." In an interview broadcast on the local TV channel, Governor Sapag refuses to go to Cutral-co until protesters "clear the road and go back home" and puts forward his own definition of what is going on and who the main actors are:

> Once they cease with the violent protest, I will go to Cutral-co. We all have the right to make claims, to petition. But the freedom of the rest of the people should not be affected. And regrettably the people of Plaza Huincul, in blocking traffic on the routes, are committing a crime. They have to think that, with that attitude, they are going to obtain absolutely nothing . . . I cannot talk to people who are committing a crime . . . I can talk to them here, in the Government House, once they cease the protest. I can't talk with five thousand at the same time. Besides, they are committing a crime. Given his investiture, the Governor cannot talk to people who are committing a crime. . . . Some of the leaders of this mobilization have political motives. You know perfectly well who they are. There is a radio station involved, and five or six leaders . . . politicians from my own party with no prestige whatsoever who are resentful because they recently lost the elections. Don't let yourselves be carried away by a group of leaders from my own party.

"On Sunday the twenty-third, Sapag treats us as if we are criminals . . . it's terrible. Picketers are furious: *hunger is not a crime!* The picketers harden their position," Laura describes. "He is ill-advised. He thinks that his political adversaries are still leading the protest, and that is no longer the case. At the beginning, politicians were at the front. Now it's the people . . . when we see Sapag on TV, we think, 'This old man is an idiot, he still thinks this is all politics.' " Laura is certainly not the only one enraged by the governor's words. The local TV station records residents' reactions to the governor's accusation. More than being about concrete demands, this war of words revolves around *who actually is in the road*. For the governor, they are people manipulated by local politicians. For residents and picketers, it is *todo el pueblo*. A resident from Cutral-co says to the cameras of Channel 2: "The governor keeps saying that this (protest) is manipulated by politicians, that this is the product of party factionalism. That's not the case. It is the people who took to the streets . . . to tell the governor that in the same way that he came to look for votes . . . he now has to face us, to tell us, 'I am with my people, I will deliver, I know your needs.' " One of the "Three Musketeers," Laura's fellow picketer Omar, tells a local TV reporter: "We want the governor to stop criticizing us, in reference to what he said last night. We want him to be as flexible as we are. We want to dialogue. We do not want a political confrontation. We are not politicians, we are nothing, we are the people. *Esto es el pueblo*. No political campaigns. The real pueblo wants to speak with him. Without politicians." The cameras also register an old resident, referring to the governor's speech, saying, "Why, Mr. Governor, are you disrespecting the people from Cutral-co and Plaza Huincul? Why? Why do you make fun of them?" I am watching this video with Laura, who asks me, "See how the people react to the governor's words? He treats us like criminals."

Less than a month after the events, the local newspaper *Tribuna Abierta* interviews five picketers. All of them agree that the "governor's insult" is a crucial moment during la pueblada:

RUBÉN: Saying that the people in the road were criminals was the last thing he could have said, it was like a boomerang, as if you go and break the window of a police station . . .

JUAN: Since then, the communities grew more determined. He had to come here, to the Torre . . .

RUBÉN: That was a terrible thing he did. It shows how much he underestimates the people. He is used to negotiating; he is a politician. That's why he wants a group of fifty people [to go to the capital and negotiate with him].

OMAR: We went around the pickets and we saw that people were really offended by the governor calling us criminals . . . People said: if I am a criminal because I am protecting what is mine, the governor has to come here and talk to us.

LAURA: Besides, hunger is not a crime.

This confrontation around the definition of who is in the road translates into concrete actions. As Laura writes, "Everybody is able to be in the pickets, in the road, but one thing is unanimous: if a mayor, a councilman, or a deputy shows up, everybody approaches him. They ask him: Are you coming as the mayor? If he answers yes, then they insult him and kick him out. If he answers, 'No, I am coming as a common citizen,' he can join the crowd, drink some mates with us; he can even tell some jokes or stories." Picketers seek to "protect the protest from politicians," as Laura says, who are always seeking to, as Rubén and Omar add, "break the protest," to "betray la pueblada." How so? "Many people tried to break the pickets with words; others were distributing wine and money." Former mayor Martinasso acknowledges the truth of the picketers' recollections: "I went around the main pickets, with my face masked, to see what was going on. It was so dark at night that nobody recognized me. You have no idea how the people were insulting me and the other officials . . . During those days, many officials and politicians attempted to buy people off, with drugs, money, or wine." In the pickets, in the roads, residents from Cutral-co and Plaza Huincul are "protecting ourselves from politicians"—as Laura, Jote, Rubén, and Juan remember—and offering to the general public, to themselves, and (not least important) to local politicians and officials a shared self-understanding: We are citizens, we are self-convened neighbors, we are the people. Nowhere is the making of this collective identity more patently reflected than in the notebook Laura carries during the days of the protest, taking minutes in the several meetings picketers have.

Laura's Notebook: In Search of Visibility

"Part of what we, the picketers, did is in this notebook," Laura tells me as she hands her *cuaderno* to me. "You can have it, take it with you." Facing one of those rare opportunities allowed to researchers, I open the notebook and begin to ask her about her annotations. Akin to reading

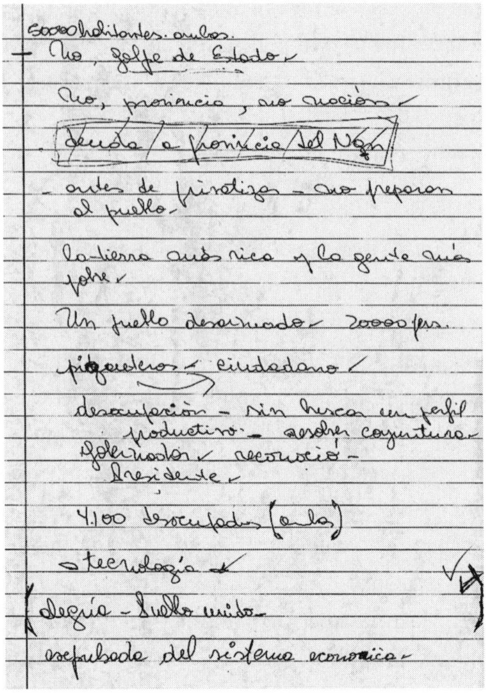
50000 habitantes. antes.
– No, Golpe de Estado
No, provincia, no nación
Deuda/a provincia/del Neuquén
– antes de privatizar – no prepararon al pueblo.
la tierra más rica y la gente más pobre
Un pueblo desarmado – 20000 pers.
piqueteros – ciudadanos
desocupación – sin buscar un perfil productivo – resolver coyuntura
gobernador – reconoció – Presidente
4.100 desocupados (antes)
tecnología
alegría – pueblo unido
expulsado del sistema económico

FIGURE 5.
Laura's notebook.

Martha Ballard's diary, the experience is "like walking into a room full of strangers" (Thatcher Ulrich 1991). With the help of detailed archival work and the aid of Laura and the rest, I was able to understand most of those writings, and I am now trying to open them up for the reader.

Laura carried this notebook with her during the seven days of la pueblada. As central as it is to understanding the picketers' actions and deliberations, it does not stand alone. Newspaper clips, video footage, in-depth interviews, and, above all, her own recollections during weeks of conversations provide the necessary documentation showing the notebook's relevance. Videos show her in meetings reading from it and writing in its pages; newspapers record the positions that, first registered in the notebook, are later made public. There is not a chronological sequence in the notebook; in fact, its twenty-four pages (mostly written by Laura herself) present a series of chaotic annotations ("Though I wanted to . . . we hardly had time to write," Laura tells me), a mixture of phone numbers, draft versions of public statements, one-line phrases, things to do, and brief proposals. Even in its messy character, the notebook offers an unmatched source for the picketers' actual discussions and doings, their organizational concerns and participation identity (figure 5).

The notebook hints at the organizational tasks ("Place labels on vehicles," "Call for a meeting with the lawyers association," "Machines to block roads," "Retirees are in charge of food," etc.) to which the pickets devote most of their time in the road. As Mary recalls, "The elderly brought us food, *yerba*, cigarettes . . . We, women, organized the food, we took care of children, we prepared mates." Laura sounds very much like that jack-of-all-trades, the underestimated housewife, when she describes her picket: "We were very organized. Women were the coordinators, they took care of kids, they got and distributed the food brought by the Centro de Jubilados. Five or six times a day, in a jeep that we had, we brought food, messages, and tires to the other subpickets."

On one page, under the title "Proposals," Laura registers the picketers' intentions regarding the media. The notebook reads: "Use the media," "Utilize the media." In most of my interviews with picketers and residents, the different local radio stations are referred to as key actors in the coordination of the protesters' actions: calling for meetings, broadcasting specific needs (food, firewood, an ambulance in the case of an emergency, etc.), warning pickets of the coming repression, and so on (batteries were distributed among the picketers so that they could follow the events on their portable radios). But the picketers also have other things in mind when talking about the "use" of the media. In another page, Laura registers the phone numbers of the most important national radio stations and TV channels. Years later, as we are going through the pages of her notebook, Laura brings to mind one of the picketers' main aims: to gain visibility, to make the protest heard beyond the confines of the two towns, and even beyond the limits of the province. "Use the media," Laura explains to me, "so that someone pays attention to us." Her annotations and comments show the profound awareness that protesters have about the role of the media; they know that demands "have to be expressed through the media to have any hope of having a publicly recognized existence and to be, in one way or another, 'taken into account' by those with political power" (Champagne 1999, 56). In her statement, however, this concern with visibility is not merely a strategic need. It is also an expression of the dialogical basis of the identity that the picketers are by now defending. If they, with the help of the media, are taken into account, their collective image will change in the eyes of the main object of their demands, Governor Sapag.

LAURA: What we were going through was completely unknown. Something big was going on in the town, but with no diffusion; it was totally unknown to the rest of the country. That's why we wanted to get in touch with the national radio stations and TV channels. We were afraid that they [the authorities] would take advantage of our exhaustion. They were abandoning us, and nobody was paying attention to what we were going through. The local newspaper paid us some attention, but that was it. It was one protest among others. Who would notice that we wanted the governor to come to town? Without the national media, this protest would be a provincial affair. . . . We were thinking, "If somebody pays us some attention, the governor will realize that we are not criminals. He will realize that all the people are here."

The media at the time, and my interviews years later, record this need to be listened to. At a time when both Cutral-co and Plaza Huincul are perceived, by locals and outsiders alike, as rapidly becoming ghost towns, the crowd's emphasis on "being seen," "being noticed" by the "governor in person," can be read as a cry against invisibilization, against the threat of disappearance. As Marcelo, a picketer, recalls, "We obstructed traffic because it was the only way in which we could be listened to." Rubén recalls, "The people wanted the governor to see and feel that we were not five subversives, that we were not criminals as he said, that we were not protesting because there was political maneuvering behind us. The people, some of whom even voted for him, wanted the governor to see that we were tired of lies and of many other things . . ." Or as Mary, her eyes on the verge of tears, clearly puts it: "My son asked me why we were in the road. And I told him, 'Look, son, this pueblo needs to be heard. The people in this town need to be aware of the things we are losing, of the things that the government is taking away from us.' I understood it that way; I lived it that way." Listening to Rubén, Mary, Mónica ("We won't move from the road because we are here, in Cutral-co, to stay"), and many others, I would even venture that the social world created around being-in-the-road offered residents and picketers alike, for seven days, that which they most totally lacked as inhabitants of a place-in-danger: a justification for existing. Being-in-the-road has the power of rescuing them from official oblivion, offers them the chance to emerge from indifference.

Who is this "we" that wants to be seen, acknowledged, recognized? The notebook provides a window into the picketers' self-defining efforts. The following are the phrases that Laura wrote on two of the pages, phrases that became the basis for her public appearances on radio and TV. Brief as they are, they synthesize the (relational and dialogical) claims and self-understanding of the picketers. The references to a coup, to the lack of arms, and to citizenship can be read as a response to the governor's (and some federal officials') accusations.

> Fifty thousand residents. No coup d'etat. . . . Before privatization, they didn't get the people ready. The richest soil, the poorest people. An unarmed people, 20,000 people. Picketers-Citizens. Unemployment. . . . 4,100 unemployed. . . . Joy-People United. Expelled from the economic system. . . . The representatives of the pickets inform the people: we are having meetings, we are more determined than ever. The governor has [in front of him] a people demonstrating that it is united, that it will not give up, and that it wants to have a dialogue.

That is the "we" that is in search of visibility: a numerous, united, and determined collectivity of citizens, without arms, and without revolutionary intentions. As Jote recalls: "We didn't want to overthrow anybody. We said so: we do not want a coup." And Laura, on TV, repeats: "We are very respectful of the authorities. We want them to listen to the people." This collective "we" has one major concern: the lack of jobs and opportunities that these two towns are suffering and the subsequent danger that this disappearance of work means for the towns' very survival. As Mónica puts it: "I love this place, this landscape. Why do I have to leave? It was a huge effort to get a house here; why shall I go away? The pueblada was about this." And Zulma: "We wanted jobs . . . we wanted an answer from the government, we wanted to have something so that our children could study. We wanted the government to know that the situation was a one-way ticket to hell [que esto se iba a al carajo sin retorno]. Those were our claims."

Finally, the notebook contains the draft version of the agreement Laura signed with the governor, and scattered phrases capturing one of her major worries throughout the protest, that is, safety: "Define a strategy," "appeal for habeas corpus," "Security." In another of her TV appearances, Laura expresses this worry in clear terms: "We just had a meeting, and the most important issue was the following . . . lawyers should present an appeal for habeas corpus for the whole population. We are without protection. Given the protection that they enjoy because of their investiture, council members should be present in the pickets, day and night, one councilman for each picket. . . . We want one councilman in each barricade, for our safety and tranquility." As the rumors regarding the coming of the gendarmes and the impending repression grow, this worry becomes the major concern in the pickets. In Laura's notebook it is registered as "Define a strategy." This, she recalls years later, "is in reference to the coming of the Gendarmería. The idea is to leave the route as soon as the repression begins. The general consensus is: We should not allow them to touch us. As soon as they leave, we will go back to the road. But we should not allow them to touch us. We want peace. We don't want violence. One of the mottoes is: 'We should all be alive at the end of this, so that we can recount the episode to our sons, daughters, grandsons, relatives, and neighbors. We have to take care of our bodies, to protect ourselves.' "

What Laura refers to as a "general consensus" or "common idea" is not actually such. Many of the people I talk to tell me about the fire-bombs (Molotovs), rocks, and sticks they have ready to confront the tear gas and the rubber bullets of the gendarmes. In point of fact, right before the judge recuses herself from the case, there are some skirmishes between the picketers in the first barricade and the gendarmes. Many picketers tell me anecdotes concerning the number of Molotovs ready to be used in case they were needed: "The truck that you can see there in the first barricade is full of *muchachos* [Molotovs]," a picketer tells me as we watch a video of the events. "We are prepared," another one tells me, "we, the kids in the front picket, are ready to go all the way . . . we have nothing to lose" (figure 6). And a third adds, "Fortunately, the gendarmes left, because it would have been a massacre. More than one of them would have died, burned down by all the Molotovs we had." Whether this determination to fight back against the gendarmes was going to be carried out, nobody knows. What we do know is that there were different ideas about how to deal with the upcoming repressive actions: to counterattack ("To the outsiders," a picketer tells me, "we said that we were going to leave the road as soon as the gendarmes came.

FIGURE 6.

The kids (los pibes). Courtesy of Juan José Esteves.

But among ourselves, we had a different idea"), or to peacefully leave the road.

In Search of Safety

If I have to define what I did, I'd say this: my aim was to protect people. —LAURA

Laura's annotations and remarks concerning nonviolence reflect, to some extent, part of the picketers' discussions at that time. But they also reflect her own anxiety about safety. Recall her first comments on the TV program a week after la pueblada. When asked about what happened, she says, "We had to ask for peace, we had to say no to violence." Years later, she tells me, "We knew that the road blockade was a crime. And it was even worse because we were obstructing the entrance to the distillery. And that's money, and once you affect money, you are in trouble. We wanted to protect people. I said that on the radio: we, the picketers, are here to protect people."

Laura's caring and protective actions were directed toward two main groups in the pickets: mothers with children and "the kids" *(los pibes)*. She still cries when remembering how she convinced los pibes to stop drinking by using an argument that, again, reflects the "we" that was being constructed in the road: "I told them that the politicians give them alcohol to use them and their families. I told them to throw away the bottles of wine so that they can be aware of their actions." Laura sheds tears every time she describes the moment when the more than fifty youngsters in her picket threw the cartons of cheap wine into the burning tires. Her staunch opposition to the consumption of alcohol ("If you bring wine into the picket, we would kick you out because that would generate conflict") is a sign of the peaceful character of the protest that she adamantly defends.

For other picketers, the refusal to drink during those seven days is also an extremely important sign of their determination and of the seriousness of their actions. Jote is in the first barricade, "the most dangerous one," when the gendarmes come. A heavy drinker ("But those days . . . nothing . . . nothing at all . . ."), his feelings about his fellow picketers and about himself illustrate how deeply linked alcohol (or the absence thereof) is with the picketers' self-understanding: "In my picket, we were all proud about the fact that we didn't drink at all, not a single glass of wine until the very last day . . . You know how these things are, when you are there, waiting and waiting, most would drink. But those days, nothing, we really respected that. . . . It was a total discipline. If someone came to bother, to have fun, we kicked him out. We came here to fight, not to joke around. Discipline, we had discipline . . . The picket was an example of the will to fight."

I later interview one of the "kids" to whom Laura refers, "the kids that still make me cry . . . they were so nice, so pure." Daniel is one of the fifty or so youngsters stoning the gendarmes before the judge recuses herself from the case. I am having a conversation with him, Angélica, and Laura in the Barrio 176 Viviendas. His comments show his understanding of the absence of alcohol (and drugs) as a sign of the seriousness of their collective struggle and Laura's key role in persuading them about that. "In the road, nobody drank, nobody used drugs. It was just fine. The kids themselves said, 'Let's not drink because we are going to lose. *Vamos a ponernos las pilas.*' And we did not drink. There were people around, I think you [referring to Laura] were one of them, asking us not to drink, telling us to stay calm. I saw Laura because she used to be around all the time."

Laura comes back to this issue of wine and protection often in the several weeks we spend together. And there is a reason for that. A reason that has to do with how deeply her protective and caring actions are linked with the story of her own life, and particularly with "the three years of suffering" that preceded the contentious episode:

> We had to protect the people; we had to protect ourselves. How so? We had to fight against the wine. Because if you drink, you can't think; and it is easy to manipulate a drunkard. We also had to take care of the violent people. How did we calm them down? *In the groups [against domestic violence], I learned that you have to approach the violent person,* and touch him, and try to caress him. That's how you calm him down. When someone is irritated, you have to approach him tenderly; the first thing you have to tell him is that you understand him. People told me that in the groups. *Those were the techniques that we learned to placate the violent husband.* Never confront him, always use words such as "understand," "comprehend." Try to fondle. The angry person thinks you are going to reject him. So if you approach him and smoothly put your arm around him, you bring the aggression to an end. That's what we did in the pickets. . . . *The things I learned in the groups against domestic violence were very useful those days.* In order to calm down the violent kids, you have to be kind to them, touch them . . . *pretty much in the same way I did with my husband when he got mad.* (Italics mine)

Laura's firm defense of nonviolent actions and her determination to look after "women and kids" are rooted in her own biographical episodes: in the extra dose of protection and care that she had to perform for her own children every time she was abandoned by her husband, and the deep marks that his violence left on her life. This suffering is actualized in the road and shapes her experience of the protest. She is in the road not only in search of a respect she lost a long time ago but also to do what gives her a sense of worthiness: to protect people. Her life (and now the protest) is all about that: finding and providing protection. In her simple words, she summarizes this circularity between the protest and her biography: "In each barricade, we express the things that were going on in our daily lives."

Meeting with the Enemy

The meeting at the Red Cross is another instance in which the picketers define who they are and what they stand for. "That's the worst night," Laura tells me, referring to the night of June 24, when a group of residents, among them the two mayors, many council members, church representatives, party leaders, members of the local chamber of commerce, and other local notables, gather at the Red Cross building and decide to send a delegation of both towns to meet with the governor in Neuquén. Laura still thinks that this is one possible solution to the stalemate in which the parties in conflict are involved: the governor refuses to go to Cutral-co, and protesters refuse to clear the road. "I really want to choose fifty persons to go and talk to the governor," Laura says, referring to the meeting at the Red Cross. A video camera spots her small body talking to the mayor of Plaza Huincul during the meeting: "I am telling him that no matter what we decide, the picketers will not allow anybody to get out." Laura recalls in front of the TV: "I personally think that this is the way to go, that it is a good idea to send a commission to negotiate with the governor in Neuquén. It is a way of solving the problem, because the gendarmes are coming. And maybe the kids in the pickets have no idea what exactly the gendarmes are. They didn't live during the years of the military repression; we, who are older than them, lived through that. I tell the kids about the risks involved, but they say, 'Sapag should come here!' In an assembly at Añelo, I cry, I cry . . . but they won't agree with me. They tell me, 'You represent us, you go and tell them that nobody comes in, nobody gets out.'"

She goes to the meeting by herself carrying a mandate with which she does not agree, "Nobody in, nobody out, until the governor shows up." Going to the Red Cross is, Laura describes, "like going to a meeting with the enemy, because the politicians are there, and they all want to go to negotiate, and I know that the picketers won't allow any commission to go out." For most of the picketers, a commission of representatives implies a betrayal of the by now "original" objective of the protest: the physical presence of the governor. "We," Rubén tells me, "put an end to that meeting from the outside. All the local leaders, the *dirigentes*, are inside. We begin to insult them . . . and we tell them that nobody will negotiate. At the Red Cross, everybody realizes the strength that the picketers have, because we are in control." What began as a protest of one faction

FIGURE 7.
Zulma's jewelry box.

of the governing party against the other is, by now, out of the hands of the initial organizers. Raúl and Omar, Laura's closest companions, take her out of the meeting: "What the fuck are you doing here?" they ask her. "If you think I am with *them* [the politicians], I'll get the fuck out of here [the meeting at the Red Cross]," she tells Raúl and Omar; "I am trying to convince these people not to try to leave town," she tells me as we watch an amateur video with images of the Red Cross meeting. "I just want to avoid violence, that's all. I know that if a group of people tries to leave, it will be a disaster. That's the worst night because I know the Gendarmería is coming and the picketers won't negotiate."

Pride

Zulma keeps empty tear gas canisters and rubber bullets in a jewelry box (figure 7). She thinks of the protest as a crucial moment in both her life and the life of the town. When asked about her mementos, she tells me, "I keep these things because la pueblada was something important for me. Maybe these things are garbage for my daughters, but perhaps they will understand them in the future. I always tell them that there are important moments in life. They say that you have to plant a tree and have a baby. I would place this protest in that same scale: you have to live a pueblada. This protest is part of my life, it's one of those things that leave a mark on you." Alicia and her daughter Clarita also keep an empty tear gas canister as a keepsake: "It's like a trophy, it's a symbol that stands for rebellion." And Mary, a *piquetera*, summarizes the thoughts of most protesters I talked to: "I feel good about what we did. At least I know that my son will have this recollection. Someday he will say, 'My mom fought for what she believed was just.'"

Cecilia lives with her six children in a tiny two-bedroom apartment built by the provincial government in the Barrio 176 Viviendas. She is a strong-looking woman in her mid-thirties. She was in the road, in the picket of the Torre Uno, for a couple of nights: "In the road, we were asking for dignity, for jobs . . . we were not asking for a gift, we were asking for work." And referring to the job programs implemented after the protest, she adds in frustration, "And what did they receive? A $150 subsidy . . . you tell me: what do you do if you have six kids with that amount? Can you eat? For how long? A week? And after that? La pueblada was useless." I come to Cecilia's house with Laura, who by now is a sort of informal but extremely efficient research assistant. The day before, I explained to Laura the purpose of the interviews, and I asked her to try not to intervene with her own stories during the conversations. I had already heard her version, and I wanted to identify other people's experiences. As I interview Cecilia, the irrepressible Laura looks at me and asks if she can ask a question. "Of course you can," I answer. The dialogue that follows conveys not only the collective self-definition of protesters but also Laura's own convictions. I later realize that she is trying to make a point with her queries; she is trying to make me "understand what it was all about," at the same time that she seeks to make sense of her own participation in the barricades. This dialogue also illustrates that, as many scholars of collective action have examined (Calhoun 1994; Jasper 1997; Wood 2001a, 2001b), the rewards of taking part in risky action are not reducible to the material gains obtained (or not) as a result of the protest.

LAURA: Do you feel proud about your participation in the pueblada?
CECILIA: Yes.
JAVIER: But you just said it was worth nothing, it was useless.

CECILIA: But I feel proud because I stood side by side with my people. I was there with my people.

LAURA: Were you part of the people during those days?

CECILIA: Yes . . . those days, yes. And the people were united, the haves and the have-nots. We were all there. The guy who delivers newspapers, the cab driver, the bus driver, the businessman . . . everybody brought food so that we could eat. Even the richest physician in town was eating a *choripan* [meat sausage] or a stew on the road.

LAURA: Did you feel that there were differences between professionals and people from this barrio?

CECILIA: No, no . . . we were all the same, all one. I was not there when the gendarmes came, but I believe that the whole pueblo was there . . . [her eyes well up]. The people got together and said, "Here we are, we are all united."

JAVIER: Why are you crying?

CECILIA (smiling): Because I am seeing her crying! [referring to Laura, who is also crying].

LAURA: That's not true [crying and smiling], it's because it is very emotive . . .

CECILIA: Because you feel moved . . .

LAURA: Can you explain that sentiment that you carry inside?

CECILIA: No, no . . . it is not possible to explain what you felt at that time . . . I feel a very big emotion, a great pride. Even though it was useless . . .

Laura feels pretty much the same: "If you look for an economic gain, it wasn't a victory," she later tells me. "But if you see the pueblada as an event in which the people didn't allow politicians to use them, the result was something good. We achieved something marvelous: we demonstrated that a people can get together, all united, to fight for something as simple as the dignity of a person; and in that sense, we won."

"When the gendarmes show up, all the people, every resident is there, at the Torre Uno," Alicia, a high school teacher, tells me, "but we have no fear because we are all together. There's nobody in town, everybody is at the Torre Uno awaiting the gendarmes. That gives you enough courage to face anything." "We have no fear," Angelica says, "we even go toward them, we are all together." Daniel adds, "We are not scared . . . a whole pueblo is fighting." And Zulma agrees: "When you are defending something that you think is yours, you have no fear. It is difficult to explain . . . but we were not afraid." The video images confirm this. There is "tension in the air," but no fear, I am repeatedly told by residents and picketers, because "we are all together."

In the letter Laura sent to a friend explaining her participation in la pueblada, the description of the moment at which the judge recuses herself from the case, voicing her decision from the top of a van, is quite brief. Laura trusts her friend's acquaintance with the episode; after all, it is the country's big news during the last week of June. The pace of Laura's writing becomes choppy, her handwriting bigger, when describing the moment when the picketers realize that the governor is on his way to talk to the residents of both towns: "Sapag comes. The national anthem. We won. The kids. The hugs. The tears of happiness. Sapag in Cutral-co."

This shared sense of collective victory is never better expressed than when residents and picketers cheer at the gendarmes' departure. Jote, holding an Argentine flag, shouts, "We won, we won . . . this is the people's victory," and people spontaneously begin to sing the national anthem.

Cecilia, Laura, Jote, Zulma, Daniel, Alicia, and the rest of the protesters and picketers do believe that "el pueblo ganó." Here "el pueblo" has, it is important to remark, two connotations that, however associated, should be analytically separated because they speak about the claims made and the identities activated during these seven days: the pueblo as locality, and the pueblo as a collective subject that excludes politicians.

On the one hand, "el pueblo" refers to location, to the towns of Cutral-co and Plaza Huincul. The repeated references to "the whole pueblo" refer, in part, to the fact that the entire towns are present in the road. And both towns are present in the road so that the governor and "the whole country" (as Laura records in her notebook) become aware of their rapid decline. Both towns are in danger of disappearing because, with YPF privatized, the semi-welfare state that the company supported is gone.

Residents' collective memories of the workings of the semi-welfare state during the times of YPF provided them with a powerful solidarity impetus to fight for what they saw as their city's interests.[6] In residents' minds, their pueblo is very special because it provides energy (natural gas and petroleum) to the rest of the country. As a young picketer remarks, just a couple of feet away from the gendarmes, "We provide the gasoline, the oil, the electricity, and . . . is this the pay we get?" Or as Alicia, the high school teacher, comments when referring to the moment when the crowd sings the national anthem, "It is as if we were saying, 'This is ours.' Because, in a way, YPF was ours. It wasn't exactly ours, but something used to trickle down to the people. Nowadays we don't get anything. To sing the national anthem is like saying that you are defending what is yours." Both Alicia and the young picketer are pointing toward this connotation of the term "pueblo-as-locality," a signification that has deep roots in the folk understandings of the residents of the area. Among Cutralquenses and Huinculenses, there is a widespread belief (itself rooted in the entrenched nationalist rhetoric that portrays residents as the "owners" of the oil in the region) that YPF's mineral resources belong to them. The motto "*We* provide the gas, *we* provide . . ." was hardly an idiosyncratic expression of this picketer; it was repeated several times during those days in the road. Laura herself elliptically refers to it in her notebook when she writes: "The richest soil, the poorest people." In other words, the collective self-understanding that was relationally and dialogically forged during those days has its roots (its material bases, I would say) not only in the current plight of Cutral-co and Plaza Huincul as towns at risk but also in the memories of the "golden times" of YPF and in the deeply held conviction concerning the ownership of natural resources.

But this moral economy did not exhaust the protest. Protesters and picketers constructed their identity and their demands in democratic terms against what they saw as politicians' obscure dealings and constant attempts to "use the people." From the picketers' point of view, who the protesters were and what they were shouting about had as much to do with the devastation provoked by state retrenchment expressed in the privatization of the state-run oil company as it did with the ruin brought about by politicians' self-serving actions. That is the reason why Laura, when talking on national TV, mentions the word "egoism" in tandem with the word "unemployment." Only a perspective sensitive to the words and actions of the crowd, to protesters' claims as much as to their self-understandings, can realize that, far from being an expression of the "false consciousness" of someone with no political trajectory, Laura's remarks point toward the actor against which picketers constructed their identity: the political class, or in her terms, "those who are in charge, those who say, 'I will do this and that if you vote for me.'" It is without the usual representatives (or, better, in spite of them) that residents are able to voice their discontent about the towns' rapid decay to the whole country: "That's something to be proud about," Laura and the rest agree.

Chapter Four

After the Road:

Contentious Legacies

The next day, after we all took a shower and got rid of the soot from our faces, we didn't recognize each other. —LAURA

The Torre Uno was built decades ago to commemorate the discovery of petroleum in the area (1918); the fake oil derrick and pump are placed not on the exact site of the discovery but at the entrance to Plaza Huincul, the tower being the first thing you see when coming from Neuquén, a long-hour drive mostly through the Patagonian desert (figures 8 and 9). A small park has recently been built around the oil well, with painted leafless trees, well-tended grass, and a multicolored cement ground. The red, orange, violet, yellow, and blue trees contrast sharply with the gray-ish and brownish landscape. The oil derrick is now lighted, and at night it looks like a huge modernist Christmas tree; the oil pump has also been recently painted in black and red. An adjacent big metal arch-way with colorful flags marks the entrance to the YPF distillery. Right in front of the oil well, a big, bright, lighted sign reads: "The tower of YPF. Historic Monument. Symbol of struggle of the pueblos of Plaza Huincul and Cutral-co." The sign was placed by the Municipality of Plaza Huincul. The memory summoned by the new park, the recycled derrick and pump, and the sign is straightforward. These are oil towns proud of their history, a history that includes la pueblada.

A few days after the protest began, Governor Sapag accused pro-testers of being manipulated by resentful politicians and urged them to clear the road because they were committing a crime. Once he was forced to go, he drastically changed his evaluation of the protest and

FIGURE 8.
The Torre Uno.

adopted a position with which he would cunningly stick for months to come. At the Torre Uno, in front of thousands of angry residents, he congratulated them for the *patriada*, the "patriotic act," because with it they had put the critical living conditions of both towns on view. They had, Sapag implied, placed both towns, and by extension the whole province, on the national government's radar screen. Now the entire country was watching, and the ball was in the national administration's court. Four months after the protest, during the celebrations of the sixty-third anniversary of Cutral-co, Governor Sapag vindicated the pueblada as a way of "making ourselves heard." He urged residents to "keep up the spirit of struggle" and warned the federal government that "we will get together again if they don't listen to us." Since the privatization of YPF, Sapag said, the protest was "latent . . . It had to happen. This people expressed spontaneously and unanimously." During the same celebration, Mayor Martinasso asserted that "we have to put pressure to remind both the national and provincial governments" about the troubles of the town

FIGURE 9.
The Torre Uno.
"Symbol of Struggle."

(*La Mañana del Sur*, 23 October 1996). Both speeches condense the government's attempt to appropriate the protest and displace the target of the protesters' claims toward the national government. "We" protested, both the governor and the mayor said, because of the privatization of the oil company, that is, because a decision made by the federal government; it is thereby the federal government's responsibility to fix the damage. In the following months, Sapag used the protest (or the probability of another happening) to make claims to the federal government: send more subsidies, more "employment plans," more food rations, or whatever resources the federal government has in order to prevent another "explosion." In the same way, many other communities in Neuquén (Rincón de los Sauces, Senillosa, and Piedra del Aguila, to name a few) threatened the provincial government with an "explosion à la Cutral-co" in order to obtain resources. Regional newspapers talked about "the Cutral-co effect" to describe the veritable demonstration effect that la pueblada had on many other towns.

La pueblada enjoys—as we can read in the words of local authorities, see in the sign at the Torre Uno, and hear in the voices of almost every resident of both towns—a good reputation. It is, as we can read in the sign, publicly recognized as "the struggle." However, the good standing of the protest does not extend to its main protagonists, the picketers. For most residents, theirs is a story that has "betrayal" as its title. The pueblada is indeed something to be proud of *despite* what picketers did (or what residents *believe* they did) afterward.

Less than a year after the pueblada, residents of both towns were in the road again. Between April 9 and 18, both towns were again isolated from the rest of the province. The protest began as a result of a teachers' strike; on the night of April 9, a group of teachers from the union organized a "symbolic blockade" on the by then "historic" site on Route 22, at the feet of Torre Uno. Different groups of residents quickly joined in to protest the unfulfilled agreements of June 1996, the "broken promises." This time there was no federal judge to prevent the gendarmes from acting. Early on the morning of April 12, they violently suppressed protesters, with the collaboration of the local police, the UESPO. During the June protest, the state police remained mostly passive, in some cases actually helping protesters in the obstruction of the traffic. They were the ones who first told truck and bus drivers that a protest was going on and that they should look for another route. This time, the police sided with the repressive forces; on the morning of April 12, while attempting to regain control of the route and the main streets of Plaza Huincul, they killed Teresa Rodriguez, a twenty-six-year-old mother of two.

"We are not piqueteros [picketers], we are *fogoneros* [stokers]. The picketers betrayed the people," protesters blockading accesses to both towns told the press during April 1997. They were shouting pretty much about the same thing, that is, demanding jobs, but they did not want to be identified with the protagonists of the June episode. This time protesters' participatory identity excluded not only politicians but also picketers. This chapter examines this new self-understanding in terms of what it tells us about the way in which the June protest and its main actors are constructed in the months that follow the episode. Why are the fogoneros so angry with their fellow protesters?

"People here think that the picketers were traitors," Mónica tells me in front of her friend Laura, the "picketers' symbol," who (to my surprise) completely agrees with her. The three of us are having dinner at

Mónica's house, where I have been staying for the last five days. Laura's daughter Paula joins us in the discussion.

JAVIER: Why do people call them [the picketers] traitors?

PAULA: Because they forgot about the people and began to take care of themselves. Supposedly they were going to defend the people, but they stopped listening to the people's needs, and they began to pay attention to their own needs. They now have their own businesses; they are in power, and they never paid heed to the needs of the people . . .

MÓNICA: Today, if you speak about Laura, there's a lot of bitterness [*bronca*]. They don't like her, because she is a picketer.

PAULA: Because she made a pile of money, she took care of herself, and she left . . .

MÓNICA: She is living in General Roca, she is doing wonderfully, with all the money she stole from here . . .

JAVIER (looking at Laura): Who says that?

MÓNICA: Everybody . . .

PAULA: The whole town . . .

LAURA: My friend Jorge told me that politicians began to bad-mouth me . . .

PAULA: Right after la pueblada my own house was a mess, people came at any time asking if Laura can get this and that for them. People came and asked for jobs, as if Laura were representing them. Presumably she was in charge of solving the people's needs . . .

MÓNICA: Everybody asked: Why did Laura leave town? All the people I know said that the picketers were fucking traitors. Laura, people said, is a fucking traitor. How could I explain to them that she was not?

PAULA: At the pub, people stopped me, the daughter of Laura Padilla, and asked: 'Are you spending all our money? And where is your mom?' People think that she made a pile and she left with the money. You know how we live, and you are lucky enough because you come during good enough times. If you come between the twenty-seventh and the tenth [when Laura's ex-husband pays child support], there's nothing. And that house was built well before la pueblada; it wasn't built with the picketers' money. Most people think that she bought that house with money she got after the protest. She was just the visible face, but she was not a sellout. And yet who will believe that? Nobody. She has a bad name here. . . . Despite what people believe, she didn't take any bribe, so she shouldn't be ashamed, she shouldn't hide herself.

I speak with dozens of residents during my two stays in Cutral-co, and I can attest that what Mónica and Paula say rings true in the ears of most of them. Most people in town despise the picketers. There is a widespread and firm belief ("conviction" would be a proper word) that matter-of-factly states that right after la pueblada, local politicians began to distribute money among the most outspoken and active picketers in exchange for their silence or departure. The "picketers' symbol" could hardly be exempt from these charges. In point of fact, being the one who signed the agreement with the governor, Laura is the object of the most (and most diverse) accusations: "She is living large in General Roca," "She obtained a lot of things and got the hell out of here." However, she is not the only target of the people's finger pointing: most picketers are. "They got new cars," "They got public jobs and forgot about the protest," "They received loans and left town." Everybody in town, as Mónica says, has something (mostly bad) to say about the picketers. Curiously enough, even the picketers themselves do. Right after the protest, the clean-faced picketers not only did not physically recognize one another but also began to turn against each other, to suspect each other's intentions.

As my fieldwork progresses, I learn that Ernesto "el Jote" Figueroa is one of the most vocal picketers during the protest. He is the one who talks to the judge when she comes to Cutral-co in command of the Gendarmería, and he can be seen in most of the picketers' assemblies and negotiations. Jote now works as a cook on the construction site of a new methanol plant that is being built close to the Torre Uno. Laura's friend Ricardo puts me in contact with Jote. When the three of us arrive at Jote's workplace, he gladly agrees to talk about his participation in the protest later that same afternoon. He is in the middle of his shift. "I am too busy now, but come home later, we'll have some mates and we'll talk . . . there are plenty of things we can talk about," he says, looking at me and at Ricardo, completely ignoring the presence of Laura. Four years ago they were together on the barricades, "fighting for the people's dignity," as both of them say, but now they hardly look at each other.

It's the afternoon when I go to Jote's home. He is waiting for me with another friend, Juan. We spend hours talking about the protest. Eventually we come to the thorny issue of the rumors about the bribes presumably received by picketers.

JOTE: That woman you came with this morning was Laura, wasn't it?
JAVIER: Yes, it was.
JUAN: She received a lot of intimidations, against her and her children . . .
JOTE: I never knew what happened with Laurita.
JUAN: She left . . . and everything was very confusing. People say that she received a lot of money, that she got bribes . . .
JAVIER: That is not true. She left because she finally got her ex-husband to return the house that belonged to her in Roca. I've been with her, she took no money from anyone . . .
JOTE: That's why I say . . . I don't know what happened. What I do know is that she disappeared. I never saw her again. When I saw her this morning, she looked familiar, but I didn't recognize her. She has changed a lot . . .

At the end of the book, I will come back to my (to some) utterly improper intervention. For the time being, it is important to focus on Jote's and Juan's comments because they encapsulate most of what picketers have to say about each other. Other picketers with whom I talk say the same things about Jote himself—"He was bought off right after la pueblada." After many interviews with picketers, I realize how deeply held this belief is; they all have bad things to say about each other. "Many of the picketers who were with us," Rubén tells me, "got bribes . . . not money, but jobs." Enrique, who was in one of the main pickets day and night, adds: "This guy was with us, and the next thing we knew, he bought a new car . . ."

As we saw, the specter of betrayal was present during those seven days. Picketers did not want politicians to be involved because they would corrupt both the protest and the protesters, "with words, wine, or money." By "corruption," picketers meant exactly what (many believed) happened afterward: politicians would try to buy off the protest. When picketers left the road and returned home, this specter took on a life of its own. Less than two months after la pueblada, a regional newspaper captured this growing general mood against the picketers: "There is a widespread disbelief and total lack of trust not only in local politicians but also in some members of the new institution people here call the picketers" (*La Mañana del Sur,* 10 August 1996).

My sense is that this animosity is, more than the result of bribes, an unintended consequence of the picketers' own goodwill efforts. As soon as the days of protest are over, they, true to their absolute distrust for politicians, try to organize to distribute the aid (subsidies and food rations) that the national and provincial governments are slowly beginning to send. Local authorities try to resume business as usual, but they now have to deal with a new actor, the group of picketers claiming a share of their decision-making power. What the picketers get is a part in the administration of the aid that is coming to both towns. They begin to list the people who are in most need, those who urgently need a job or whose children need daily assistance. Together with the daily trips to the municipality in search of "solutions," poor residents begin to visit the picketers' homes or their meeting places to formulate their demands. That's why Paula (Laura's daughter) says, "Right after la pueblada, my own house was a mess; people came at any time asking if Laura could get this and that for them. People came and asked for jobs, as if Laura were representing them. Presumably she was in charge of solving the people's needs . . ." Jote puts it in the following terms:

JOTE: Right after la pueblada we, the picketers, created different working groups to attend to the different demands that the people had. And they, the politicians, turned the whole town against us. Suddenly we were managing all the subsidies, all the employment plans . . . We had no skills whatsoever to carry out the distribution; you have no idea of how difficult it was . . .

JAVIER: So everybody was now demanding solutions from you instead of from officials?

JOTE: Exactly, and we were providing solutions to the extent that they [the officials] were giving us resources.

The newspapers at the time register this new development, saying that the picketers are "a sort of parallel government" (*La Mañana del Sur,* 11 July 1996, 6). Before they become aware, picketers themselves turn into the objects of popular claims and thereby, in the eyes of those claiming food or subsidies, tainted by the presumption of corruption that pervades local politics.

The fogoneros themselves cannot escape the accusation that they formulate against the picketers. Soon enough, rumors of corruption and bribery are also affecting them. The fact that one of the most important local officials (the current mayor's secretary of government) was one of the main fogoneros gives residents enough evidence to arouse distrust. Again Paula conveys this widespread feeling when she says that "they [the former protesters] are in power, and they never paid heed to the needs of the people . . ."

The question that we should ask is not whether picketers were bought off (some of them might have received bribes, although no conclusive evidence is available) but whose interests are being served by the rumors of betrayal. Whatever the source of the rumors, it seems to me that a "divide-and-conquer" logic is operating here, with a result that any visitor to Cutral-co and Plaza Huincul can feel as soon as she talks about both protests: as I've been repeatedly told, "It is worthless to protest; don't you see how the piqueteros and the fogoneros end up? They forget about the people."

The aftermath of the 1996 protest is marked not only by the astute "uses" of the protest by the local and state government but also by the spread of rumors concerning the picketers' treachery. In the months that follow, picketers denounce threats and armed aggression. Together with the bombs that are placed in some local politicians' homes, the months that follow the protest are months of both rumors and fear. "El ambiente se enrareció" [the atmosphere got weird], I am repeatedly told by former picketers, local officials, and the public prosecutor.

It has been more than three years since Laura last saw Raúl and Omar, the other two "Musketeers." She is very aware of the rumors circulating in town about her and knows that both Raúl and Omar might also be thinking that she is a sellout, that she "betrayed them." Nonetheless Laura helps me to locate Omar's home and offers to introduce me to his family. Because it has been a long time, I prefer to wait for her outside while she makes the necessary arrangements for a time and place to talk. After more than twenty minutes, Laura comes out, crying, speechless. She grabs a cigarette and tells me, "This is very sad, let's go . . ." Ten minutes later, again on the verge of tears, Laura says:

> Omar and Raúl were fogoneros . . . They became involved because nothing happened with the promises made during 1996, and they were angry about it . . . This is so sad. They've been threatened, people tried to beat them, they've been in jail because of their participation in the protest. They've been told not to participate anymore in any of

these things. They don't want to talk about it. Many cruel things have been said about them; people said that they got a lot of money . . . Omar's wife told me that she thinks that Raúl is in a wheelchair. She thinks that he doesn't walk after a beating. She asked me not to come back. This is so sad . . . I know she is not lying to me.

Most picketers recall that right after the week in the road, threats and persecutions were part of their daily lives. Some of them have nasty experiences with the local police, and some others have stories to tell about people who took active part in the protest and then "had to leave town." Threats and physical attacks do occur after the protest—the public prosecutor remembers not only "El Chofa's" alleged mission to "kill Laura" but many other episodes. Together with the rumors about betrayal, these (other) rumors created a mist of suspicion around the picketers. Whether or not they are true, one thing can be said for sure: they keep some people, like Omar and Raúl, silent and secluded.

The rumors about Laura have one thing in common. They all refer to the fact that she left town. Why did she leave? How did the protest change her life? Laura did indeed materially benefit from this protest, but not in the way most picketers and residents think, not one secretly provided by a local official or politician. She got her house in General Roca back. She also acquired less-tangible benefits that have been denied to her for years: respect and recognition.

After her appearance on national TV and in both national and regional newspapers, Laura acquired a huge notoriety in town. This renown had effects that she could not have predicted but drastically transformed her life:

> One thing I noticed is that after la pueblada, the judge who had my file, and who had told me a million times to go to hell, asked me to come into his office and to tell me what was going on. The prosecutor who had never paid attention to me before called me to find out if I was receiving child support or if I had been threatened. At the courthouse, I stopped being "the troublemaker" and began being "la señora." "Please, Miss Padilla, come in. How can we help you?" they told me. The way in which I was treated changed radically.

Her husband had not answered any of the letters she sent to him. In those letters Laura asked Juan either to return the house that they both had in

General Roca to her so that she could move back there with her three children, or to use the rent money to pay for child support. A month after la pueblada, her husband answered Laura's letter for the first time, informing her that the lease on the house was expired and that if she wanted she could move back in, but she would have to deal with the person renting the house on her own. "I broke into the house, I changed the lock . . . and that's how I got the house back . . . La pueblada gave me my house back. I'd been struggling in court forever, but to no avail. Only after the protest, after I was on TV, Juan answered my letters. I guess out of fear. . . . that was the only time I got him to answer. La pueblada in that sense was useful; do you think that he would have answered had I not been on TV?"

As soon as she learned that she had the house back, she began making plans to move back to General Roca. In a bigger city, in a nicer house and neighborhood, her children could have access to the education that Laura still believes can make all the difference: "Paula was finishing high school, and in Roca she could go to the university . . . and after all, that was our house." In December, Laura and her children moved back to General Roca. Months later, the civil courts sentenced Juan to pay child support; "With that $400 a month, I began to breath a little bit." On April 13, 1998, he was given a suspended sentence of two years and two months of prison for having claimed a fraudulent bankruptcy to avoid making child support payments. Laura now receives $690 a month in child support. Since going back to General Roca, she has formed a group against domestic violence to work with poor women. Once a week, she, together with two lawyers and a journalist, promotes the activities of the group on a local radio station.

As for the rumors, she doesn't seem to care what "people who I never met say about me . . . I know who I am and what I did. I would go crazy if my friends have doubts about me. I don't care much about the rest," she tells me. And in a letter to a friend, she summarizes it all; what the protest is about, who the picketers are, how she feels about the whole thing, and how significant the protest is to her own life:

> The picketers were not career politicians, or people coming from a family of politicians. They were not running for anything. They only obeyed what the people, by majority rule, decided in the meetings. They never betrayed the people in the pickets. They were only their

voice. The force lay in the people who, day and night, stayed in the pickets . . . Until the end, they did not take any cash (afterward, there were, I have to admit, some sellouts). They had no experience in [political] negotiation. They [politicians] destroyed them [the picketers]. For example, people say that I received a lot of money, and I left town . . . The only thing I can say is that nobody can take away from me the pride of being there and of signing the agreement, when no one dared to do it (coward men). Until now, it was the most important event in my life; actually, the second, the first was to be a mother.

Laura enjoys being called "la piquetera" because it conveys what, for her, the protest was all about: "I like what we did, and I liked being called the picketer. I feel like, those days, I earned the respect I deserve. I felt respected, not by my husband but by the authorities." No other statement can better encapsulate what she was looking for in the road and how that search was closely linked to her life story.

Part Two

The Queen of the Riot

FIGURE 10.

Nana dancing in the streets of
Santiago del Estero, February 1982.

Here I am totally covered in sweat. To me the Carnaval was something else. It was like fighting to get something, I don't know what. To me, the Carnaval was to go in and consume all my energy. Because I danced for two and a half hours straight [figure 10]. I didn't stop even for a minute. That's why I was a revelation. That's why I was considered the best dancer. I would dance four kilometers back and forth every night, three nights a week. I would start a little bit overweight, and I'd end up being really thin, like a little stick. I danced all the time, and I would dance everything. I could be short of breath and terribly thirsty, but I would go on. At that point the little, cute, and very well made-up girl that everyone had seen at the beginning would transform into a monstrosity. My hair was a mess. I was all covered with sweat and would smell of anything you could imagine; anything but the perfume of the Carnaval. Even my butt would sweat. That was what the Carnaval was to me: giving myself away completely. —NANA

On December 16, 1993, Government House in the city of Santiago del Estero was burned (figure 11).[1] During the morning, thousands of public employees concentrate in the main square of Santiago to claim their un-paid wages, some three to four months in arrears, and to protest against widespread government corruption. In a city whose economy revolves around the salaries received by public employees (almost half of the wage earners are public employees), three months without payment are bound to affect everybody. High school and university students, house-wives, retired elderly, informal sector workers, and unemployed youth join municipal and provincial government workers in the rally in front of the Government House. Angry protesters throw bricks, stones, sticks, bottles, and flat paving stones at the government building while trying to enter the house. One of the stones hits the face of the police chief while he is apparently trying to talk with some union leaders to calm the protest down. As the chief, his head covered with blood, passes out, the police fire tear gas and rubber bullets against the crowd, which backs off toward the middle of the square. Soon the police seem to have run out of ammunition. In less than ten minutes, thousands of protesters become, as a local newspaper report describes, "the owners of the battle-field"; they are now "in charge of the situation." Hundreds of projec-

FIGURE 11.

Government House, Santiago del Estero, December 16, 1993. © El Liberal

tiles, among them some Molotovs, enter through the building's windows while policemen run from floor to floor "without knowing what to do," and visibly affected by the tear gas that the wind is returning to them. Fire takes hold in parts of the building. The police, now lacking any means for forceful response, seem totally overwhelmed. Governor Lobo refuses to abandon the building. At 11:30 A.M., the front part of the house is completely on fire, and the chief of police convinces the governor to leave the palace: "Governor . . . there might be a massacre here; leave the building with the cabinet members, and we will escort you." Just after the governor leaves, the twenty-seven infantry guards also abandon the scene, and the final sacking of the government building begins. Forty minutes later, the courthouse, just two blocks away, becomes the target of more than one hundred protesters. They break windows and enter the building, where they take computers, typewriters, and court case files and burn desks and chairs.

At 1 P.M. a group of demonstrators attacks and loots the local legislature, throwing the legislators' chairs out of the windows and, as the local newspaper reports, "destroying everything they find." Protesters now head toward the home of Governor Lobo "with the firm intention of burning down" his house. As they break into Lobo's house, a group of infantry guards arrives at the scene, preventing the assault. But the crowd moves faster than the police; an hour later, they are sacking and burning the homes of several prominent public officials and former governors (Crámaro, Iturre, and Juarez). Armchairs, tables, underwear, carpets, appliances, clothing, doors, and windows are the "principal trophies" of the crowd. One of the homes that suffer the most devastation is that of former public works minister López Casanegra, who initially tries to defend his property. Another group of demonstrators heads to the home of one of the leaders of the opposition (Zavalía), who shoots at the crowd and stops protesters from breaking into his house. It is 4:30 P.M. when a crowd of 250 attacks the residence of former governor Mujica, burning both his house and his car. Protesters take furniture and appliances out of his house while neighbors applaud and celebrate the destruction, a destruction that, according to the newspaper report, "serves as a way of venting the discontent against this politician." Later that afternoon, hundreds of demonstrators break into the homes of former legislators Gauna and Granda; the latter unsuccessfully tries to defend his house. As the troops of the Gendarmería Nacional arrive in Santiago, the homes of a member of the Superior Tribunal de Justicia (Moreno) and the leader of the largest teachers' union (Diaz) are also destroyed and burned. At night, the headquarters of Matelsan—property of former governor Iturre—are attacked, doors broken, and furniture destroyed while neighbors "cheer the attackers." The homes of former undersecretary of media and institutional relations Brevetta Rodriguez and legislator Riachi are also sacked and burned. Finally, at 9:30 one of the buildings of the Ministry of Social Welfare is assaulted. An hour later, the National Senate authorizes federal intervention in Santiago del Estero. The national government sends in hundreds of troops from the Gendarmería Nacional and suspends the powers of the executive, judicial, and legislative branches, imposing its own officials as trustees. The next day, after more attacks and lootings of local officials' homes in the neighboring city of La Banda, the protest is over.

Who are these "angry protesters"? What are they shouting about? Why public buildings and then private residences in a seemingly synchronized action? Who, if any, coordinates protesters' actions? What do the destruction and sacking mean to them? Two days before leaving Santiago (August 2000), I ask Nana to draw me a map of what she did on December 16. Instead of going to politicians' private residences, she chooses to stay around the main square, "enjoying the moment," as she puts it, and frantically moving around, "so that not to miss anything." Her recollections are so vivid, her desire to tell her story so fervent, that she mixes past and present tenses in the references—an "inconsistency" that I have kept in this edited version.

Despite the tear gas, the rubber bullets, the running, and the injured comrade, December 16 has, for her, all the features of a public celebration: "I enjoyed the moment walking through the streets. We looked and walked around the burning courthouse. . . . We were celebrating, calm. I never smoked a joint, but I think it was something similar to that . . . Yes, because we enjoyed it, like sitting down to smoke a cigarette and drink coffee with a good friend . . . We were sitting down, enjoying all that, feeling the heat of what was burning at the Government House," Nana remembers, encapsulating the way in which most of the protesters I talk to think and feel about the uprising. After describing her actions, Nana situates her experiences in a local context and gives a particular meaning to them: The Santiagazo is, for her and for most protesters, about a wage claim, but it is also about less-tangible rewards: "That night, when you could still smell smoke from the burning, I was thinking . . . Well, we had to put so much of our hearts into it, to generate all that mess, so that at least they talked about Santiago in the capital city. Just so that Santiago appears once on the cover of the *New York Times*, because we knew that, too. We are the first province, the poorest, the one that is left behind the most, where it is so hard to educate our children, to raise them healthy, where it is so hard to achieve a dignified future . . . A big mess had to be made so that someone wrote about it and became interested in us."

"In order to understand December 16, we should go back to January," a leader from the Teachers' Union explains to me; "It all starts at the beginning of 1993," Nana tells me. In the many hours I spend talking with dozens of protesters, they all refer to the "whole situation" that precedes the uprising and helps to explain its occurrence. This "whole mess" comprises a local state that is not only unresponsive but deeply corrupt; unprecedented disruptions in everyday routines that make "life impossible"; and a street mobilization that has been growing since the beginning of the year, draws unparalleled numbers of people to the streets, and demands incessant coordination efforts by the leaders of the protest but at the same time bypasses the established leadership. An editorial published in *El Liberal,* the main local newspaper, on September 7, which in hindsight proves to be oddly prophetic, captures the increasing wave of contention. Entitled "A Field of Protest," the editorial reads: "It has been a long time since the different social sectors of our province have transformed Santiago into a field of protest." Street protest is part of everyday life in this province, the editorial describes, and warns the protests' leaders that they have a "huge responsibility in claiming what the people need and preventing . . . violent episodes." Among these potentially violent episodes the editorial mentions the "burning down of the main square."

Nana and most protesters locate these three processes—increasing government corruption and incapacity, daily disturbances, and growing street mobilization—in a long time frame, and they also refer to a set of developments that, hinted in the image of the "field of protest," escaped the purview of most observers at the time: as contention escalates, protesters learn to deal with violent repression and collectively agree both on who they are ("the honest people") and on where the responsibility for their plight lies ("the corrupt political class"). Based on archival work and in-depth interviews, chapter 5 provides a straightforward empirical description of the widespread socioeconomic and political crisis that predates the riot, paying particular attention to this learning process and to the creation of the boundary between "we, the people" versus "them, the political class."

Chapter 6 seeks to understand the riot as a lived experience. How do protesters understand their actions and themselves? This is the first time in the history of the town (and, in fact, in the history of twentieth-century Argentina) that protesters have paraded around town sacking and burning down public buildings and private residences. How do demonstrators "decide" to break into the government building, the courthouse, and the legislature? Do they actually "decide," or is entering those "symbols of corruption"—as a protester describes them to me—something already inscribed in the protesters' repertoire and thus part of a collective practice that excludes deliberate and conscious action? Why do protesters set all these public buildings on fire, destroying everything that they could get their hands on? How does fire become part of their repertoire? How do they "decide" to proceed to the homes of politicians and officials? Again, was this a deliberate, conscious decision?

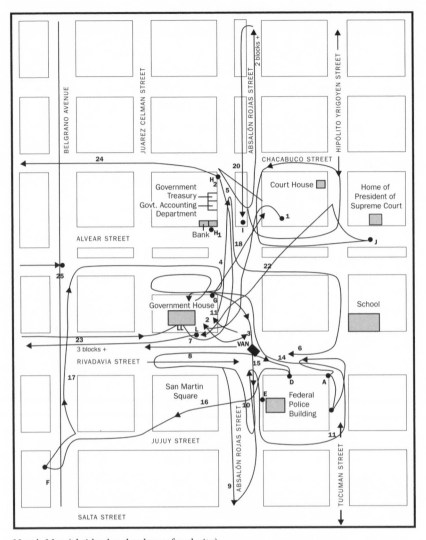

Nana's Map (abridged and redrawn for clarity)

Key

1 A few minutes before leaving [the union locale], we painted the flags with the slogans we used that day (I painted skulls). Then we went out, showing the posters, toward the house where the compañeros awaited us.

2 I stood close to the balcony, next to the leaders. We were requesting Lobo [the governor] to come out.

3 The clamor [*agites*] began, there were clashes, and all the "peaceful protest" went to hell. The first tear gas of the day began (just a little early).

4 We escape through wherever we can . . .

5, 6 A few minutes later we recover from the suffocation and come back following new roads, because the cops block the way.

7, 8 Once there was some distance, due to the police blockade, there were moments of rage. People were throwing back the tear gas, stones, bottles, etc.

9, 10 Running, we came and went. It was all too intense. I was meeting people from other unions, people of all kinds.

11 We found another route to go back to the house.

A A paper bonfire we use to calm the burning feeling from the tear gas.

14 The people go into Government House singing the national anthem.

15 We go back to the sidewalks, and then all the officials leave in the firemen's truck. There were some shots that sounded strange. I go to the street on the side, looking for shelter from the shooting (D).

E A compañero falls, injured (from police gunshots).

16 I go to the Santiago Clinic [with him]. (F).

17 After this guy (my compañero) enters the operating room, I go back, again having to avoid the cops. I arrive through the area behind the house. . . . The house is occupied through the front.

G People begin to burn the house.

18 After a couple of minutes, we decided to go to the courthouse.

20 People run because of rumors that the federal cops are on their way.

I We return.

J Cops try to arrest kids with souvenirs. I insult the cops and they let the kids go.

22 I go back to Government House.

L I sit with my friend Guillermo on one of the benches in the square to contemplate the scene. He buys a painting of San Martín (stolen from Government House).

23 I go with him while he puts the painting away in his car one block back.

LL I enter Government House, on the first floor. I stand on the Agreements Table, and I tear down the chandelier.

H1 Some compañeros from the union (courthouse employees) are drinking beer and celebrating. I share with them.

H2 I look for my motorbike.

24 I go back home at Barrio Rivadavia.

25 I come back from home. I move around the area a couple of times.

Why some politicians and not others? Why, if there is so much rage and fury against them—if they "can't take it anymore," as another participant in the uprising explains to me—is nobody hurt? Or to paraphrase E. P. Thompson's simple but still essential question: being hungry, angry, their lives disrupted and threatened, what do people do?

In this chapter, I take a closer look at the protesters' itinerary during the riot in order to delve into the meanings that the looting and sacking have for the perpetrators: what is the "celebration" of which Nana and many others talk about? To foreshadow some of the results of the reconstruction of the protesters' experiences, I suggest the following: protesters do not deny the wage claim that was at the root of the protest, but their actions and words during the uprising tell a partially different story, a story full of images of parody and degradation that points toward a feature of the protest that transcends the material claim and emphasizes the protesters' struggle against corruption. In particular, I pay attention to the carnivalesque dimension of the riot. Protesters' words and actions also convey a story of a collective "we" in action, a "we" that, far from being a headless mob, knows where to go, whom to attack, and why to do so.

A Personal Protest

For Nana, the events of December 16 are a personal issue. "I take the sixteenth personally," she repeatedly tells me in our first interview at the courthouse employees' union hall, and later adds, "After that, I was never the same again." In that first meeting, I am struck by her determination to tell the story of that day and by the vibrant character of her recollections. When the union's secretary arrives, it is the turn of the all-male leaders to give me their description and evaluation of the events. Her detailed recollections give way to the dirigentes' general remarks about the period preceding the riot, about their own leading roles in the collective struggle, and about the riot's impact on local politics. During this second part of the interview, Nana remains mostly silent. As we finish the interview, I am craving more of Nana's recollections and wondering how I can have an extended conversation with her. I need not worry. As she climbs on her motorbike, she gives me her work phone number and tells me, "Call me, there's a million things I can tell you about December 16. It's not that I disagree with them [the union leaders], but *I have another way of looking at things.*" The next day I call her, and we begin a long series of conversations about the events and about her participation in the riot.

One day, as we are concluding our talk, I ask her about a photograph of her I saw in the newspaper while browsing the archives of *El Liberal.* Although it is a remark intended to elicit her memories of the days preceding the riot, her answer opens up a sort of Pandora's box: "And the funny thing is that the guy who takes my picture is the same guy who used to take pictures of me when I was a dancer. . . . I was a dancer at the Carnaval . . . I was crowned as the Carnaval's best dancer."

Coincidentally enough, and prompted by the "funny anecdotes" that participants in the uprising have been telling me about that day and by the images I am observing in photographs and videos hinting at the protest's celebratory, even ritualistic, character, at this time I am beginning to think about the carnivalesque dimensions of the events of December 16. The Santiagazo is certainly not the first protest to have elements of hierarchy inversion, parody, open-air cursing, and degradation typical of carnival. Finding that "the queen of Carnaval" is among the rioters, I think, will make that dimension of my story more real. However, in subsequent interviews and conversations, I realize how limited this view is. Nana's story is much more interesting and will add much more than a touch of "local color" to my reconstruction of the events.

After I find out that she has been "the best dancer in the Carnaval" (and certainly impressed by the coincidence), I ask her if she is willing to "keep talking and tell me more about you, about your childhood, your children, in other words, the story of your life." At this time, I am interested in her life before she becomes—in her own words—"an activist of the Santiagazo." After hours of talk, I end up understanding something more complex, more theoretically challenging, than that, namely, the complex ways in which the narrative of her life meets and meshes with her account and other protesters' accounts of the Santiagazo. Hers is certainly "another way of looking at things," but at the same time it is emblematic of the way in which many Santiagueños experience the uprising.

The "anecdotal" fact that she is "the queen of Carnaval" is much more than a factual coincidence; as we will see, it points to a common theme underlining both the narrative of her life and protesters' (herself included) experiences. This common theme is the public search for recognition. Both her life and the lived protest are about a pent-up quest for respect and dignity. And both narratives speak about the obstacles that this search encounters. "I am thirty-six years old, and I have been eating crap for thirty-six years. Many times I get depressed, and I think about this society in which everything you are is denied. If I am a part of the Santiagazo, and you are talking to people who tell you that the Santiagazo didn't exist, it is almost like saying that Nana is a farce, that she doesn't exist. Many times I fall, I go to hell. . . ."

In a single remark, Nana points to the existence of a contest over the meaning of the episode and links this contest with her own biography, with the meaning of her own life. This "denial" to which Nana refers is that of the dominant accounts of the protest. In talking about the "explosion," most media (both national and local) and local officials adopt what Natalie Zemon Davis (1973) called the "riffraff theory." The Santiagazo is fabricated as an unplanned and economically determined outburst.[2] The explosion is constructed as a sudden reaction after a brief period of mounting anger, a generalized violent explosion without restraint or reasoning, a "moment of madness" (Zolberg 1972) in which madness overshadows everything else; no goals other than filling their stomachs guide the protesters' actions, no history informs the burning and sacking. In some (mostly local) accounts, rioters are portrayed as an amorphous mob led by callous "subversive agitators." "A sad day," as the main newspaper puts it a year after the uprising, in which the "enraged mob," the *revoltosos*, the *turba*, has its day. The Santiagazo is labeled a bread-and-butter outburst; it is constructed as a revolt of the belly. "The so-called Santiagazo did not exist. It didn't change the destiny of Santiago del Estero; it was a peak of fever, a couple of more degrees in the heat of Santiago . . . it was all about wages; after that, everything went back to normal," a local judge tells me, summing up much of the official memory on the protest.

We know that the meaning of collective action is conflictingly manufactured (Amin 1995; Brass 1996; Roy 1994). Before, during, and after the episode, protesters and authorities tell stories (to others and to themselves) intended not only to explain what they are doing but also to construct and broadcast who the parties involved are.[3] Those stories are crucial to understanding the fight over the categorization of popular collective action and the identities of its protagonists. The "fighting words," furthermore, matter not only because they are the stuff through which the riot is continually constructed. Protesters' stories are also crucial for the construction of the sense of who they are, that is, their self-understandings, their situated subjectivity. Contending stories, then, are central in the construction of the riot *and* of the rioters.

For someone who takes the riot personally, who thinks of the riot neither as a moment of madness nor as a moment of sadness, a denial of its significance constitutes a rejection of her self. How does Nana live this, for her, "long-awaited" protest? Why does she take it in such personal terms? As I said, I think that Nana is illustrative of *some* crucial aspects of the riot's lived experience, a sort of Weberian living "ideal type" that accentuates and synthesizes some important meanings that the protest has for its protagonists. She alternatively defines herself as "the queen of Carnaval" and "the activist of the Santiagazo." It is only by looking at her life story that we can understand why this uprising marks her in such a way; we can begin to comprehend why, as she tells me several times, she "takes the Santiagazo personally." Chapter 7 centers on the history of Nana, her childhood, her public life as the Carnaval's best dancer, her private and difficult relationships with men, her strenuous life as a mother of six always on the verge of economic disaster, her personal memories of the Santiagazo, and the ways in which all these elements are linked.

Chapter 8 will focus on "what pisses me [Nana] off": the official denial of the riot. Particular attention will be paid to the process by which local elites created a particular version of the events, neglecting the experiences that I seek to reconstruct in the pages that follow, and to the contentious dialogue that protesters' recollections establish with this official memory.

Much like the reconstruction of the lived pueblada, my account of the experiences of the Santiagazo closely follows Nana's trail. However, hers, like Laura's, is a guide for (not the sole source of) my description and analysis. Nana's recollections take me to conversations with the leaders of the teachers' union, with public administration and court employees. As I spend part of my days in the local newspaper archives, I talk with journalists who covered the events, who, in turn, take me to other protagonists: the judge in charge of the arrests during December 16, the physician who can be seen in many photographs trying to save a woman trapped in the second floor of the burning Government House (and who will later be accused of being a "professional agitator"), and many other participants—most of whom have not only stories to tell but also quite interesting "souvenirs" of that day. My fieldwork in Santiago is (much like in Cutral-co) also punctuated by some detective-like episodes. During my first stay there, a policeman calls my hotel and asks me for an interview. He has read a report on my research in the local newspaper and wants to share "his version" of the events with me. After some initial (and given the context utterly reasonable) hesitation (after all, this is Santiago del Estero, where the current spy chief, a policeman who was in charge of a clandestine detention and torture center during the last dictatorship, conducts routine espionage activities on union leaders, peasant organizations, politicians, and priests), I meet with Mario, the cop, in the lobby of the hotel where I am staying. The conversation not only provides me with an important version of the events, a version I later confirm with another policeman; it also marks a turning point during my fieldwork where I begin to pay more attention to some hidden aspects of this, to many, historic day.

Chapter Five

The Lived 1993: The

Coming and Making

of the Explosion

Santiago del Estero is a landlocked province bounded by Chaco and Salta on the north, Chaco and Santa Fe on the east, Córboba on the south, and Catamarca, Tucumán, and Salta on the west. A wide plain gently sloping from north to south, the province is crossed by only two rivers, the Dulce and the Salado. The capital of Santiago del Estero (Santiago del Estero) and the neighboring city of La Banda have a dominant bureaucratic role, and the highest concentration of social and community services in the province (more than one-third of the population lives in both cities).

Santiago in the 1990s

In many ways, Santiago symbolizes the relegation of the Argentine interior. Every single study locates Santiago as one of the provinces with the highest levels of "unsatisfied basic needs" (27.4 percent of households put the province in second place, after Jujuy), the lowest income levels ($232.60 per inhabitant puts it third after Chaco and Formosa), and the lowest life expectancy (69.8 years, sixth after the poorest provinces of the Northeast and the Northwest) (PNUD 1996; Fundación Gobierno y Sociedad 1999; Zurita 1999c). The province has, according to a report from the United Nations Program for Development (1996), the second-worst "index of human deprivation" and the second-largest percentage of children living in poor households (42.2 percent).

Out-migration, public employment, and governor Carlos Juarez's patronage can be said to be the terms that better describe social and political life in the province.

Close to half of those born in Santiago are now living outside the province, making outward migration the dominant demographic feature of Santiago (Zurita 1999c), and a potent element in the provincial imaginary; the fact that "sooner or later, everybody leaves" conveys that "there's not much future here."

As of 1994 (and little has changed since then), the primary sector, consisting of agricultural and livestock activities, contributed 14 percent of the value of the total output of goods and services (horticulture, cotton, soy, sorghum, and, of lesser importance, cattle raising). Industry is hardly significant (the secondary sector contributed 18 percent of the value, mainly in food, beverage, and textile production). Although Santiago is the province with the lowest urbanization levels in the country (despite the fact of the rapid and persistent urbanization of Santiago–La Banda), the agricultural sector is not the most important source of employment. It is the service sector where the majority of the employed are concentrated (33 percent). The overwhelming majority of the total economic activity is concentrated in the tertiary sector (financial, transport and communications, commerce, tourism, and mainly government services). As Zurita (1999c, 48) puts it, "Santiago del Estero is a case of dependent development without industrialization; public and service sectors are central in urban areas, the agricultural sector is segmented in areas devoted to export and a huge sector of subsistence peasantry."

How significant is public employment in the province's occupational structure? The last available study shows that public employment is at the center of provincial life—and a crucial factor in understanding the riot by public employees (Zurita 1999a, 1999b). Close to 46 percent of wage earners are public-sector employees. In 1994 the unemployment rate was the lowest in the country; a not so surprising value if we factor in the effect of public employment. It has been calculated that the unemployment rate without public employment will increase to 20.2 percent of the economically active population from the registered 3.4 percent. In the past decade, this state of affairs has been rapidly changing, with rates of unemployment increasing fivefold between 1990 and 1997 (from 2.8 percent to 12.4 percent) (Fundación Gobierno y Sociedad 1999).

With an oversize public sector, it is no wonder that 70 percent of state spending goes to the salaries of public administration personnel—one of the highest percentages in the country. With few resources of its own, the province is highly dependent on resources sent by the national government ("fondos ATN") and the funds sent through "coparticipation," a form of revenue sharing established by the federal government.

It is somehow difficult to describe political life in the city of Santiago without falling into ethnocentric stereotypes such as the ones that journalists from the capital city regularly use when referring to Santiago, "magic realism" being the one most often applied. What most journalists don't see is a powerful system of domination based on patronage. Public employment drains off many of the resources available to the province and provides dominant political elites with a potent instrument of control: clientelism. Jobs in the public sector (and public housing) are distributed according to blatant clientelist criteria, making the fear of losing one's job a powerful "incentive" to attend rallies and show support for candidates.[1] Local sociologists refer to the *modelo juarista* (in reference to the five-time governor Carlos Juarez) as a system of power based on this strict clientelistic distribution of public jobs and other favors and services. This model makes Santiago del Estero the archetypal example of "patronage and underdevelopment" (Verbitsky 1993; Tasso 1999b).

"El Tata" Juarez, "the only successful endeavor in a province plagued by frustrations and failures" (Tasso 1999a, 5), is undoubtedly the ultimate caudillo. His first term as governor was when Perón was at the peak of his power in 1949. Juarez was reelected governor in 1973, in 1983, in 1995, and in 1999. Now in his eighties, he publicly admits that he is "condemned to this job" (of governor). In the last election, his running mate (and now vice-governor) was his wife Nina Aragonés, who, as I was repeatedly told by journalists, union leaders, and residents of Santiago, is the one "who now gives the orders." She is the leader of the powerful Peronist Women's Branch, a group of her followers that controls access to public jobs, attendance to rallies, and distribution of public housing and other goods and services provided by the government.

Se viene el estallido

Juana is an organizer at a Catholic Base Community. She takes part in the massive demonstration on December 16, 1993, heading back home as police reaction escalates early in the morning. She watches the burning and sacking of the public buildings and politicians' homes on TV, stating, "We watch with the people from my community with great excitement." It is worth quoting Juana's recollections of the months before the riot, because they synthesize many crucial elements of the events as seen from the protesters' points of view:

> Well, let me tell you that *before* the December 16 thing happened, the public workers, all those workers who depend on the province government, hadn't received their salaries. It had been at least three months without payment of wages. People did not have money for medicines or food. The businesses did not let you buy on credit anymore. All the mutual aid societies were closed. *It was a terrible chaos.* I had a business at home. . . . There were demonstrations, people complaining. Soup kitchens [*ollas populares*] were organized in the streets. We were constantly going to the demonstrations, together with the people from the communities. We used to write "justice" on the Argentine flag and put a black ribbon on it showing that we were mourning for all that was going on. . . . At the time, we were feeling euphoric because we were demanding what was ours. I was an independent worker, but my husband depended on the provincial government. In a certain way, the whole situation affected me too, because sales went down, and I went broke.

According to a book published by *El Liberal* compiling the opinions and analyses of the most important local journalists, the "news published during the last thirty days (before the riot) explained the explosion." A close reading of this newspaper's reports during the year before the riot is even more helpful. These speak about generalized public nepotism; intense political factionalism within both the government party (Partido Justicialista) and the main opposition party (Unión Cívica Radical); and a local government that—in part because of these fierce factional disputes—is "paralyzed" and threatened by the possibility of federal intervention. They speak clearly about a rapid dissolution of the dominant coalition and decisive changes in political opportunities and constraints. Although in less detail, these reports also expose the escalation of protest by public administration employees and their unprecedented levels of participation in street protests, and the effects that the lack of payment to public employees and the paralysis of the local government are having on the city's population at large, that is, the "terrible chaos" to which Juana refers.

Newspaper reports give even less attention to some other crucial dynamics occurring *within* this increasing wave of contention, dynamics that Juana's testimony hints at: through their repeated encounters with state repression, protesters are learning to react ("The police would always repress us . . . We would go back and stand in the front row again"); protesting organizations are multiplying brokerage efforts to bring together all complaining parties ("We were constantly going to demonstrations, together with the people of the communities. . . . We all got together"); the leadership is increasingly unable to control its followers ("It was impossible to hold people back"). Embedded in these relational processes that take place outside the polity but in contentious dialogue with it, the thrill protesters felt (some of them for the first time) in the street ("We were euphoric") is also a relevant—although more elusive—dimension that facilitates understanding the fury and rage of December 16.

Decreasing Government Capacity: Factionalism and Corruption

"Power vacuum," "institutional crisis," "paralyzed government"—these are some of the descriptive headlines that the main newspaper uses to speak about the state of the local administration at the time. Less than two months before the events of December 16, the governor— besieged by fierce factional disputes within the governing Justicialista Party and pressed by the national government to implement fiscal adjustment—resigns, leaving his place to the vice-governor. During almost two months, while unable to appoint his cabinet members, the new governor, Fernando Lobo, receives strong pressure from the national government: to obtain fresh funds to pay the wages of public employees, the provincial government is being forced to sanction an adjustment law (known as Ley Omnibus). The adjustment law implies the layoff of hundreds of temporary workers, the reduction of public administration wages, and the privatization of most public services. All the while, the threat of federal intervention—with the consequent removal of all local officials—hangs over the governor's head like the sword of Damocles. In other words, for the local government, it is a no-win situation: the only way to calm the mounting mobilization from public employees claiming their overdue wages—or so the national government tells local officials—is to fire many of them and reduce their wages. This is a decision that, as any observer can predict, will not pacify the protest but increase it to unpredictable dimensions—as happens when the law is finally passed in the local parliament on November 12. As of that day, protesters add the derogation of the adjustment law (a law that the leader of the retirees repeatedly calls "perverse and immoral") to claims for their overdue wages.

The local government is portrayed not merely as paralyzed but also as deeply corrupt. Corruption scandals involving millions of dollars break open almost every week on the front page of the main local newspaper during 1993. Serious irregularities are denounced in the distribution of public housing and public land (mainly used as goods to be distributed before elections in a blatant illustration of what the newspaper labels "political clientelism"). The soup kitchens serving poor neighborhoods are also the object of obscure dealings; they are closed because the funds sent by the federal government have mysteriously disappeared. More than a million dollars has been paid for public works that were never done; hundreds of vehicles bought by the provincial state have vanished into thin air; the local social security system's program for the retired is in complete disarray because of money squandering by prominent officials.[2] Officials have a free hand in public funds partly because of the local justice system's inefficiency or—as the newspaper often implies—outright complicity. A few days before the "explosion," Brevetta Rodriguez, the undersecretary of media and institutional relations, who, in connection with other public officials and the governor, has been indicted for signing a contract between the government and a ghost publicity company for U.S. $300,000, is released by the judge after twenty days as a fugitive (*El Liberal*, 23 November 1993). According to many local commentators (Dargoltz 1994; Curiotto and Rodriguez 1994), the judge's decision is the final blow to the courthouse's public image: justice is obviously complicit with entrenched powers.

For the past months, these local notables have been accusing each other of being "corrupt and robbers" (as a former Peronist governor, himself involved in serious venalities, defines the personnel of the new—also Peronist—administration). They are also portrayed as greedy; they are, according to the local newspaper, "the best-paid public officials in

Argentina, despite the fact that the province is among the country's poorest."

Crucial as they are to the collective drawing of lines of culpability, corruption cases are not merely material to read about and discuss with friends in coffee shops and during street rallies. Adding injury to insult, they also affect everyday routines and cause serious threats and suffering to many Santiagueños. Days before the riot, many learn through the newspaper that top officials and local politicians are presumably involved in the operation of a clandestine meat market. Almost half of the meat that the city's population consumes is being distributed without the proper controls, posing serious health risks. To make matters even worse, many areas of the city lack potable water because government officials seemingly squander the money budgeted to buy the chlorine to treat the water system. All the while, city dwellers are learning that infant mortality and malnutrition levels are skyrocketing, that there is a serious health crisis throughout the province, that a cholera epidemic is about to break out, and that energy cuts are leaving entire neighborhoods in the north part of the city without electricity and water. There are no classes in primary and high schools because of the teachers' yearlong strike. By December, the average student has only attended school for fifty days (classes in Argentina begin in March and resume after the two-week winter recess in July).

Although widespread corruption figures prominently in protesters' recollections, it is this disruption of everyday routines caused mainly by lack of payment to public administration workers that they emphasize the most. "We had not been paid for the past three months," Osvaldo, a local artisan who makes percussion instruments, tells me. "But you are not a public employee," I reply. "Yes, but my wife is . . . and the social security system (funded by the provincial state) was suspended, and I couldn't go to the doctor . . . We were so angry." In a city where almost half of the wage earners are public employees (public administration, teachers, police forces, health workers, etc.) (Zurita 1999c), three months without payment have a pervasive impact, as Juana (mentioned in the previous section) admits: although she is not a public employee either, "The whole situation affects me too, because sales fall and I go broke." She is not alone; since September commercial sales suffer a 30 to 90 percent decline, and an unusually large number of businesses file for bankruptcy.

Many interviewees summarize this generalized feeling for me: "This city lives at the rhythm of public administration; if something happens there, everybody feels it." In other words, residents of the city of Santiago del Estero experience an intense disruption of their everyday routines and expectancies, an abrupt imposition of suffering, together with a deep sense that repair through institutional channels is not only not forthcoming but—given the "rotten state" (*todo podrido*, as many protesters define it) of the provincial administration—extremely unlikely: a "terrible chaos" indeed.

Escalation

National analysts focus mainly on the economic genesis of the riot: the implementation of structural adjustment is diagnosed as the main cause behind this and other less-violent "popular explosions" in the interior of the country. Local analysts give more prominence to the political history of this outburst and pay particular attention to the harsh factionalism within the polity and the corruption cases that periodically taint local elites. But the bulk of national observers and local commentators do not focus on the processes that are occurring *outside* the local polity, the growing tide of contention that starts at the beginning of 1993. According to the national newspaper *La Nación,* for months the city is an "active volcano" about to explode mainly because of the intense street mobilization of teachers, public employees, and students clamoring for wage increases. Local journalists are somehow more attentive to the previous climate of street mobilization, mentioning the multitudinous rallies organized by an opposition caudillo against the 1991 electoral fraud (demonstrations that presumably fuel the violent climate that makes the riot possible) and the protests of teachers, retirees, and other public employees. Yet for the most part, the riot is seen by both national and local journalists as an "explosion" *(estallido)* of people who are "tired," "enervated," or "mad as hell" and one day blow up, shouting: "That's enough, we cannot take it anymore." Although disagreeing about the causes of this "explosion," almost every interpretation concurs in the extraordinary and sudden character of the outburst.

Six years after the riot, the events of December 16 and 17 look anything but sudden. Throughout 1993 we witness an escalation of contentious challenges that each time employed more violent direct action

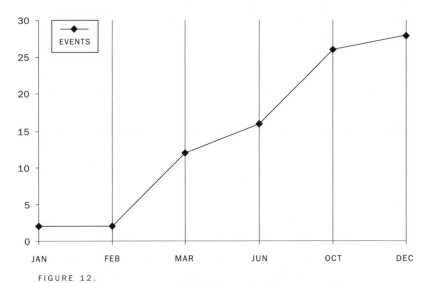

FIGURE 12.

Graph of strikes and street demonstrations from January to the first two
weeks of December 1993, as registered in *El Liberal*, the main local newspaper.

against the authorities. After the fact, the riot seems to be the (socio)log-
ical end point of this cycle of contention. The chart in figure 12 illustrates this increasing wave of mobilization (demonstrations, marches,
and strikes). Protesters and some local observers examine the riot as part
of this increasing surge of contention. Nana recalls: "What happened
on December 16 had been developing for many months. I think that it
was a very long path throughout the year of 1993. I remember that those
who started the whole thing, taking crowds into the streets, were the
teachers. With their demonstrations, with their flag spread in the hands
of fathers, mothers, students. . . ."

This increasing mobilization is, as Henri Lefebvre might put it, "inscribed in space" in the form of a decreasing distance between protesters
and the objects of their demands. The spatiality of the contentious actions preceding the riot caught the attention of Jose Luis, a local photographer and cameraman. Here's how he describes that contentious year:
"This thing that happened in December was something that I had been
following since the beginning of the year . . . one day they had arrived at
that street, the next day the demonstration got to that other corner, and
later it got to . . . I mean, the thing was in crescendo. The demonstra-

tions became more explosive each day. Every day there was a different one . . . every day."

For Jose Luis, the wave of protest is not only becoming more "explosive" but also "getting closer and closer to Government House." Contentious collective action prior to the final "explosion" involves the liberation of certain urban spaces (traffic blockades), the selection of specific places to burn tires (politicians' homes and public buildings), symbolic sieges of public buildings, and attempts to break into some others. Contention also involves symbolic protests such as blackouts whereby all the stores are asked to turn out their lights as a symbol of dissatisfaction with the government.

In March, two thousand schoolteachers rally throughout the city and "symbolically take over Government House and the legislature" (*El Liberal*, 23 March 1993). On April 13, high school teachers surround Government House (the local paper calls it a "siege" of the building), protesting against the transference of schools from the federal to the provincial government. Teachers have repeated clashes with the police in subsequent months while trying to gain entry to Government House in order to "speak with the proper authorities." During the year, other public buildings are also the object of "invasions" by angry public employees. On June 23, municipal employees interrupt a session of the local council with "insults, shouts, and threats" against a proposed reduction of their salaries. According to a newspaper report, workers threaten to jump the barrier that separates the public from council members, telling them: "You are not going to leave this place . . . you are corrupt, shameless . . . you should give up your salaries." The police intervene "to calm down" the protesters. A week later, the same group of workers stones the municipal building, breaks windows, burns tires in front of it, and tries to enter the building by force.

The first week of September also has state employees getting "closer and closer" to Government House. On September 1 and again on September 4 the house is "virtually besieged" by demonstrators (this time, they are students, state employees, retirees, teachers, and members of the transport union). They throw stones, break windows, and burn tires. For the first recorded time, protesters try to burn the building's main front door. This same week, state employees and municipal workers storm the local council, cut the building's electricity, and demand the presence of council members to discuss a "just income policy." Protests are becoming increasingly violent and closer to the "center of power" as protesters begin to couple their demands for unpaid wages with complaints against generalized corruption. Retirees, who are organizing a hunger strike in the main square, also attempt to "invade" the building, shouting, "We are hungry . . . don't protect the dirty crooks and corrupt ones" (*El Liberal*, 20 November 1993). Days before, the leader of the strike tells strikers: "If we need to immolate ourselves, we will do it . . . Let's march [into the building] and break the access door if that's necessary."

The legislature building is also the object of "symbolic sieges." On October 15, "visibly irritated teachers, encouraged by union leaders, storm Government House and the legislature . . . insulting officials, breaking glasses and tearing apart papers from the desk of the undersecretary of labor" (*El Liberal*, 16 November 1993). A week later, teachers are again trying to enter the house but are stopped by the police, who are "growing in number . . . to guard the increasingly threatened Government House" (*El Liberal*, 23 November 1993). The most violent clashes with the police occur when the local parliament passes the Omnibus Law: public employees try to enter the legislature during its session, throwing stones, bottles, and eggs at the police. They are stopped with tear gas and rubber bullets. Three policemen and two protesters are injured.

Participants in the riot and many observers mention high school teachers' unions and retirees as the most active groups. It is worth quoting at length the way in which members of both groups describe the events leading to the "sudden explosion." Their stories speak about their awareness of the structure of political opportunities, their decision to take advantage of these opportunities (and to make them happen), but they can also be read as indicators of other relational processes that were taking place within this wave of contention.

RENÉ (leader of the Teachers' Union): We could draw a picture of the year of 1993. It was very important to us as the teachers' union, which was one of the most combative organizations at the time. It is not a coincidence. In 1993 the transference of national schools to the province was taking place. . . . Our union grouped together precisely the schools that were going to be transferred completely. Obviously we started to get organized in order to resist that transference. Because we understood that it was the way of the national state to abandon or get rid of its role in education and of its obligation to support it—an obligation that cannot be delegated. And we could then see how its first operation was to throw the bundle to the provinces. We could also foresee that after that, the provinces were going to throw the bundle to the *municipalidades* [city governments], and finally the system was going to end up privatized and killed. Then we started to get organized. In January 1993 we were only seven or eight people in the streets with a megaphone and a placard [laughter]. The column in the newspaper said that we were an insignificant group of people who stood by the door of the market, in the heart of downtown. We were denouncing the transference of the national schools to the provinces, which was going to imply a great loss in the quality of education. Because, as we said, the province was manipulating the education matter with political favoritism. . . . In 1993 we started to resist the transference. And because that was the year of the elections, we thought, "Now that we have already started moving, we should take advantage of the whole situation."[3] Then that group of about ten people started to go out in the streets, and it started growing. We began by going out every Saturday, and the day came when we were a very good number of teachers, with no differences among us, who were starting to complain. And we said, "We have to take advantage of this, because being a year of elections, there will be some response here."

In describing how few they are at the beginning, how "ridiculous" they look, and how they grow in number and force throughout the year, the recollections of the leader of the retirees are similar to those of the teachers.

ANTONIO (leader of the retirees): We, the retirees, started to confront the government before December 16 with hunger strikes in front of Government House. This started at the beginning of 1993 . . . with demonstrations and screams. We were asking to be attended to, asking for help with our debts, fighting against the privileged retirements. No one took care of the common retiree. But that wasn't the case of anyone who had been a deputy. . . . When we started, there were only five or six of us. People laughed. We became strong through conviction rather than through numbers. It was so much so that we built a tent in front of Government House to start our hunger strike. We fought the police. I have a picture of a police dog biting me. We were the precursors. Not only hitting the government, but also the leadership of the union that was doing absolutely nothing. . . . We started to scream and scream, making a fuss at the retirement cashier.

"Learning Fire" and Locating Targets

Throughout the year, contention begins to blend conventional forms of protest (such as strikes, gatherings, and marches) with new ways of acting (obstructing traffic, tire burning, symbolic sieges of—and attempts to break into—public buildings): an incremental innovation within usual forms of collective action that is reflected in protesters' stories in the form of anecdotes and "first-time" experiences. In those stories, we find that in the day-to-day practice of contention, protesters' routine suffering of violent repression fosters a truly collective learning experience. Throughout the "long path of the year of 1993," Nana remembers, "the atmosphere gradually turns into something heavier and denser." By December, street gatherings, marches, demonstrations, and strikes have turned the whole city into "one vast, boiling cauldron" (Tocqueville, quoted in Tarrow 1998, 29); "Seen from the sky, it is almost sure that Santiago looked like a bombed city" (*El Liberal*, 2 September 1993). Nana distinctly recalls how in the face of what public employees are going through without their wages and their increasing street mobilization, the widespread nepotism of the political elite is visibly insulting. In blending the escalation of protest to issues of corruption, her recollections are close to those of the leader of the retirees quoted earlier: "And to the demonstrations of the previous months and all of what is developing, you have to add the nerve of the people in the government. They buy new cars, showing up with imported ones, wasting money. They go out to clubs at night . . . champagne, women, and all that kind of stuff." As mentioned, this is a process that can be reconstructed through a careful archival analysis of the main local newspaper. But Nana also recollects a set of processes that fell outside the purview of even the most attentive observers. Nana remembers how, together with other street protesters, she begins to experience repression and to react to it, every time in a wiser way:

NANA: At the time we started to suffer the tear gas. There were compañeros who appeared with the forehead and the arms and legs wounded. We started to see . . . let's say it was like a *training and learning*. In each demonstration we had to have something with which we could oppose the effect of the repression we were subjected to. There were bonfires where we burned paper and palm tree leaves. And then we threw the tear gas back at them—well, but that's just a way of saying it. The compañeros threw the tear gas back, even when they burned their hands. But they would throw them back . . .

JAVIER: You said that during that year your compañeros had learned to . . .

NANA: To defend ourselves . . . And *it was learning* because the first time we had to run away, escaping from the gas. Many of us were late. I remember thinking that I was never going to be able to breathe again, because the feeling of suffocation was so impressive. Many were left lying on the floor of the square. Especially the elderly and the women. . . . That was in September, long before the sixteenth. We escaped. After that, it wasn't like the first reaction where we all ran away for three or four blocks, and many went back home while some of us went back. Instead, the following times, we would withdraw when *we knew* they were raising the weapon to fire the gas; *we were more alert*. We would withdraw a little and then come back. Or else we would take something with which to make a bonfire, because some said that the smoke soothed the effect of the gasses. I always had a handkerchief with me, but it was never enough, because I could feel the stinging pain in my tongue, my nose, everything. The kids would cover their noses with wet handkerchiefs. And we tried to react collectively and help each other. It was not the same as in the first days, where we didn't know where the hell to run to. I remember that many people stepped on each other . . . I couldn't understand what the hell was going on. We would run into each other and step on each other. Later on . . . well, that didn't happen anymore. *There was some sort of common agreement* of protecting us from our own selves. We could not hurt us, or twist our ankle or push each other . . . (italics mine)

On November 20, the local newspaper publishes a report on the grave effects that the burning of tires is having on the local population's health. "With a government besieged by the economic crisis . . . the protests of different unions have been massive during this year. Almost all of these demonstrations use the burning of tires as a way of protesting." Burning tires, which according to the report "represents a serious health risk because of the toxins it produces," becomes a normal way of carrying out protest; making fire is becoming something not only thinkable but even routine.

René and María are two middle-class women from the teachers' union. It is hard to explain why, but their demeanor, appearance, and recollections of the days before the riot make them unlikely candidates for the "exercise of fire." At that time, they are engaged in the more traditional ways of protesting: "We go out to the street, hand out flyers, talk on the megaphone." However, even they are burning tires. At the end of our long interview, I ask them about this other way of making their claims heard. Their hesitation and nervous laughter convey the idea that although their "doing it" looks unthinkable from today's standpoint, it is pretty normal in the chaotic 1993, because "people don't know what to do anymore" to make themselves heard. When closely read, the following testimony illustrates how fire is a product of the lack of response from the government authorities; this particular performance within the protesters' repertoire is part of a contentious conversation between the ever-louder protests and the ever-more-oblivious elites.

MARÍA: Some days before, in each area, the public workers burned tires.
JAVIER: Did you do that too?
MARÍA: No . . . [hesitates]
RENÉ: I think that we did burn some tires. [laughter]
MARÍA: Yeah. [laughter]
JAVIER: I mean, because it is hard for me to imagine the two of you burning tires.
RENÉ AND MARÍA: Yes . . . [laughter]
MARÍA: *People didn't know what to do anymore.* When we had classes . . . every now and then we would go to teach, and the kids, the children from secondary school [junior high], would fall asleep because they hadn't had much to eat. They had probably had only bread and mate. The church denounced the deaths of three children as a consequence of hunger. Then all the nurses from the regional hospital would go out and block the street and make bonfires with anything they found. Half a block ahead, the workers of the education council would go out and burn something. I don't remember us doing any of that . . . On the sixteenth, we had a press conference at 10:30 at our place. There

was a school right next door, my school [laughter]. The teachers had gone out, blocking the street with chairs, making noise, because *we did not know what to do anymore*. . . . Someone passed us a tire . . . that was the only time [laughter] . . . then we put the tire in the middle of the street, by the door of the vegetable store, and all the teachers came and put papers inside and burned them. We had a fight, a domestic but happy thing that shows people's mood, with the owner of the vegetable store, who came out and started to fight with us and to sprinkle us with water [laughter]. We were in that fight.

In another interview, a year later, I ask René if burning tires was a "usual" practice at that time. Her answer speaks not only about the routinized character of that collective practice but also about the importance of relationships in this learning process: "I don't even know how to make fire for the barbecue . . . I don't know, things just happened, other teachers showed up . . . well, there was this guy, Castrilli, *he had experience . . .*"

Smoke from burning tires is contaminating the air of Santiago, fire is being inscribed in protesters' repertoire, and "targets" are being collectively agreed on. Far from being random, the targets that the "innocent horde"—as a local judge called protesters—attacks on December 16 have clearly been located beforehand: the burned and sacked houses are the residences of officials and politicians that, according to newspaper and TV reports, are involved in public nepotism.

Anger is moralistic (Katz 1999); people do not get mad until (and unless) they have some person or group to blame for their predicament. In the streets, demanding their wages and shouting against corruption, protesters locate culpability: the offices and private homes of the "political class." This explains the "precision" with which the crowd moves from one home to another—and that some observers use as "evidence" of the work of "subversive agitators." Protesters know their targets in advance; they are reading profusely about them during the months that precede the final "explosion."

Media reports unanticipatedly construct a blueprint for protesters.[4] "The targets were perfectly visible. This is a small town, everybody knows each other, and the media always remark who is who. . . . *It was as if everyone understood that we had to go there*," Mariano, a participant in the events, explains to me six years later. Toto, a policeman, tells me: "At the time, many media were commenting on the amount of money

officials made." And Carlos explains by way of example: "The legislature was the place where the most anger accumulated." "Burning it was
a necessity," Mariano summarizes.

"People rebel because they are not paid, that's beyond question," another protester asserts, "but it is also true that they *naturally* burn the
buildings of political institutions, and if people burn them down, it is
because the buildings don't mean anything to them." I argue that the
opposite is true: protesters "naturally" burn them because those buildings and homes mean too much. Rather than empty places abandoned
by officials and politicians, public buildings and private houses are in-
tensely meaningful places. During the previous months, they have been
filled with significance and established as objects of rage: as Nana puts
it, "[Government House] is a historic monument of trash and corruption. . . . I want to enter that corrupt house." I am not arguing that by
December 16 protesters have a "map in their heads" of the places they
are going to attack, burn, and sack but contending that the space of the
city is, in a way, reconfigured by protest and that certain places acquire
the status of focal points of protesters' actions and anger. Not every invaded home is previously visited by marches or demonstrators, but all of
them become concrete places where the responsibility for the suffering
of the Santiagueños can be located. Well before December 16, the targets
of protesters' rage are already part of a potential itinerary, and the use
of fire against them is a "normal" practice inscribed into the protesters'
repertoire.

New Actors, Brokerage Efforts: A New Self-Understanding

As some are unexpectedly burning tires, others take their claims to the
streets for the first time. As reported by *El Liberal* on November 6, 1993,
many workers from the public administration—while shouting in the
streets and the main square—tell reporters that "this is the first time in
the history of this office that there's a public demonstration." New actors
are aligning themselves on the challenging side of the field of protest.
By the end of November, local writers, poets, singers, and actors demonstrate for the first time in the central plaza against "corruption and
injustice" with a show entitled "Black November." The week before the
riot and in a measure "without precedence in the history of commerce

of Santiago del Estero," the Business Chamber decides to go on strike, demanding a "solution to the economic crisis and measures to repair the moral order." Stores, supermarkets, and service stations close their doors for one day.

Catholic priests and nuns join protesters in the main square, offering their mediations and expressing their solidarity with the "innocent people who—having no responsibility whatsoever in the unclear use of public money—are deprived of their salaries" (*El Liberal*, 13 November 1993). As Carlos, who, together with hundreds of protesters, enters Government House on December 16 (and can be seen in many pictures trying to rescue a woman who is trapped by fire on one of the upper floors), says, "There were demonstrations in front of Government House every day. The last two were strongly suppressed. One of them had a strong police response, and the other one—I went to see them both—was very peculiar because it represented the *new thing* in politics. I saw a cordon of nuns and priests separating the police from the unions. They were making a cordon to prevent the police from reacting."

"We were accompanying this process with hunger strikes in other towns," a priest explains to me. Local newspapers report on the presence of priests in the hunger strike carried out by retired elderly in the months before December 16. As Enrique Hisse, a priest who is now one of the leaders of Memoria y Participación (a political party created after December 16) describes, "I joined the retired in the plaza, supporting their hunger strike. I have become much more involved since then. After that, there was an episode of police repression, so next time we, priests and nuns, made a cordon, a barrier so that people didn't get hurt . . . Our feeling at that time was that there was no way out. We used to talk with some friends and couldn't figure out a solution to what was going on."

Some priests and nuns not only express their support; they join protesters in the streets, sometimes to protect them (as during the many encounters with police repression), other times to teach them how to organize a street protest. As the leaders from the teachers' union recall: "We had the support of a church group that was very combative and committed with the needy people. So we talked to the priest and told him, 'Look, we want to organize a street blockade, how can we do it?' 'Leave that to me,' he replied. We wanted to block the street to make a mess in the traffic, but we didn't know how! So we made a procession, and we sat on the road. He organized it in a very smart way . . ." In showing their support, in protecting protesters from police repression, and in teaching inexperienced protesters new ways of acting, church members are legitimating the protest; a validation that, coming from church authorities in a deeply Catholic city, carries impressive symbolic weight.

While new actors are "doing this kind of thing for the first time," the most active unions are engaged in brokerage efforts to bring all the protesters' organizations together. René recalls: "We form a group of various teaching unions that includes almost all of us . . . almost all of the teaching unions of Santiago [three] and the group of dissidents from the largest union that, just as always, is with the government" (the group called Intergremial Docente). What looks from the outside to be an explosion of "fed-up people" is, in fact, a bundle of social relations making claims in collectively learned ways.

On November 11, nine unions (Obras Sanitarias, waterworks; Asociación Bancaria, bank employees; CISADEMS, AMED, SADOP, teachers; ASEJ, courthouse employees; ATAD, UOEM, public administrators and meat workers) create the Frente Gremial de Lucha (Union Front) to mobilize all "the workers' forces" against the adjustment omnibus law. In its opening document, the Front blames "the three branches of the government" (executive, legislative, and judiciary) for the plight of both public employees and citizens in general and demands the investigation and punishment of "those responsible for the economic and social chaos." Coupling claims for unpaid salaries with resistance against public corruption, this opening manifesto contests the charges that the provincial government is making against protesters. Rather than blaming "outside subversive agitators," the Front places responsibility for the escalation of violence squarely on the shoulders of the ruling elites.

René and María recall that "the Union Front is created given the need . . . when the problem ceases to be a teachers' problem, because the government owes the salaries to everybody . . . I don't recall how it is formed . . . someone says, 'Why don't we get together?' So the people from the Courthouse Employees Union come, because we have a friend there, a contact person there, and he asks us, 'Why don't we have a meeting and see if we can do something together?' It seems like a good idea. So we talk to some other people, they talk to some other unions, and that's how we come together in the Union Front. . . . [The unions that formed the Union Front] are not usually close to us; they don't work with us. But at this time *we are kind of close*" (italics mine). During these

meetings, they recall, "We decide what to do, we make joint pronounce-
ments, we organize rallies."

These organizing and brokerage efforts occur amid widespread expansion of workers' militancy: "People who had never before gone to
assemblies were showing up," Nana recalls; and Mariano adds, "Those
were the largest meetings that ever occurred." This eruption of popular participation in meetings and street gatherings begin to surpass the
established leadership, both from unions and from other organizations.
As Juana from the Catholic Base Community puts it, "It was impossible to hold people back"; as Roque, head of the courthouse employees
union, admits, "Probably yes . . . at some point the people got out of
control"; or as María and René (CISADEMS) clearly explain:

MARÍA: I felt that in some meetings when we said, "Let's go out in
    mobilizations," some people said, "Forget mobilizations, let's go kill
    them . . ." There were a few expressions that we had never heard be-
    fore. "No peaceful demonstrations. Let's go break everything!"
RENÉ: So the temperature was rising. The atmosphere was building up.

In another interview, they both tell me how "surprised" they were when
"people with whom we were sharing our workdays, the meetings and
the debates, were out of their minds. . . . In the meetings the people encouraged us, they told us, 'No peaceful protest, let's burn everything.' "

While some union leaders are losing their ability to control their followers, others are becoming the objects of claims themselves, especially
those who are close to the government and grouped under the General
Workers Confederation (CGT). The protest is also directed against them.
As Antonio puts it: "We built the tent and started the strike . . . not only
against the government but also to condemn the pseudo-representatives
of the workers . . . the workers also started the protests, forcing them to
listen."

Within the major teachers' union (AESYA), members accuse its president Robert Diaz of negotiating "behind the back of the union's con-
stituency." Diaz's house is one of the last to be attacked and burned on
December 16. "He deserved it," René points out, illustrating in a single
remark what "everybody in Santiago now knows": that the attacks on
the homes of local notables mark a calculated retribution. "We wanted
to punish them," I am repeatedly told by participants in the events. "But
it was not a matter of being cruel to someone in particular," Mariano

points out, telling me that when they enter the house of Deputy Granda, this local notable is inside. "Nobody touches him, they sack and burn his home, but they don't even touch him. *They want to take things away from those who have been pilfering the province for so many years* . . . But it is not a matter of being cruel to someone in particular."

At the beginning of 1993, public employees are making claims as employees from this or that branch of the public administration or from this or that union (courthouse employees, teachers, retirees, etc.). Teachers demand better (and on-time) salaries and better school buildings; health workers demand their salaries and their *aguinaldo* (annual bonus); university professors complain about their meager salaries and the bad working conditions. By June, public employees organized by their own unions (the various teachers' unions, the Health Workers Union, the Court Employees Union, the Waterworks Union) are claiming their unpaid salaries, occasionally converging in the main square in rallies and demonstrations. By September, demands and actors are converging in the street, but not yet in a single front. As the main local newspaper reports on its front page: "Workers mobilized. Hundreds of workers and high school students concentrate in front of the government house, in a peaceful demonstration, claiming a 'just income policy' and the continuity of the academic year." During this month, demonstrations are organized by different unions and groups of employees from different state dependencies (ATE, Dirección General de Catastro, Dirección General de Arquitectura, Centro de Cómputos, Escribanía de Gobierno, Registro Civil, Dirección Provincial de Turismo, Industria, y Comercio, Registro de la Propiedad Inmueble, Consejo General de Educación, Recursos Hídricos). Although they converge in the street, internal disputes about who organizes and represents the protesters are rampant: groups of protesters point out that "they come by their own and are not assembled by ATE [State Employees Union]." Union leaders make clear that no union other than their own is coordinating their protest. A report from *El Liberal* explains the fragmentation of the protesting parties: "The development of the protest carried out by employees of the public administration showed an assortment of different groups of workers. These workers, with their own leaders, demanded 'each by their own' notwithstanding their similar demands . . . Recursos Hídricos and IPVU tirelessly repeated that the decisions they made were exclusively theirs; teachers . . . stressed that they were coming on their own."[5]

However, by November 15, the newly formed Union Front is calling for a massive gathering in front of Government House and the court-house to have an interview with the governor and to demand "the punishment of those who are guilty of corruption and robbery." Union leaders are now signing joint declarations, organizing common street demonstrations, and collaborating in each other's protests in different ways. Leaders from the Dirección de Energía, for example, ask the co-operation of Agua y Energía Eléctrica to cut the energy supply of the city as a form of protest: "With this [collaboration] we intend the pueblo Santiagueño as a whole to express its solidarity, because it is not something that affects only the public employee, it is a matter of the whole society" (*El Liberal,* 16 December 1993). Or as the teacher quoted earlier puts it when referring to the creation of the Union Front: "[At one point] it ceases to be a teacher's problem."

By the end of 1993, the claimants (who at the beginning of the year were pretty much "on their own") are "the people." During the course of 1993, through contentious interaction, individual public employees become "the people of Santiago versus corrupt power holders." Embedded in the set of relations and interactions I have described, a new collective self-understanding begins to take shape: a category of persons becomes a short-lived political actor. This is the "we" that will "explode" on the morning of December 16.

Chapter Six

The Lived Sixteenth:

The Feast and the

Remains of the Riot

On December 16, moving from one "target" to another seems the "natural" thing to do. Here's how a protester describes what he calls "the procession" through downtown on the day of the final uprising:

> When we were in Government House, the public employees were clapping at the fire. It seemed *natural* to move on to the Congress. And while we were going there, the *feeling* was that it had to be the same. It was at the Congress where the most anger had accumulated because the workers had gone there to ask the legislators to vote against the Ley Omnibus that would be bad for them and that had been so controversial . . . The people clearly knew that the legislators were not doing anything to defend them. So it seemed *natural* to them that, having already settled the differences with Government House and the courthouse, the Congress was next. (italics mine)

Another protester talks about this "natural" character of the crowd's actions in terms of "necessity": "It was as if it was understood that it was necessary to go to the Congress, because there was still the anger caused by the repression that happened the day that they approved the Ley Omnibus."

After being in the legislature, some protesters return to their homes or go back to the main square, but "a very dynamic group begins to move around by mopeds and bicycles," another protester recounts.[1] This "very dynamic group" arrives at a politician's home and is joined by neighbors in the burning and sacking.

The Itinerary

Much like the public buildings, the residences that protesters attack, sack, and burn on December 16 have also been, in a way, defined as targets in the previous months. As I said before, the "precision" with which the crowd moves from one home to another does in fact illustrate the previous process of reconfiguration of the city's geography in terms of the localization of the sources of corruption and suffering, sources who, in the words of another participant, "deserved to be burned down." "How do you decide where to go?" I ask Marilú, a public employee. "Here, in Santiago, everybody knows each other, and we know where people live . . . Someone says, 'Let's go there because he has also been stealing from us.' Because that's how it is here in Santiago; we all know each other." Although the great majority of the local political elite is portrayed as corrupt, not everybody's house is looted. Some attacks are negotiated on the spot. Mariano recalls that when hundreds of protesters reach the home of deputy Washerberg, "the guy is freaking out with his sons in the back part of the house. His wife comes out of the house to defend him, 'Please, don't do it . . .' She is crying, kneeling in front of us. In any case, Washerberg opposed the Ley Omnibus, and he voted against it . . . So after his wife cries so much, five gallons of tears, they don't enter his house."

Others, whose homes "deserve to be burned down," are spared for logistical reasons: "The next target," Mariano adds, "is the home of Corvalán, a union leader close to the government. They don't burn his house because he lives in a housing compound; they fear that his neighbors' houses will also be reached by the fire." And others are (partially) saved from the attack because of the scattered police action: "We are trying to break into Lobo's house when the cops come," Raúl recalls; and Mariano adds, pointing at the interaction between the size of the town and the intermittent repression in the making of the protesters' itinerary:[2]

> *Santiago is a small town.* Everyone knows each other, everyone knows who's who. We leave the Congress and go to the governor's house . . . From there we take another street and go to [government official] Cramaro's house. It is a very nice house, with a lot of wood and many nice things inside. They enter and trash it. Some cops come in and take us out, running. We then take the Avenue . . . and the groups go to [former governor] Juarez's house either by foot or by bike . . .

[former governor] Iturre's house is a spectacular house, with a swimming pool . . . They also loot and burn it. After that, someone says we should go to [deputy] Granda's house. . . . He is inside, alone. They go into the house and don't even touch him. But again they loot and burn it. They start to take things out, silver trays and teapots. . . . *It is a moment of joy.* It is like stealing from the fellows that have abused power for so many years. (italics mine)

After protesters enter Government House, and except for minor deterrence attempts scattered throughout the city, the police leave protesters alone. Through mutual signaling (signaling that comprised negotiation, logistics, and protection from potential repressive action), protesters move from one place to another. In this mutual signaling, local radio programs play an important role, broadcasting the crowd's actions "as if it were a soccer match." The places that protesters attack have, indeed, different histories and meanings (whereas the plaza and Government House have long been centers of political life and thus of protest, the home of local politicians have become sites of contention only during 1993). That day, however, claims against corruption and wage demands get concretized in all of them; public buildings and private homes provide concrete representations to protesters' rage. What follows is Roberto's description of the interaction between a few police agents and the protesters as the latter are trying to break into the minister of public works' residence. The description portrays not only the actions of protesters and policemen. Most importantly it illuminates the meaning of this particular house and hints at the way that protesters are "feeling" at the time, a feeling summed up in the "moment of joy" Mario talks about:

People start to gather in front of his house, a man who built a mansion in one year, right in the middle of downtown. He is an exhibitionist. And he takes bribes and benefits. The people are crowding in front of his house, like trying to say, "Here we are." And the crowd starts to knock on the door. The police come. There are two police cars that come to save him. But you can tell from the cop's faces that they are also enjoying the fact that the man who has probably also screwed them is in that kind of a situation. There are two thousand people in front of his house. It is wonderful to see that scene, because at a certain point, the police force that is controlling the situation can't hold it any longer. They have to shoot at the people again, and they are not going to do that, because by now *it is almost a party, a chaos.* There is nothing left to defend in this province. The government is gone to hell. What are the police doing? And then we find out that the fellow is in the house and that they [the cops] have to get him out. *A pact is made.* The crowd, the youngsters at the front, tells the cops: "You can get him out, but you have to leave after that." *They are feeling strong* . . . and the police are weakened: they can't shoot—they are ten fellows against two thousand. [It is like] a situation almost of indulgence, of buddies. . . . "Let us get him out," the police say. "All right, get him out, but you leave the house for us"; you could hear that. So the police say, "Yes, yes." The police greet us like saying: "Do whatever you want, there's no problem." And they leave. People enter the house, one of the nicest houses, and steal everything. (italics mine)

The Feast

After an unsuccessful attempt to protect Government House with tear gas and rubber bullets, the police leave the scene, showing up only sporadically to protect some of the victims of the attacks. Protesters then have the chance to enjoy moments of amusement and joy, moments that contrast with the tension lived in the main square. When repressive controls relax, the "party" and the "celebration" about which Roberto and Nana talk begin. "There are many interesting anecdotes. We laughed a lot. Do you want me to tell you those stories?" Roberto laughingly asks me. And Nana adds, "We laughed like crazy. It was hilarious."

The main streets of Santiago become the stage for an unforgettable collective performance. "For once, Santiago was ours," Nana tells me. And Marcelo, at that time an aspiring journalist, recalls the festive atmosphere of the sacking: "There are many people who went there as spectators. When we were in the terrace it was something happy, funny. People were sitting in the terrace with sunshades because it was really hot. They were watching what was going on. And they said to each other, 'Look at that one, how he leaves with the suitcase,' or 'That one . . . with the piggy.' They took out chairs, doors, suitcases with clothes in them . . ." In participants' accounts, the observable spectacle merges with the experiential feast. There is both a "bond of sympathy" (Rude 1964) between those who join the crowd and those who line the sidewalks or sit in front of a TV set, as well as a constant exchange between the roles of spectator and active participant. As René puts it:

> At around 3 P.M., we see on TV that the politicians' houses are still being burned. And both the TV and radio are transmitting as if it was a soccer game. "Now they are going to the house of such and such" [laughter]. And then on the TV we see that they are burning (Governor) Juarez's house. And you can see spectators who look satisfied at the scene. I am with my aunts at home. I put them in my old Citroën, and I go there to see. Half a block from the house, people from this downtown area are clustered in their cars to see what is being done. . . . People are celebrating . . . Me too [laughter] . . . of course . . . [because] they [the officials] are destroying us . . .

María adds, "We see it like a popular spectacle, a thing of the people, really spontaneous and comprehensible." In an interview with Manuel, another active participant, I mention the title of the newspaper report that describes the uprising. It is entitled "The Saddest Day." He responds, "No, not at all. It is a day of happiness and explosion . . . a lot of anger. . . . It is a sad day *for them*, because the government palace and the legislature are burning." The uprising is lived as a pleasurable and amusing experience.

ROBERTO: At Casanegra's house, the upstairs bedroom's windows have bars, and the kids already looted everything.[3] They are starting to burn it, and you can see the flames going up. There are some kids left upstairs who are not going to be able to leave through the windows because of the bars. You can see them staying there, looking through [laughter]. And there is a crowd outside; all of them worried to see when the kids are going to get out. A woman raises her hand holding a beautiful pink shoe in it. Through the bars you can see a guy who knows her and is throwing her some stuff. She shows him the shoe and says, "[I need] the other one!!" [laughter]. That guy is risking his life, and she is asking for the other shoe. How wonderful! We are laughing like crazy.

Nana at the time is in the main square. She can't actually believe what is going on but takes pleasure in it. After running back and forth, after the stones and the tear gas, she is now wandering around, "enjoying the moment": "I stay at the courthouse and then head back to Government

FIGURE 13.
A protester's trophies.
© El Liberal

House. I enjoy the moment walking through the streets. We look and walk around the courthouse. . . . We are celebrating, calm . . . I never smoke a joint, but I think it is something similar to that . . . Yeah, because we enjoy it, like sitting down to smoke a cigarette and drink coffee with a good friend . . . We are sitting down, enjoying all that, feeling the heat of the burning Government House."

Another union activist, Andres, also compares his sensations at the time with "smoking pot or . . . at the time we are chatting with a friend and we are saying that it is as if we are making love to someone we desire for a long time." He, Nana, Roberto, and many others have been waiting for this moment for a long time, since it all started at the beginning of the year.

Newspaper reports mention in passing the applause and cheers of bystanders, describing the apparent happiness of protesters as a "contradiction": "Given the critical moment in the life of the city . . . it might seem a contradiction that the persons who were observing the actions of demonstrators were, at the same time, celebrating, applauding pro-

FIGURE 14.
Man saluting
the crowd from
the balcony of
Government House.
© El Liberal

testers as they went by with their 'booty,' and showing a state close to happiness" (*El Liberal*, 17 December 1993). In protesters' voices, the "celebration" takes center stage.

A cluster of images of parody, open-air cursing, and degradation points to a carnivalesque dimension of the uprising. A man dressed in Nina's clothes parades like a model in front of the former governor's mansion and leaves with his "trophies" (see figure 13); another man sits in the governor's chair, his arms open, saluting the crowd from the balcony of Government House (see figure 14). "That really impresses me," René says; "That is the image that strikes me the most," Juana states. Downstairs people are spraying the walls with curses and threats to established authorities: "Traitors. We'll kill you," "God forgive me. Archbishop, you are a son of a bitch" (the archbishop supported the approval of the omnibus law), "Juarez, Iturre, Lobo, Mugica, hijos de puta." In these graffiti, protesters are not only identifying the objects of their claims and discontent but also putting forward an understanding of who they are: "In Santiago, there are no more sheep," someone sprays on the wall of the house, capturing a general collective feeling. No more sheep, meaning no more cowardly people, no more (stereotypically) calm and submissive Santiagueños. No more sheep, meaning "We, aggrieved, honest people, are not going to take it anymore, enough is enough." On the walls of Government House, the protester leaves—for other protesters, for the elites, for the media, and for us, the analysts—one of those publicly available symbols in which the meanings of the protest and the self-understandings of protesters are embodied.[4]

Episodes of ritual defilement, of comic degradation and inversion, and of passing suspension of boundaries, also abound. "This guy," Roberto describes, "pees all over Juarez's and [his wife] Nina's bed . . . spread all over . . . so funny." And Toto, a policeman, adds, "There is this fool man who goes into one of the homes and comes out with a raincoat and a hat, à la Humphrey Bogart . . . people are laughing like crazy. It is like a show, people are celebrating." Or as René recalls, "At Juarez's house there are people I knew, and we greet each other while we watch the fire. And there are people who come out carrying chairs . . . Then with my car, we take one street to go back, and we see a police car going in the opposite direction, with four or five policemen in it. They honk and greet us. I do that, too, for the first time in my life, because I usually reject them. I honk, and we greet them. Like brothers, I don't know [laughter]."

During this festive trashing, participants highlight the fleeting conformation of a community of demonstrators. "One thing that catches my attention," Roberto says, "is that there are no fights among the people who are sacking those houses. Each person takes something, and no one bothers him." It is not a Hobbesian "war of all against all," because as Gustavo—at that time a journalist—recollects, "nobody even touched what someone else was stealing." For him, the protest is "a party, a catharsis, and a revenge." The transient community formed among protesters transforms fight and punishment into festive action, and for one day, it turns the world of local hierarchies upside down:

We see a huge fat man coming—very impressive—with a sofa, a jewel. It must be a unique piece, a beauty. The fat man is carrying it all by himself, walking through the middle of the street, like the owner in his own house. And all of a sudden he turns around and sees a police car, filled with policemen from the infantry. It stops, and it is obvious that they have to put him in jail; the fat man can't deny he is stealing [laughter]. So the policemen surround him, make him put the sofa down, and make him sit. The fat man doesn't really resist them. He uses the whole backseat of the car and sits down with his back facing the driver. And off he goes. When the car turns around, the people stop it and say, "Give us the fat man back, give us the fat man back!" [laughter]. You know, they exchange him. The cops get the fat man out of the car and take the sofa. . . . People clapped [laughter].

For participants, December 16 has many elements of carnivalesque egalitarianism. That day is lived as "a privileged time when what oft was thought could for once be expressed with relative impunity," a special time that Peter Burke (1978) sees as characteristic of popular rituals, experienced as the "temporary suspension of all hierarchic distinctions and barriers," which Bakhtin defines as central in the carnivalesque (Bakhtin 1984, 15; Stallybrass and White 1986; Steinberg 1998). Far from being a space of forgetting, this Carnaval allows protesters to vent their anger against clearly identified wrongdoers.[5]

The Remains of the Riot

Six years after the events, I go to Santiago del Estero for the first time. In my first day there, a local historian introduces me to Osvaldo, a fifty-year-old artisan and musician, who "was in the square on December 16, and can tell you all about it." At first reluctant, Osvaldo describes his own itinerary during that day, giving particular emphasis to the objects that people take with them from public buildings and private houses, the things that, as another protester later tells me, protesters "want to take away from those who have been pilfering the province for so many years." These objects include armchairs, dining tables, carpets, appliances, typewriters, fans, heaters, bicycles, computers, telephones, firearms, air conditioners, VCRs, clothing, and underwear. People take those objects with them (or "steal" them, as a local judge told me) and are still keeping them as "souvenirs of that day." Each of the protesters I talk to during my fieldwork has with him or her some keepsake from December 16: a crystal from Government House's chandelier, a piece of a deputy's chair, the front door of the governor's house, a diskette from a judge's office.

A leader from the courthouse employees' union describes the moment at which the crowd enters Government House and the possessions with which protesters leave: "It is like an unreal thing. Thousands of people in the Government House are destroying everything. . . . Everyone take something. Typing machines, whatever. Telephones . . . some kids take four chairs and the Ministry's chairs . . ."

What authorities describe as looting, protesters refer to as "keepsakes" and "souvenirs." As devoid of material value as these objects may look (to us), participants in the riot keep them as "trophies":

ROBERTO: I took a souvenir from the Congress: two door handles that I still have, the armrests of one of the deputy's chairs. I was taking them as keepsakes. I also took a car's plates.

NANA: While I am walking around, a kid gives me a telephone he took from the house. I put it under my jacket. I put it here, holding it in my arms. And I start running because, once again, people are saying that the cops are coming at us. I am running with the telephone in my hands. If I drop it, the kid will yell at me. Who knows why he took it. Maybe he wanted a souvenir from the house . . . like many others who took souvenirs.

A Man with His Flag

Juan stands with the Argentine flag from the governor's office, in front of Government House (figure 15). More than six years have passed since that day when we meet to talk about the episode. Juan—a public employee with more than ten years on the job—is forty years old and has three children in their late teens and early twenties. He is happy with his job because it leaves him some free time to do what he loves the most—acting in an amateur theater group. An excerpt of our interview follows. In pointing at protesters' feelings, at their shared self-understanding, and at the relational character of this collective identity, Juan penetratingly summarizes much of the "lived uprising" and wonderfully encapsulates the meanings of the "keepsakes."

JUAN: We wanted to go in [to Government House] so that we could kick everyone out; we didn't want anyone to stay there. We really didn't want anyone to stay there, so that it stays in the record. So I went into Government House. I took a handkerchief; I remember there was a

puddle where I moistened it. I tied it around my head, covering my
mouth, and went in. Inside, it was hard to breathe, I felt like my eyes
were popping out. And the smoke, the smoke inside . . . I could see
that everybody was taking computers, TVs, typing machines, furniture. I didn't care about those things; I was just going there with one
goal, to get the flag, the flag from the governor's office. . . . I remember
that when I entered, there were six or seven guys inside the office. The
guys were picking up chairs, and two of them were trying to move
the desk; others were taking a TV, still others, a telephone. And there
were both the nation's and the province's flags. Then I went and stood
facing the nation's flag. I couldn't take both with poles and everything. I took it out and left the building with the flag in my hands. I
couldn't stay inside anymore.

JAVIER: What did you want it for?

JUAN: I don't know. You know I am a little bit of a bohemian. Having
the flag was like saying, We have won the war. It was the most valuable trophy that we could ever have. For me it was the Argentine flag.

I mean, having the flag, having regained the flag, meant something glorious to me. We have won this battle, the flag is ours. In other words, how could I explain what one feels when one takes a symbol like this? When you see a war movie, in the U.S., what happens all through the movie? There is always a flag. Look carefully, and you'll see that in all the movies there is always a flag. In an office, in formations, in a ship, the flag is always there. And taking the flag meant we had won a war. Because to me that moment was a war. I felt I was fighting against the rubber bullets and the tear gas, and that I had taken a position. That position meant I had to rescue the flag. . . . You can't imagine what it was like when I came out of the house with the flag. . . . You can't imagine the applause. People applauded a lot, and they were all touching the flag and kissing it, like they were finally realizing what had happened. At that time, I looked up and saw a compañero who was on the balcony sitting in a chair, like he was taking over the place of governor at the time. . . . One day I am going to put the flag in a frame, with corduroy on the background and the pole at the bottom. I have it hidden. I don't want to show it because I could go to jail [laughs] . . . It is a symbol of having won a small war. I don't know if I should call it a small war, though. At the time it was a great war . . . the Santiagueño took the Government House and kicked out a group of corrupt politicians who were manipulating his life.

JAVIER: Ten years from now, your son will ask you about the flag, because it will be on a frame . . .

JUAN: [laughs] At that time, I will make him sit down, and I will tell him the exact same story I am telling you.

For months after December 16, Marilú keeps the front door of Juarez's residence (senator at the time of the riot, and now governor) in her patio. "How come you kept the door?" I ask her. "Maybe I did it so that I could say, 'I had been in the explosion.' So that I could say, 'This is from the explosion, I was there.' I didn't tell many people about this [the door] . . . It was a beautiful door, it might have cost a fortune . . . I don't know, maybe in the future when I get married, I will tell my husband or my kids about this. And we might remember this as I am doing right now with you. I don't usually talk about this."

Nana, Roberto, Mariano, Marilu, José, and many, many others have "souvenirs" of December 16: a crystal from the chandelier, an armrest, a painting, a tile, a door, a flag. Much like "winks to epistemology, or sheep raids to revolution," those objects speak to larger issues "because they are made to" (Geertz 1973, 23). The souvenirs speak to a particular set of meanings that the riot has for protesters. As we conclude our informal conversation, Osvaldo, who toured the city of Santiago on his motorbike during December 16, tacitly acknowledges the "trophy" he (or someone he knows well) took with him and hints at one possible meaning of those keepsakes: "Can you imagine how nice it is to shit in Nina's [the governor's wife] toilet?" he asks me as we conclude our conversation. "No, I cannot imagine that," I think, but the image stays in my mind. Protesters invade, burn, sack, and trash the "symbols of power and corruption," as Nana puts it. Not content with that, they tear them apart and take a piece of the remains with them. They are still around, reminding us about the lived feast.

Police Inaction and Souvenirs from the Cops' Point of View

As it is clear from the previous account, the actions of the Santiago rioters are facilitated not only by city geography but also by the geography of policing. I interview Toto and Mario at two different stages of my fieldwork. Their different stories illuminate not only the reasons behind police action but also many other aspects of the uprising.

Toto is an uncommon cop. He was chief inspector when the riot happened, and while on the force, he pursued degrees in law and sociology. He is now an ex-cop, lawyer, and sociologist. A highly articulate man in his late fifties, he was very excited about my work and came to talk to me as soon as I called him, myself having been prompted by a university professor who had Toto as a student.

> That day there was no government; the man sitting on the balcony of Government House represents just that. Anarchy and disorder, that was it . . . How nice it would be to have a picture of it. The police were working without any enthusiasm, *a media máquina*. There was a lot of discontent in the force because of the unpaid wages. There were many versions about a strike that was on the way. You know, the police force is a vertical institution, but that day no one was giving orders, *no había mando*. We didn't have precise commands. People

passed in front of the central precinct shouting, "We are going to burn down the Congress," and no one did anything about it. Our only concern was to guard the precinct. We learned about the burnings and sacking through the radio . . . Before the explosion, there had been many strikes, and there were various leaders and factions within the police force, because the prior governors were not strong enough [referring to Governor Mujica and Governor Iturre] . . . internally there was a lot of despair. And there was also a lot of anger and resentment because of unfair promotions, and some personnel who were left behind. Note that the first thing that the officials from the federal intervention did was to pay the police and to strengthen the institution.

"That day cost me my career," Mario, a police chief in charge of security for the government building on December 16, told me after introducing himself. Within months of the uprising, he had been fired from the police force over a series of episodes related to the burning and sacking of public buildings and private homes. Now unemployed but still very angry with "those at the top of the institution," he has found someone to "set the record straight." In fact, Mario called my hotel after the leading local newspaper published an article headlined "The Santiagazo Seen from a Sociologist's Point of View," which reported my presence in the capital of Santiago del Estero. Over the phone, he said, "I want to tell you the whole story, my version of what actually happened." We talked for more than three hours. At the end of our conversation, I had the sense of having gained a privileged access to a private but very relevant version of the events—a story that might otherwise have been lost. For Mario, the riot and its aftermath were not merely about claims but also about his dignity and recognition as a policeman.

Mario was "studying" the maneuvering and coordinating taking place "before December 16." He was "doing intelligence because I was interested in what was *behind* the wage claim, the motives, the people who were involved" (italics mine). Mario was "going beyond" his "jurisdiction to identify the groups that were usually demonstrating in front of Government House," and relations between them. "I attended union meetings and took pictures. I had very good information about the most active unions, about the coordination between different groups." Although he acknowledges that he "knew something big was coming, and that the burning of Government House was the people's objective, the whole responsibility for what happened rested with the police. The police did not take the situation seriously." What the local judge and some journalists report as the product of foreign agitators or alien "activists" was, for Mario, the product of intense coordination and planning carried out by protesters during the previous weeks. "Activists, yes . . . if by that you mean that some people are more active than others, but they were all from Santiago," he insists. Another police chief with whom I spoke agrees: "There were no activists . . . this was not a sudden thing; it had been developing for a long time."

Mario provides me with a great deal of detail about the reasons he thinks the police did not effectively quell the protest: they lacked ammunition, and what they had was of very "bad quality" (it dated from 1978); the tear gas was so old that it would not blaze, allowing protesters to "return the gases to us." But mainly, he points out, it was because the infantry "received an order to abandon the place," and "we, the people from my precinct, were left alone. We didn't even have clothing; our clothes were destroyed, we were dressed as civilians. We couldn't do anything." He vehemently opposes the explanation that points to the police's own wage claims as the reason for their inaction (see chapter 8) and hints, without explicitly saying so, at an underlying moral economy of the police force that was being threatened at the time and might explain why they did not react in the expected way.[6] "[The wage claim] is an excuse . . . we could have done something to protect the house. We tried to calm people down, but we didn't have guns. We were totally disarmed. We didn't even have proper clothing. . . . Although we didn't have the means, we could have prevented it. I was angry at the lack of capacity and leadership of my superiors, not of the subalterns. . . . Politics has always been involved in the police force; all the promotions are done through politics."

They "didn't have clothing," he repeats throughout the interview. "They didn't have guns," he stresses, "and the ammunition was old." To make things worse, "the superiors were appointed through politics." For Mario, the events of December 16 were not so much about wages as about organization (of protesters) and an already lost *dignity* (of police agents). On that day, the lack of ammunition, clothing, and leadership exposed the lack of recognition that they—the "subalterns, not the superiors"—had as cops. Because they had already stopped being cops, they consequently did the logical thing: they left the scene.

Mario's dignity as an officer was challenged again right after the riot when "my superiors ordered me to find the things that were stolen that day and the following day." A "very nice Spanish pistol . . . that was the first thing Governor Juarez ordered me to recover. I got many things back from the sacking of his house: classic furniture, a very beautiful desk, Nina's fur coat; many, many things." He showed me a list of the things he found: typewriters, fans, heaters, bicycles, computers, telephones, firearms, air conditioners, VCRs, clothing. During our interview he also displayed the pictures that he and his fellow officers took during the sacking of the politicians' homes and that later allowed him to track down the missing items. "It was not so difficult to find the stolen objects," he said. The problem arose when he found that the most valuable objects (Nina's fur coat, her gold jewelry, her expensive clothing and shoes) were in the possession of officials close to the governor. "Juarez's bodyguard had his Spanish pistol . . . and a deputy's lover had Nina's fur coat," Mario told me and, seeing my surprised face, rapidly added, "Yes, yes . . . I was playing with fire." But he kept on in his search for the stolen goods. "As a good cop, I followed orders," and he began receiving threats. "People at the police force told me to stop because I would be fired." He did not stop, and later that year, "they implicated me in the theft of a cider truck, saying that I was going to buy all the stolen cider." He then opens another folder, not the one with all the pictures of protesters stealing things from politicians' homes but one with newspaper clips that report the "scandal in the police force. A cop involved in a truck theft." Predictably, he was fired, "fired for playing with fire," he tells me. "December 16 was the beginning of the end of my career as a cop," he summarizes, "that's why I wanted to tell you my version of what happened."

Chapter Seven

Nana's Life: "Thirty-six

Years of Crap"

Doing ethnography has dull moments, but it also has some cherished ones. The moment Nana handed me the crystal from Government House's chandelier is one such. Going through the newspaper archives and finding a photograph of her shouting during a demonstration is another precious occurrence. "This morning I was reading the newspapers from those days, and I saw a picture of you with the caption: 'Young woman insults journalists.' You were standing sideways," I tell Nana in one of our conversations. "Young woman insults press people aggressively . . . Yes, it is me," Nana answers laughingly, and explains: "I am shouting and bitching because I'm offended by the fact that the journalists are behind the cops, because I would like them to stand by our side, being workers, and not taking pictures for the *escrache* (so that we can be identified later). When I ask them to give me my picture, they refuse. And the funny thing is that the guy who takes my picture is the same guy who used to take pictures of me when I was a dancer. . . . I was a dancer at the Carnaval."

Ethnography not only has precious moments but, as any experienced fieldworker knows and patiently waits for, has breakthroughs. The moment Nana tells me that she was a dancer in the Carnaval Santiagueño for many years, a whole new dimension of her story begins to emerge.

Yes, I was a dancer at the Carnaval . . . I was the best . . . Well, that's what they used to say. That was in the time of the dictatorship, when my mind was still young . . . I was always news . . . "the best dancer in the Carnaval." It was a prize that was established after I started performing. "How nice the way that girl dances, we should have a prize," they said. Then they established a prize for the best dancer of the Carnaval. . . . When I was eighteen years old, I could go anywhere, and people would always whisper when they saw me.

In this chapter, I would like to return to "the problem of biography" with a look at the story of one protester, Nana. Why her and not, say, Roberto or María, who played more central roles before, during, and after the uprising? I did not choose Nana because she is a "typical" Santiagueña (whether that is possible at all, I'll leave the reader to judge); on the contrary, as we will see, there's nothing "typical" about her as a person. I choose her because "the queen of Carnaval" accentuates and synthesizes the shared meanings that the uprising has for its protagonists. Nana is, in this vein, a sort of living ideal type that condenses the meanings of vengeful popular celebration that, for many protesters, the Santiagazo encodes. Her experiences of the riot not only sum up those of most protesters but also are deeply linked to her own life story. Nana, the "activist of the Santiagazo" and the "goddess of Carnaval," offers us an unusual chance to explore the intersection between the lived riot and the biography of one protester.

"Thirty-six Years of Crap"

What follows is the interview transcript I edited and constructed to take the reader through the main viewpoints that jointly make up Nana's point of view on her life, which she often defines as "thirty-six years of crap," and on the events that "marked" it. I spent many hours talking with Nana, sometimes with a tape recorder, sometimes without it (all the quoted excerpts come from recorded conversations). Much as in Laura's case, the criteria that I used for this reconstruction are a composite of elements endogenously provided by Nana's story—the events to which she devotes more time and thought—and those that, although sometimes briefly mentioned, I consider essential to understanding the genesis of her "other way of looking at things." The Carnaval, her first two marriages, her children, the love affair that "broke my heart," and, later, the riot are the events around which the recounting of her life revolves. The time she devotes to retelling and thinking about them marks them as the signposts in a "difficult, hard, very hard" life. Underlying this "shitty life"—as some other times she defines it—is a need to be different, to be noticed, to not "be one of the crowd," a need to be acknowledged and backed up; a need that she seeks to satisfy (with varying degrees of success) in many arenas: on the stage, through (later acknowledged as harmful) romantic involvements, at home, in the streets dancing, and later protesting.

Childhood Memories:
"I Suffered Hardship . . . I Was the Privileged One"

My childhood was modest, I suffered hardship. My children don't have absolutely everything, but they do have their own bedroom, and each one of them has their own bed. I had my bed but not my own bedroom. I shared a bedroom with my brothers. And earlier, when I was younger, the house used to be a big room that served as a bedroom for all of us. My dad would sleep with my mom in one corner, and my brothers and I slept in the other one. . . . I probably have had more privileges, being the first daughter. Out of the few things we had at home, the few things that we would get were always for the little *nena* [female child], the only female, the oldest . . . I didn't really have a hard time.

In this picture I am eight years old (figure 16). It is at my First Communion. This little house was in the Barrio Triángulo, almost at the border with Pacará.[1] It is a very modest, popular district. The house was really modest. We used to rent at the time. The house later crumbled because of the flood, and we had to leave it. I had my First Communion party . . . as always, there was no money. But every time something happened to me, my old man used to play the lottery, with the number of my birth date. That time he won. And we used that money for the party. My brothers complain that I am the only one who gets birthday celebrations. My father is a very irresponsible man when it comes to expenses . . . celebrating the nena's birthday could mean that we wouldn't have money for food, but he would have the party anyway.

Nana spends part of her childhood in the countryside, with her grandparents and her aunts, because her mom is working as a rural teacher. When her brother is born, her mother quits the job to take care

FIGURE 16.

Nana's First Communion.

of the children. Her father is at best an intermittent (and rather unhelpful) presence in her life, anticipating, in a way, the role that fathers will later play in her life as a mother of six.

> When we were kids it was basically my mom who raised us. And she did that without any money, because there were some months in which my dad would not bring a single peso home. . . . Mom still feels a little resentment toward my dad because he put pressure on her so that she left her job. My mom always says that if she had kept working, we would have had a different life. She says, "Now that I am old, I would still have a salary." She always complains. She's been hurt; she's been hurt for years. My dad left her alone for a long time. That's what I remember best. My dad would leave. And a lot of gossip would arrive at our home. Women would come looking for him. My mom wanted to kill herself in front of us. Those were really bad things, hard things. When I was young I lived under the constant strain of thinking, "Maybe I'll get back home, and my mom won't be alive." I was constantly frightened. Because she would get caught up in her hysterics and would end up lying on the floor. And that would happen for one day, two days, a week.

School:
"I Wanted People to See Me, to Notice Me"

Nana's sorrowful recollections cease when she begins to talk about her school days, about the days when she made her first "public appearances." It was in school that Nana first made it to the place she believes is "her destiny": the stage. The recollections of her school days are almost completely dominated by the "attention" she looked for and obtained as her school's main performer. Note how, when talking about her first steps in a public setting, she objectifies herself to the extent of speaking in the third person. Note also the pressure of economic necessity in determining her life chances and the presence of out-migration as a (frustrated) possibility, a presence that should not come as a surprise in a province with the highest levels of out-migration in the country.

> Here in Santiago people recognize you in the streets either because you come from a rich family or because you have had some condition; either you are intelligent or a good student or you are outstanding in some respect. I was a good student, though not "super-excellent." However, through acting in the school plays, I received a lot of attention. That is before I started to be a dancer in the Carnaval. I wanted people to see me, to notice me; I didn't want to be one of the crowd. That's how I am. . . . In primary school I was a very good student. The teachers would take me to their houses. Two principals took me to their houses to spend weeks there. I was like a daughter to them. I felt loved, just as if I were one more member of the family. They gave me advice. . . . In school I was always really spoiled. And in public events, if there were eight performances planned, the teachers would request that Nana participated in seven of them. Because I was the one who knew how to sing, how to recite, how to dance chamame, chacarera, tango . . . My life was the stage, and it is still the stage today. . . . When I entered secondary school, being Nana was more difficult because the school was big; it had fifteen hundred students. The teachers talked about me. Every time my mom went, they said nice things about me. . . . While I was in secondary school, I danced in the Carnaval. That was when I was in the third year. . . . Later on, when I got into the university, sometimes it bothered me that people saw me like the little whore of the Carnaval. When I agreed to dance

in the Carnaval, I knew I was going to be labeled "whore" . . . but I didn't care because I believed in myself, in who I was. . . . Dancing and parading was a way of exercising my real vocation: theater. Since I could not leave for somewhere else to study, that's what I did. I am not a lawyer or a social worker or a judicial employee. No, I was born to be an actress. The problem is that I could never actually do it, because my parents couldn't send me to study that, because they didn't have money to pay for it. Some ex-teachers tested me in school and said that I had an artistic vein that I had to exploit. They used to say that I should go to the Theatre San Martín to study, in Buenos Aires, because, as they'd say, "You were born for the stage." My schoolmates thought that I was going to be at least a variety actress. I was the woman they fantasized about . . . they thought about me constantly, and they grew up in terms of knowledge and wisdom [laughing]. Two or three of them confessed that to me, that for everyone in school I was the sex symbol.

Nana's Carnaval: "Giving Myself Away Completely"

December 16 and the Carnaval are organizing principles in Nana's narrative. Given that her participation in the Santiagazo was the reason why I approached her for an interview in the first place, it should not come as a surprise that the year 1993 is, especially during the first interview sessions, overly present in her narrative. As my interest in (and my explicit inquiry into) other aspects of her life increased (her life as the queen of Carnaval, her relationships with men), the Santiagazo receded from view only to come back as a sort of defining moment in her life when things changed "once and for all." Her story is told with the story of the Santiagazo in mind, and vice versa, the story of her participation during the events of December 16 is told with the story of her life in mind. This constant back-and-forth between her past (childhood and Carnaval) and December 16 ("shuttlework," as Portelli [1991] calls this typical way of handling time in oral narratives) indicates the mutual imbrication of both narratives. This shuttlework is expressed in the constant shifting between present and past, a shifting that (much as with the references in her map presented in the introduction), I decide to preserve to highlight the intensity of her recollections and their reciprocal intersection.

NANA: I danced in the Carnaval's best years, between 1979 and 1983. It was beautiful. For me, it was like touching the sky with my hands. I had entered the Carnaval because I always had my artistic roots. When I started dancing, people would talk about the girl dancing at the end. The next year, they asked me to be the first in one *comparsa* [parading group]. When I danced, I moved from the front to the back of the comparsa all the time. I wasn't going to dance just in one place. When I came dancing down Belgrano Avenue,[2] there were long lines of kids and their moms waiting for Nana, either to take a picture or to give her a flower. The little kids would go to wait for me, and they'd give me letters and asked for autographs. It was really great. Also, three or four male dancers would look after me, making sure nothing happened to me. To me, dancing in the Carnaval was almost like fighting in a battle. It was almost like being part of a mobilization, from before or after December 16. That's what the Carnaval always was for me. All the effort and the blood that I'd put in it was because of that. . . . But when I start participating in the union struggle a little bit more, when I start being with the workers more and more, I feel more complete, more whole. Maybe because for all those years I was looking for my true destiny . . . the other side of the truth . . . the other history. Don't forget that in the time of the Carnaval, the dictatorship hid the *desaparecidos*, the repression. I was a part of something that I didn't realize until later: the Carnaval was used to cover and hide all of that.

JAVIER: You had no way to know at that time . . .

NANA: I had no idea. . . . I was so naive . . .

JAVIER (referring to figure 10): Tell me about this picture.

NANA: Here I am totally covered by sweat. To me the Carnaval was something else. It was like fighting to get something, I don't know what. To me, the Carnaval was to go in and consume all my energy. Because I danced for two and a half hours straight. I didn't stop even for a minute. That's why I was the revelation. That's why I was considered the best dancer. I would dance four kilometers back and forth every night, three nights a week. I would start a little bit overweight, and I would end up being really thin, like a little stick. I danced all the time, and I would dance everything. I could be short of breath and terribly thirsty, but I would go on. At that point the little, cute, and very well made up girl that everyone had seen at the beginning would transform into a monstrosity. My hair was a mess, I was all covered by sweat and would smell of anything you could imagine; anything but the perfume of the Carnaval. Even my butt would sweat. That was what the Carnaval was to me. Giving myself away completely. . . . But the truth is that the picture doesn't show what people used to say about me, both men and women, and even children. It was something more impressive. It was like I would enter a place and everyone would lay eyes on me. And they'd say, "There comes the queen of the Carnaval." When I danced, I was not in the Carnaval, I wasn't moving down Belgrano Avenue. I was making my childhood dream come true . . . Since I was a kid, I dreamed about being a star, an actress, a dancer. I remember that when I was young, I had a very small closet with a small door that had a mirror. And during the siesta—since it was very long, and I wasn't allowed to go out and play with anyone— I would perform in front of that mirror, I was the princess. I enjoyed wearing costumes and taking a plastic glass, thinking that it was a golden cup and that I was drinking some very expensive drink. And maybe it was actually water or grapefruit juice.

"Slow, Really Slow" Gender Suffering:
"I Was Really Lonely, Because I Had No One"

Nana has a unique point of view on the life of Santiago. This singular perspective comes simultaneously from the positions, at once marginal and central, she has occupied in Santiagueña society: a woman from poor origins who works at the courthouse and deals on an everyday basis with lawyers, local politicians, and judges; and a woman who, in her attempts to become an artist (dancer, writer, singer), has been in touch with the (mostly male) local intellectual elite. As part (though never full member) of this universe, she has had romantic involvements with university professors, musicians, and a now prominent politician.

She presents herself as a rebel, an uppity woman, as someone who challenges the stereotype of the "submissive and passive" Santiagueña. And to a great extent, she is this rebel who, in her own words, "takes no shit from nobody." However, this heretical status contradicts other themes very much present in her story, mainly her relationships with men—that is, the "shit" she silently took from most of them. The fathers of four of her six children never contributed much to their support. One of them "simply disappeared" when Nana's third child was less than a year old and she was pregnant with the fourth. She never saw him again. The father of Nana's first two children (living with him "was like living alone . . . like a jail") subjected her to different sorts of violence while they were married ("he *only* raised his hand at me [a euphemism for being beaten up] three or four times"). He still lives in Santiago but seldom visits his children and never gives Nana money for raising them: "He sees them only twice a year and doesn't provide much." Years ago, he had an accident and is now on a wheelchair. It was after the accident, Nana tells me, that he began to try to "come closer" to the children, only after the children made the first move: "Fernanda [her daughter] was kind of resentful of him." Despite both fathers' lack of support, Nana says that she always attempts to portray them in a good light: "I try to give my children a good image of their fathers. I tell my children, '[Your fathers] are far away, they don't show up, but they are your fathers.' " She never attempted to claim the right she has by law to obtain child support from both fathers. "I don't want to bother," she repeatedly told me, and proudly added, "I am not the kind of woman that will fight over those things. . . . I am their mother, and I can take care of them." Abandoned as she was three times by different men, she took refuge in her four children; victim of pernicious forms of violence, she fought back with motherly devotion, suffering, and silence, forms of "soft violence" that women are many times condemned to use against men (Bourdieu 2001, 32), weak "weapons of the weak" (Scott 1985), true, but weapons nonetheless.

One of those weapons she used against men was romantic affairs with other men who, in turn, subjected her to other forms of (this time, symbolic) violence. In her story (and this seems to be the aspect she is less aware of), it is men who "destroy" her, and men who "save" her; men who offer her a life worth living (making her feel like a "goddess"), and men who take this life away (as if she were "in jail"). An extreme form of this search for existence *through* men (a form of masculine domination par excellence) is her remark (her confession, actually) that she would have liked to have a baby "by" (not "with") Jorge, the man who saved her from "the jail" of her first marriage, the man who "discovered" her, the man with whom she felt "alive again . . . like a goddess," and the man who later abandoned her for another woman, making her "lose fifteen kilograms. It was really hard to lose him."

It is important to notice that as her life increasingly becomes a "mess" (mainly because of her relationships with men), she grows more solitary, ending up alone with four kids, ignored by her family, and with no support from her workmates, who, she believes, think she "deserved the life [she] got." Although everybody shunned her at the workplace, her job at the courthouse provided a last refuge of stability and security.

It is also important to realize that the recollections of her troubled relationships with men took the form of a long monologue that lasted approximately two hours. It was one of the only two occasions that she cried during the many hours that we spoke—the other one being when she recalled the time her last baby got sick. At the end of those two hours, Nana reflected on the impact that these relationships ("all my suffering") are *now* having in her life and, most importantly from her point of view, in the life of her children, who are now slowly beginning a painful (and in the case of two of them rather uncertain) search for their fathers.

NANA: When I got married (I was twenty-one) it was because I had no other choice than to go live with my husband. Had I been a little bit wiser, I'd have gone to live on my own. But I wasn't enlightened enough. When I got pregnant with Matías [her first child], my mom said, "Either you leave or you have an abortion." My mom didn't give me a choice, and my dad behaved under her pressure. Living pregnant in my mom's house and being controlled was not a possibility. So I decided to go with my husband because I had no other choice. . . . When we—my husband and I—moved in together, I did it knowing that it wasn't going to work because he was the macho type. [He was one of those men who] are really nice and wonderful until they know they have caught you. He caught me, he got me pregnant, and then he started to change. It was then when he showed me the other face, a face totally different from the one I had known. He was a lot older than me. About ten years older . . .

JAVIER: How was life with him?

NANA: I wanted to separate because I could not handle living alone anymore. I was always waiting for the moment when he would get tired and leave. He wasn't going to leave because he had a wife and children. Socially, he had a family. For me it was a very heavy weight on my shoulders, because there was nothing between us. We talked to each other as if we were neighbors. I was polite because I was very clear about where I didn't want things to end up . . . I mean . . . I didn't want to get to violence, to be beaten up.

JAVIER: Did he ever hit you?

NANA: Yes, he did . . . that's why I closed myself up and made a plan to leave; it was like a jail. It was horrible. It was ugly because I was not the person I am today. I was twenty-one or twenty-two years old. I didn't know what to do, where to go to. I didn't want to tell my mom because she was never on my side. . . . I was very young and was terrified because of how violent he was with me. It wasn't really about physical violence. The truth is he only raised his hand at me three or four times. It was psychological violence. I lived under constant threats. I had the idea that one day I was going to split. I didn't ask anything from him. We lived under the same roof, and I paid for everything: rent, electricity, gas, taxes. He only gave money for food. He could leave anytime he wanted. He had no schedule. I didn't care where he was. He had all the freedom he wanted, under the sole condition that he left me alone. And we spent about two years like that, until I ended up separating when Fernanda was eight months old. Women tend to allow men to beat them up. . . . When I told him I wanted to get separated, he responded, "I am not going to be embarrassed in front of all my friends just because it is your fancy. I have already been separated once." In my house no one knew anything about it, nor did anyone at my job. No one knew anything. . . . I had developed a protective shell, trying to have a good time while he decided to leave the house because there was no reason to stay. I saw him as a violent man, and I saw that he would scold Matías or spank him. To me it was clear that he was violent, that he was hitting him.

A few months before I decided to pack his things and put them all in the street, I met Jorge. He was a guy who had recently arrived to Santiago. He was *porteño* [from Buenos Aires], medical doctor, musician. Today he is the undersecretary of social welfare, I think. He was like a god to me at that time, because I had never met any guy like that before, someone with so much strength and so many things to say. [He was] an artist. I loved to be close to him. I had no intention to seduce him, that wasn't like me. But he did. So I ended up having an affair with him. Having such an intimate relationship helped me share with someone all of what was going on. And, well, he was one of those people that when you say, "I am like a paper bag with no sugar inside," he tells you that you are a very important person. He'd tell me that I had many things to give. He'd say, "You are no paper bag without sugar inside, you have so many things to give." He fed my ego. He made me discover the other side of me that I didn't know. I started writing poetry. He discovered me. He made me go out, grow, and not be scared of life. He made me fly and dream and realize that I could fly and dream really high. To him, I was a superwoman, a supermom. . . . Many times I would have liked to have a kid by him. He was the most important man in my life at the time. . . . You have to think that I came from being a dancer, of being in everybody's mouth, being admired, known, or acclaimed. And all of a sudden it was like someone had cut my wings off, or like I had cut them off myself. I was hidden, very small. Jorge used to tell me that I had to get angry and talk . . . "Don't let him hit you, try to tell him that you have the right to have your own life." It wasn't him who told me to put his things out by the door. But yes, with time, I started putting more and more pressure so that he left, so that we found the best possible solution to things. One day I actually put all his things outside the house. . . . When we split, my husband told me that since it had been me who had decided to separate, he wasn't going to give me money for the children. With the separation, a new stage in my life started. I felt like a goddess because I had a guy who lived in Santiago and could be with me any time I picked up the phone. I would leave home or my job for a couple of hours, and I'd come back with a full dosage to say "I am important, I know I am worth a lot, I know I can do things." . . . Jorge left my life the same way he left his wife's life . . . he left with another woman. I lost fifteen kilograms. It was really hard to lose him.

While Nana was working at the courthouse, she was also hosting shows in the local casino. "That's where I met Julieta's and Juan's father. Marcelo was an artist, a photographer, from Carlos Paz (Córdoba)." They both traveled to Córdoba to test their luck as artists (her as a show host and him as a photographer):

From the economic point of view, we weren't doing so well. We had gone there with the idea that we would do a Batman. I made the Batman costume, we hired a weight lifter, and we made him wear it, so that little kids would have their pictures taken with him in the square. The Batman idea didn't work. And on top of everything, it always rained. We were in deep shit, and sometimes we wouldn't even have money to eat . . . We'd eat boiled polenta without salt. The children were having a hard time. The shoes that they had brought from Santiago were old and full of holes. We couldn't pay the rent anymore, and we moved to a shitty, horrible pension. It was a long room where we piled everything. And one day I found out I was one or two months pregnant. We had to go back to Santiago because I had to get back and work in the courthouse. We didn't even have enough money for the ticket back to Santiago . . . We got a couple of gigs. Marcelo put some money together and got the tickets so that I could go back with the children. We had talked to my parents so that me and the kids stayed there until Marcelo came back with enough money to rent something. I came back. We talked on the phone . . . the phone relationship lasted one month, maybe twenty days. One day I started complaining, asking him to come, to hurry up. I told him I wasn't enjoying living with my mom because the problems had started: "When is Marcelo coming back? When are you leaving? We don't have enough space here!" she'd say. One day he hung up. He was very angry, and he didn't call back for a week. When I finally managed to get in contact with him, he said, "This doesn't look like love to me. Having you ask me on the phone why I haven't gone there. Having you get angry. I think we will have to talk." So I asked him if he was thinking of not coming back. And he said that maybe he wouldn't. "Do whatever you want," I said, "but keep in mind that I am here, alone, with all the kids and pregnant." "Oh, no!" he said, "I give you all the freedom to do anything you want about the pregnancy, because I will not take responsibility for it." That's when I sent him to hell. I never talked to him again. It must have been two months since we came back. I moved to a room I rented from someone I knew, with the three children and the belly. I moved with all my things piled in a baby's cart. I was walking with the children and the baby's cart with all my things. . . . It was a very hard time, a horrible time for me. I had my belly, my children who kept asking when Marcelo would come back, and I had Julietita, who was almost one year old. Marcelo called me on the phone to tell me that he would come to Santiago on April 15 for Julietita's birthday. He said that we were going to try to put order into things, to talk so that we could fix everything. I said, "What about your issues with the baby?" and he said, "Well, we'll talk about it." He was coming on April 15. He never showed up. To me, every day was April 15. I waited for him every day. It was a long, slow—really slow—suffering, because the days never went by. He wasn't coming, and never came. At the beginning I cried a lot . . . I was really lonely, because I had no one [crying]. I had no one but my children, the belly, and God. I believe God exists because He has somehow been with me. My dad was never very close to me, and my mom had asked me to leave home. She had kicked me out, and I didn't see her again for a long time. . . . Marcelo's story was very sad, ugly. At my job no one said anything. It was almost like they were thinking, "Screw her. She left with a guy, he dumped her and left her with two children . . . she must have done something wrong."

All my suffering . . . now, I believe, is screwing me up, it's hurting me. Because that time with Marcelo, I had to build up a wall, so that my son was born and I could have a happy family. I had to keep all the anger and the pain to myself [crying]. And today it's like I don't want to keep it anymore because it destroys me, it destroyed me. . . . I lived, and I have to realize that I lived according to what I felt. I never cared about what people could say. I went right into the wolf's mouth, even when I was afraid of not knowing my way out. And, well, I found my way out, and I am complete. I thought I was never going to be affected by it. And maybe it affects me because Julieta started crying in school or at home when she was nine, because she needed her dad, because she wanted to meet him. I don't know what I am going to do with Julieta's crying until she decides to go look for him. When I lived all the things I lived, I didn't think that I would feel so guilty now . . . because they depend on me, and it is hard for me not to be able to solve this problem, this situation where she can't see her dad and where she's suffering because of that. It is also sad to know that Fernanda is angry at her dad and that anger does not have a solution because I already talked to Lucho [Fernanda's dad] and he hasn't tried to talk to her or protect her."

Her Days. "I Live Hoping My Luck Will Change"

Nana's everyday life is characterized by never-ending financial acrobatics and unceasing and frantic time management. She makes $800 per month, and her husband Cesar makes $300 per month. Half of their combined income goes to pay debts (the mortgage on her house, the loan on the motorbike, and other minor debts). She makes pizzas and empanadas and sells them, with the help of their children, to the neighbors. This commercial venture adds $50 per month to their budget.

Julieta, Fernanda, and Matías pay $35 per month in school fees. Matías is the only one who pays for the bus fare, which adds up to $12 per week. I have to give another $12 a week to Fernanda, Julieta, and Juan so that they can buy stuff at school. They don't spend it on bus fare because I take them all to the school on my motorbike. I pay $160 a month for the motorbike, but I save money in fare . . . so it makes sense, it's more convenient to have it. . . . I get off work at 1:50 P.M. and pick up Juan from school. I drive home, and I exchange him for the two youngest [Nalé and Naomi]. I drive back to Santiago, leave both of them at the kinder, and pick Julieta and Fernanda, who are waiting for me at their school. I come back home at 3:30 and start cooking. Cesar goes to bed around 6 A.M. (he works at a private security company patrolling the streets of Santiago every night) and wakes up around 11 A.M. He gets Nalé and Naomi ready to go to kinder. Twice a week, when I come home, I take Matías to the gym so that he doesn't spend more money on bus fare. During winter, I come back, and I am so cold that I go to bed, for an hour or so, and drink some vodka or ginebra. Or I go and take some sun in the patio, or I clean my children's rooms. . . . During weekends, I am exhausted. I live hoping my luck will change. My children's luck must change. But mine should change too. . . . I want to give my children other things. And I fight, I fight and I work. And only I know how my body feels when I prepare pizzas and do other things. And I walk and walk, and the exit I want is not there. I want to give my children access to the Internet, I want them to have money so that they can go to the Waterfalls [in reference to the graduation trip that her daughter Fernanda won't be able to take with her friends because of lack of money]. I want them to have at least a few of the things that are necessary. I want them to be able to practice a sport with no problems. And that if they want to come home with their friends, they can find a place, small as it may be. There are some days when I come back home and realize I can't paint it, and that makes me angry. It may be a female thing. Because my husband seems to be more comfortable with how things are; he seems happy. During the school year, when there's not enough money, I go crazy. And then I buy Valium. Sometimes that helps. The other day I didn't want to buy Valium, and I really got out of it, stupid, very sensitive.

Marked: "You've Become an Old, Bitter Woman"

This year I have let many sad things out. Ugly things that happened and that, at some point, I had to cry over them . . . things that happened to me, things related to what I would have liked my life to be and what it ended up being. I still do things however I can . . . Sometimes I wonder why I never was more rational, why I never said, "No, I am going to try to find a guy who can be a stable partner, a stable marriage." Instead of first thinking about building a room for a baby, I had the baby. I had nothing to offer the baby but myself. And, well, maybe I ask myself: What would my life, my children's life, have been like had I acted in a less impulsive manner? I am not saying it would have been better or worse or anything; I simply ask myself these questions; maybe it is because I went through a lot of pain, I was always alone. I had no place to live, I was out in the street and no one cared because, after all, no one even knew. Ever since December 16 I lost my naïveté in many respects. On one hand, it hurts me, because I became a different woman. My daughters tell me, "You've become an old, bitter woman; you are always too serious." There are facial gestures that I have now and I didn't use to have. Today it is almost like those gestures show independent of me. Sometimes I am walking down a street and I think, "My face is really hard now. Change your face. Relax!" I am always on guard. Or I go around on the motorbike, and I always have a harsh answer here [in her throat], an insult, if someone cuts in front of me or says something to me. I didn't used to be like this. I was a very patient woman. I wasn't absolutely naive, but I did have the face of someone who is naive. Now I have a hard face, because I live stressed. Since the sixteenth I live wondering, because that remained very much alive inside of me.

Nana seems to have found in the contentious 1993 a way of keeping that public search for recognition that characterizes her life going, a way of being once again on another kind of stage. The streets of Santiago became, much like in the Carnaval, her streets. Recall her description of her actions during December 16 and the notations she made on the map, and compare them with an account of her actions during the Carnaval: "To me the Carnaval was something else. It was like fighting to get something, I don't know what. To me, the Carnaval was to go in and consume all my energy . . . moving all over the place, back and forth, back and forth." And recall her memories of her sensations during December 16 ("like smoking a joint") with her recollections of Carnaval dancing: "When I was dancing, I was not at the Carnaval, I wasn't on Belgrano Avenue, I was making my dreams real . . . the people from the comparsa said I was somewhere else, I was in some other world."

When I, intuiting some link between her active participation in the riot and her former life as the queen of Carnaval, pressed forward with the implications of the carnivalesque, Nana clarified which Carnaval we should be talking about: the Carnaval as lived experience, the Carnaval not as a "spectacle seen by the people" but as the world that "they live in" (Bakhtin 1984, 7); *her* Carnaval.

JAVIER: If someone writes a book about the Santiagazo, someone . . . I mean me . . . saying that it has some similarities with a Carnaval . . .

NANA: If someone writes a book saying that the Santiagazo was a Carnaval . . . it will hurt me. It will hurt because we are not a majority but a group of Santiagueños who are proud of the Santiagazo. We see an unfinished symphony in it. . . .

JAVIER: Why would you be mad if someone says that this is a Carnaval with all the good things and the limitations that a Carnaval has? Why would it hurt you?

NANA: Because the Santiagazo . . . to see it as part of the Carnaval where you get wet or dirty, or where people do things that you don't approve of, no! To see it as part of the Carnaval I lived, in which I considered myself to be the goddess of dance being in limbo, because I was doing what I liked. I was at my best, and I enjoyed it. If I have to compare it to my Carnaval, that which sweated me out and drained me of six kilos per night, dancing, that Carnaval, yes! It was not the cute girl or the nice ass that moved us. It was a beast that was dancing and ate everything. Yes, that Carnaval, yes! *Because I left my soul in the Carnaval . . . I left my soul in the Carnaval.*

She Got inside the Riot, and the Riot inside Herself:
"I Took All This Very Seriously"

The day before our last interview, the main local newspaper ran a full-page story on my presence on Santiago and about my (to many in Santiago, controversial) opinions about the riot. The next day, I recorded the following dialogue with Nana; it summarizes her point of view on the uprising and on her own life, illustrating how the story of the protest and of her life are somehow exchangeable, and how, in her narrative, the Santiagazo clashes with the "thirty-six years of crap" and opens her life to a new beginning.

NANA: After the sixteenth, I don't wear makeup. I can go out without any makeup. I can let my gray hair grow. I went on for three or four months with my hair in two colors. I don't wear miniskirts anymore. I became a commando woman, a battle woman. I took all this very seriously, ever since the sixteenth.

JAVIER: You have a very personal version of the sixteenth.

NANA: It is mine. It is this dreaming woman's version.

JAVIER: Yesterday, when the interview came out in the paper, I thought you wouldn't like it.

NANA: I liked it. With what you said in *El Liberal,* you are proving me right. You are vindicating Nana's sixteenth.

JAVIER: Why? How so?

NANA: Because for me the sixteenth is still going on, it still exists. Whether it is in a souvenir or in a complaint or in a group of families burning tires to prevent their eviction. And there are those who think, like Nana, that there are still vestiges of December 16 . . . To me, the sixteenth was the battle that I won. I bring that up and rub it in the faces of all those who I have a chance rub it in to. It is one way to have memory, to say, "Don't forget what we were able to do. If we were able to do a December 16, we can organize ourselves to do something organized, we can change our history." I can forget about the world in order to fight for something like this.

JAVIER: Forget about the world like in this picture [the picture that shows her dancing in the streets].

NANA: Yes, exactly.

Nana's biography meets and meshes not only with the uprising but also with the (contested) memories of it. She is determined to keep the memory of the uprising alive: "December 16 is still going on . . . it will come back. . . . It is an unfinished symphony." And she also takes this "mission" in very personal terms: "I am thirty-six years old, and I have been eating crap for thirty-six years. Many times I get depressed, and I think about this society in which everything you are is denied. If I am a part of the Santiagazo, and you are talking to people who tell you that the Santiagazo didn't exist, it is almost like saying that Nana is a farce, that she doesn't exist. Many times I fall, I go to hell. . . ." By the time I record this conversation, I am indeed talking to people who dismiss the uprising as an unimportant (or worse, nonexistent) event. These are the people who say that "the Santiagazo didn't exist" and in whose faces Nana wants to rub the "vestiges of December 16." It is to this memory (and to the contest over it) that I would now like to turn my attention.

Chapter Eight

Contested Memories

For nothing is absolutely dead: every meaning will someday have its homecoming festival. —MIKHAIL BAKHTIN, *Estetika*, in Holquist, *Dialogism*

"I ask you to carry out an exhaustive investigation to identify the *common criminals* that sacked my country house on December 16 and seized firearms, a television, a VCR, a sound system and other things. Impunity created alarm in the area. . . . For the good of Santiago I wish you success in your duty" (italics mine). This is the text of the telegram Senator Juarez (now governor of Santiago) sent to the military officer in charge of the secretary of security of Santiago del Estero, Brigadier Antonietti, on January 12, 1994. Juarez was not alone in calling the rioters "common criminals" and in demanding an "exhaustive investigation" to recover the stolen goods. A few weeks after the riot, the victims of the rioters' rage silently journeyed to the main police precinct of Santiago to report the "damage" and "robbery" caused by "the vandals." The victims or their relatives presented formal accusations (intentional damage, qualified robbery, intimidation and unprecedented violence, use of firearms, etc.), listed the stolen things, and, in some cases, gave the names of people who, they thought, had been the perpetrators of the looting and, they were told, were in possession of their belongings.

As Mario, the policeman who called my hotel, remembers, the frantic search for the stolen goods began right after December 16, 1993. Dozens of cops, following the trail provided by the victims of the looting, began to comb the city. Because "in this small town everybody knows everybody," the police did not have a difficult time finding the most valuable things. Two days after the explosion, the son of the minister of public works was "identifying" the recovered goods in the office of a local judge; for him, as for many others, these objects were definitely not "souvenirs."

The court file shows the victims' detailed lists of goods (clothing items, books, lamps, doors, carpets, electronic equipment, even a "beige toilet bowl"!) and, in some cases, their suspicions about the objects' whereabouts ("a family named X, living at the intersection of Z and Y, has jackets, doors, windows, and other furniture," a former official declares to the police). The text of the report also provides a window into the victims' initial labeling of the uprising and the protesters. A former member of the parliament whose house was destroyed says that "this was a popular rebellion" against democracy, that "the vandalism was planned and orchestrated by political leaders." Among those "vandals," another targeted official asserts, "we could observe three or four individuals who were directing the movements." Elites' classificatory efforts were not restricted to a court case, though; in the months and years that followed the riot, they engaged in a real labor of constructing the event and its protagonists.

On December 17, as the troops from the Gendarmería Nacional arrived in Santiago and began terrorizing its residents with menacing parades around the city, the principal federal trustee (interventor), a man from the national finance minister's inner circle, put forward the official interpretation of what had happened: "This is a case of plain bad administration, of moral and ethical problems, of inequalities and political cronyism" (*New York Times,* 18 December 1993; *Clarín,* 18 December 1993). The finance minister, the main propelling force behind the structural adjustment program carried out by the national government, agreed: "Local corruption and inefficient administration" caused the riot; "no adjustment was carried out in the province" (*Página12,* 28 December 1993; see also *Clarín,* 19 December 1993). "This was not a test case for the economic plan," the federal interventor pointed out. The cause of the "violent episodes was not merely the overdue salaries but a very bad administration . . . and a moral crisis" (*La Nación,* 20 December 1993).

While emphasizing local administrative disarray, the official account also stressed the presence of "activists." The president was the main proponent of this line of interpretation: "This was not the work of the citizens of Santiago but of leftist agitators . . . of subversive agitators," President Menem confidently asserted (*La Nación*, 28 December 1993). The federal government pointed at local corruption *and* outside agitation as the main causes of the "explosion," insisting that national economic policies had nothing to do with it. As the finance minister put it (*La Nación*, 19 December 1993): "The cause is the total chaos in provincial finances," and "fifty rabble-rousers that agitated in Santiago."[1]

Why, how, and with what consequences the events of December 16 happened merge in local journalists' accounts of the episode. In what follows, I take a close look at local examinations of the riot. Local journalists pointed to corruption and the ostentation of a privileged political class as the elements at the roots of the rebellion. According to Rodriguez (1994), the people punished a corrupt political class who were devoid of principles and of any sort of moral authority. In the book Rodriguez later wrote with another journalist, they agreed with the diagnosis made by the then finance minister, explicitly challenging the interpretation that put structural adjustment at the root of the riot: "It is an outright lie to say that the December 16 and 17 explosion happened because of the adjustment imposed by the national government, because there has been no adjustment whatsoever in the province of Santiago del Estero" (Curiotto and Rodriguez 1994, 94; for a similar argument, see Díaz 1994).

Together with a chronological report entitled "The Saddest Day" (which talks about protesters as an "enraged mob," as "vandals," and highlights the presence of "agitators") published on December 16, 1994, *El Liberal* presented the testimonies of six women and three men who, as spectators to those events, expressed their feelings about what had happened a year earlier. As expected, that "sad day" is remembered with sorrow. "I felt very bad because of what was going on," Susana said, "I was very worried for my family, mainly for my three sons. I believe that the people shouldn't have acted so violently and shouldn't have destroyed the public buildings." Ester stated that she was "angry and afraid," Eugenia that she "lived the events of December 16 with pain and bitterness." "I prefer not to remember," said Sandra, "because it was something really sad," and María recollected the "terror" she felt: "It was frightening." December 16 is a "bad memory" for Gustavo, "because it was useless." "A sad story," says another public employee, "but it was good for the province because the people reacted."

It was also a sad day for Luis Lugones, the judge whose office at the courthouse (Tribunal Five) was one of the main targets of the revoltosos, and who was in charge of the 144 persons arrested on December 16. Six years after the events, how does he remember these events? What story does he tell about December 16?

In his opening statement of our two-hour talk, his interpretation of what happened on that "sad day" mingles with an account of his actions before, during, and afterward: "I do not regret anything I did," he tells me. Why should he be repentant? He was in charge of one of the most noted corruption cases in the province: this involved Brevetta Rodriguez, the undersecretary of media and institutional relations, who, in connection with other public officials and the governor, signed a contract between the government and a ghost publicity company for US$300,000 (*El Liberal*, 23 November 1993). After twenty days as a fugitive, Brevetta Rodriguez showed up at Lugones's office but was released the next day, a release that for many local commentators was the final blow to the courthouse's public image (Dargoltz 1994; Curiotto and Rodriguez 1994). "Since bail was posted [*excarcelable*], and since I am a loyal defender of constitutional guarantees, I removed him from prison," Lugones told me in August 1999. "The people did not understand," he commented, "because they were guided by the media. It was the media who kept on making things more difficult, who kept fanning the flames."

He "did the right thing"—a phrase repeated often during our interview—"with the Brevetta case as with those arrested" for sacking and looting politicians' homes. In justifying his decision to liberate the Santiagazo's 144 arrestees (88 men, 7 women, and 49 male minors), Lugones explained that "they were in danger, since the people inside the prison center had learned that their files had been burned and were going to punish those responsible." He was "actually protecting them," he insisted.[2] Those arrested were "very humble people, incapable of acting by themselves: they were a herd." This "innocent flock" was actually incited by "agitators," the judge didactically informed me. The "crowd consisted of those who provoked, who were the ones who set everything on fire, and those who took advantage of the situation" (looters who stole a chair or a desk, some of whom were arrested by the police and later released by him). The "agitators," he continued, "were a mix of people from other provinces like Tucumán or Córdoba and local union leaders." They were a "tiny and isolated minority. Three hundred people are not the whole society . . . only fifty of them said, 'Let's burn everything.' They came prepared with gasoline. These activists came with little pieces of paper indicating the houses that they were going to burn. . . . there were political interests behind it."

It is equivocal, writes historian George Rudé (1964, 212) about the rioting crowd, that "any clear-cut distinction . . . can be made between the bulk of those who join the crowd and those who line the sidewalks or even stay at home. . . . there is an evident bond of sympathy and common interest linking the active few with the inactive many." Judge Lugones would deeply disagree. Apart from those who "agitated" and those who "took advantage," he said, the majority of people "watched the whole thing on TV with great sorrow, because a historic monument [Government House] was burned." Sorrow and sadness are commanding themes in his story, chiefly when he recalls his own feelings on learning that the courthouse was burning: "I felt a tremendous pain, because it was our house."

What caused the riot? The judge and most local journalists have a ready-made answer that blends the identification of a claim with the emergence of mobilization (a conflation that political-process theorists have long proved to be mistaken) (e.g., Tarrow 1998; McAdam 1982). According to this point of view, the riot was caused by the three-month lag in payment of public wages—nothing more, nothing less. The government stopped paying its employees for three months, and by December they were "mad as hell"—a journalist told me—and (we might add, paraphrasing the classic film *Network*) were "not going to take it any more." Thus, another journalist put it, "fury, disenchantment, irritation, and the need to steal took over the city" (Gallardo 1994, 39). Unpaid salaries were also at the root of the lack of suppressive police response to the riot. True, the police were overwhelmed by the onslaught of protesters (the police report on the riot mentions the sheer number of demonstrators, their "aggressiveness," and the lack of necessary antimutiny ammunition as reasons for the less-than-vigorous attempt at containment), but "as everybody in Santiago knows," many journalists told me, police wages were also unpaid. This plus the fact that many of the policemen had relatives among the protesters explains the absence of any sustained police response on the day of the riot. The executive director of *El Liberal* told me what his friend then-governor Fernando Lobo privately acknowledged after the riot: "I didn't pay the police. That was my mistake." And according to many a journalist, that explains the lack of repression and the "freedom" enjoyed by rioters on that day.

In addition to unpaid wages (of public employees and the police), widespread corruption fed the anger, fury, and "irritation" that "the people" felt at that time. As one journalist explained: "The Santiagueños got tired of so much corruption, felony, impunity. . . . They exploded because they were fed up . . . with the deplorable spectacle of politicians, union leaders, and officials who were sharing the booty" (Jozami 1994, 26). As another journalist from *El Liberal* put it, government corruption was one of the "driving forces behind the protest" (Luna 1994, 56). Much like the judge, many journalists who reported on these events created a taxonomy of participants, distinguishing protesters from "vandals" (Garay 1994, 24; Díaz 1994, 54) and highlighting the presence of agitators: "A lot of strange faces, some of them with accents from [the provinces of] Buenos Aires, Tucumán, Córdoba" (Gallardo 1994, 38); and "among the 1,200 people who went to the demonstration of public employees, only 100 at the vanguard assaulted and burned" (Díaz 1994, 49).

Caso Scrimini: The Dominant Elites Find the Activist

Less than two years have passed since the Santiagazo.[3] The federal intervention is about to give way to the new elected governor, Dr. Carlos Juarez. He will be the governor of Santiago for the fourth time (he was governor first in 1949, then from 1973 to 1976, and from 1983 to 1987). In the 1995 elections won by the Peronist Party, a newly created party, Memoria y Participación (MyP), obtained enough votes to elect one deputy to the local parliament. MyP is a coalition composed mainly of groups from the Left, members of Catholic base communities, and other small progressive groups. MyP recognizes the events of December 16 as a *gesta popular,* a popular epic action, and as the party's founding date. Carlos Scrimini, the elected deputy, is a physician from Córdoba. A man in his fifties, he had extensive political experience as a member of the Communist Party during the 1960s and 1970s. He was the president of the student organization Federación Universitaria de Córdoba in 1969, at the time of the Cordobazo, one of the greatest working-class uprisings in postwar Latin American history (Brennan 1994). In that capacity, Scrimini took an active part in the "street wars" led by unions and students groups during that period.

On July 12, 1995, the local parliament by majority vote decides not to accept Scrimini's deputy credentials. There are "enough proofs," a member of the Peronist majority informs, of Scrimini's "moral inability" to become a member of the parliament. He "has been an instigator and active participant in the looting and burning of public buildings and private residences during December 16," the Peronist deputy says, and a local judge accuses Scrimini of "apología del delito, sedición y motín" [incitement to rebellion and mutiny].

No charges are brought against Scrimini before he is elected to a seat in the parliament. It is only after the election, and when he publicly defends the "epic actions of December 16," that the Peronist majority decides, with the complicity of a public prosecutor and a local judge, that Scrimini is "one of the seventy persons who burned and sacked Government House, the courthouse, and the legislature." Curiously enough, it has taken the prosecutor more than a year and a half to identify (and bring charges against) Scrimini. Photographs and video footage show Scrimini and hundreds of other Santiagueños in front of public buildings and private residences, shouting against politicians and officials; pictures show him rescuing a woman who was trapped in the burning government house. Those images, together with Scrimini's public declarations saying that during December 16, they, the protesters, "intended to take power," are enough proof, according to the prosecutor, to accuse Scrimini and thus prevent him from becoming a member of the parliament.

Many in Santiago understand this episode as an act of political persecution (*Nuevo Diario*, 14 July 1995), but many others (especially those occupying dominant positions in local politics and media) use the *caso Scrimini* to put forward their version of the events of December 16, their causes and their protagonists. The dominant elites find in Scrimini the activist, the "instigator" they are looking for; he is, in this regard, a perfect activist: someone who has participated in the Cordobazo, someone who has a Communist past, and someone who is willing to say that he was "proud of the Santiagazo." In accusing and banning him, the dominant elites are not only violating constitutional laws (as most legal experts agree) and proscribing someone because of his political beliefs; they are also taking advantage of the opportunity to criminalize the protest and to reduce a mass protest to the work of seventy "perfectly identifiable instigators."

Well-known journalist Oscar Díaz's articles in the pages of *El Liberal* illustrate this association between the caso Scrimini and a particular version of the events. That day, Díaz argues in "A propósito del 16 de Diciembre," needs "a judicial classification." That "classification" comes with the decision to prosecute Scrimini. Díaz praises the judge's decision because it will help "to heal a wound that hurts us all." For him, "the 'people' in its sociological sense" did not take part in the Santiagazo. "At best it was an explosion about wages, an explosion which was infiltrated by marginal political elements and by foreign vanguardists." Whatever the sociological sense of "the people" is, it is quite clear that for Díaz (as for many in *El Liberal*), "marginal elements of society" and "activists" made the explosion happen. As usual, only the latter have names and can be criminally prosecuted. "The representative of Memoria y Participación," reads another article in *El Liberal* on 22 May 1995, referring to Scrimini, "was very active during that day. He was leading [*al frente*] the sacking and destruction of the government house, the courthouse and the legislature . . . in a well-orchestrated operation." Other publications ridicule Scrimini's presumed actions during the riot. The deputy in charge of accusing Scrimini in the parliament illustrates, in a single remark, the link between a version of the protest and the charges against the activist as it operates from the dominant point of view. For Abalos, the whole process against Scrimini is "technical and juridical . . . people want to politicize the whole thing." For the elites, the riot was not about politics but about the violation of the juridical order; it was a crime. Thus the need to find a criminal.[4]

An innocent crowd led by activists—a "passive instrument of outside agents," as George Rudé would put it (1964, 8)—vented their anger at their unpaid salaries, the judge explains; and at the generalized corruption, most of the journalists add. They agree with the executive director of *El Liberal,* who puts it very clearly when he writes: "To a great extent, it was the work of at most 300 activists, and a similar number who, at least in the beginning, escorted them with cheers and gestures of support" (Castiglione 1994, 2). Local politicians whose homes were or were not burned also credited outside organizers—that "mythic culprit blamed so regularly when 'innocent masses' rebel all over the world" (Roy 1994, 133)—for "acts of vandalism."

Those occupying dominant positions in the local political and journalistic fields construct a "dominant framing" (Steinberg 1995)—that is, an interpretive scheme that simplifies and condenses the many different dimensions and meanings of the riot—to explain the events of December 16, 1993. This dominant framing has, for its defenders, "the force of facts" behind it. After all, less than a year after the uprising, Governor Juarez was elected for the fourth (and in 1999 for the fifth) time by "the same people" who burned down his house. "See, nothing changed," I was repeatedly told.

According to this discursive construction of December 16, since nothing much changed in Santiago del Estero, nothing much actually happened that day: it was a "mere wage claim." As Judge Lugones explains, for those who "stole a chair or a TV set, what happened on December 16 meant nothing, nothing at all, maybe a couple of bottles of wine to drink, that's all." The "so-called Santiagazo did not exist. It didn't change the destiny of Santiago del Estero." He interprets December 16 as a non-event, not as a "historical fact that leaves a unique and singular trace, one that marks history by its particular and inimitable consequences," as Dumoulins defines an event (quoted in Tarrow 1996, 587), but as a "peak of fever, as a couple of more degrees in the heat of Santiago. After that, everything went back to normal." It is against the background of this framing (or better, in dialogue with it) that protesters construct partially different stories about the same events.

Contested Memories

"Before the police left the scene, there was a brief encounter between the cops and the people. You didn't know whether to bitch at them, punch them, or forgive them. The people finally applauded the cops, and they left [figure 17]. When that happened, we didn't know what to do," Roberto tells me. "I began looking for the people of the Union Front to tell them to take charge of things . . . Nobody knew what to do . . . I was already inside Government House when I saw that the *muchachos* were beginning to burn things. At the time it seemed horrendous to me. I told one of them, 'Don't be stupid . . . such a beautiful house.' But they didn't pay attention to us, they were unstoppable. While I was talking to one of them, three or four others were already burning everything . . . They were unstoppable." Against the alleged presence of agitators, this confusion conveys a sense of spontaneity of action that is explicitly emphasized in the interviews. All my interviewees make explicit reference

FIGURE 17.

Protesters applauding policemen. © El Liberal

to what I call the official framing by later objecting to parts of it: "It was spontaneous . . . there were no people from other places, *as it is said.* We all knew each other. It was the mood of the people," María, a leader of the teachers' union, tells me. And her compañera René adds, "Everything was spontaneous . . . we went to the courthouse, but there wasn't any organization. We heard that people were going to the courthouse, so we went there. On my way home, I stopped by the legislature while people were throwing things out of the windows. I didn't see any strange faces there. There were no activists, *as people say.*"

Aware of competing understandings about the uprising's driving forces, all the active participants I interview explicitly deny the existence of agitators and resort to the metaphor of contagious anger to explain why they did what they did: "It was a spontaneous thing; it was an event that occurred because of the situation in which we were living," says Juana, who at that time was an organizer in a Catholic Base Community. Or as Nana puts it, showing deep familiarity with the dominant narrative, "*Some say* that it was just the work of vandals. Maybe there actually were some vandals here or there, but those who initiated everything, those who broke the policemen's blockade, were not vandals but workers. They were working people. We did not hire any *barra brava* [gang] to break the policemen's blockade. We did it ourselves. We formed circles and started jumping and threw ourselves against the cops, turning and whirling, like kids do in the clubs, so that we could break it . . . so that we didn't have to go on facing them." In point of fact, Nana and the rest highlight the *lack of organization* as a major problem of the riot.

Whereas the "fever" referred to by the judge serves to convey a certain irrationality of the crowd and the innocent character of the "horde," the contagion and spontaneity that protesters talk about fulfills another function. Much similar to the U.S. black students' sit-ins analyzed by Francesca Polletta, the repeated reference to (and explicit emphasis on) spontaneity offers protesters "some defense against the charges that the demonstrations were led by 'outside agitators'" (Polletta 1998b, 149). Acknowledging but at the same time contesting the official version of the events, Nana asserts,

> This was something done by Santiagueños from Santiago del Estero; there were no groups of rabid fans [soccer hooligans] of any club here. *This is what pisses me off the most about the Santiagazo; people say it was organized by this one or that one.* I think that if there had been anybody trying to put this together, it went out of his or her hands. Totally, totally, totally! I wish I could give you a whole list of people . . . They would all say the same. People like me who have no interests and no reasons to risk their heads. To risk it like my comrades, because the bullets were coming for any of us.

Although they insist on the spontaneous character of the revolt, Roberto, María, and René acknowledge that—as Mario, the cop, knew so well—there were incessant organizing efforts *before* December 16. In fact, when asked about the riot's origins, all the protesters locate the day in a longer series of events: "It all started at the beginning of 1993." As I already described, their organizing efforts comprise the formation of the Union Front, which brings together several unions and an almost-weekly participation in rallies, marches, demonstrations, sit-ins, and teach-ins throughout the year. In these contentious gatherings, protesters not only meet each other in the street and realize that "I am not alone, it's incredible," as Nana says, but also learn, as I examined in chapter 5, to deal with mounting police response—"We learn how to return the tear gas grenades to them." Even a casual observer of regional events would note that this action is anything *but* spontaneous, that the "riot" is "bound to happen." Why, then, do the participants so fervently assert the spontaneous character of their mobilization? What is the meaning of this assertion within the context of their recollections?

Perhaps this insistence on spontaneity means something other than sudden or surprising revolt. Spontaneity, as remembered today, means that the protesters are both following a moral imperative to react and expressing their decision to break with a deeply held belief in provincial apathy, a mythical—but not for that less real—conviction about the unchanging passivity of the Santiagueños, about their submissiveness and indolence.[5] As María from the teachers' union puts it, "I like what we did. If we hadn't done it, we would have been unworthy. Despite the fact that it was only an explosion." On the one hand, as an assertion of initiative, the idea of spontaneity denotes a challenge to the official framing of these events that locates agitators as the driving force behind the "popular fury." On the other hand, as an assertion of the worthiness of the protesters' actions, spontaneity expresses an effort to realize a moral vision—as James Jasper (1997) would put it, a vision that transcends while encompassing the material claim. Here is how Nana explains her actions: "[I did it] because I wanted to complain, because I didn't think what was going on was fair. Yes, *what people say* is true, you wanted to be paid, but you also wanted to end the disgusting government that we had. To finish somehow with feeding so much corruption."

The Santiagazo is spontaneous, protesters say, because it is not merely a wage claim: it is also a moral protest, direct action against those they feel are doing wrong. "It was like a punishment. I got back home, and I felt proud about what had happened. I thought we had just given a punishment," Nana tells me. For her, it is not merely about wages; it has a larger meaning: it is about justice *and* about respect.

> That night, when you could still smell smoke from the burning, I was thinking . . . Well, we had to put so much of our hearts into it, to generate all that mess, so that at least they talked about Santiago in the capital city. Just so that Santiago appears once on the cover of the *New York Times*. Because we knew that too. We are the first province, the poorest, the one that is left behind the most, where it is so hard to educate our children, to raise them healthy, where it is so hard

to achieve a dignified future . . . A big mess had to be made so that someone wrote about it and became interested in us . . .

Nana is here referring to the article "With Fire and Fury, Argentine Poor Make a Point," printed in the *New York Times* on December 18, 1993. It is clearly not possible that on the night on December 16, she "knew that too." Should we then discard this testimony (and that of many others who mix up times and events) as wrong information? This is hardly the first testimony that is not fully reliable in point of fact. Historians know that more than telling us what people actually did, "oral sources tell us . . . what they wanted to do, what they believed they were doing, and what they now think they did" (Portelli 1991, 50). Oral sources have another kind of credibility: their importance rests not so much in its "adherence to fact, but rather in its departure from it, as imagination, symbolism, and desire emerge" (51). This is the oral source's forte rather than its drawback—"errors, inventions, and myths lead us through and beyond facts to their meanings" (1). Thus this "wrong" tale is extremely valuable because it provides a window into the interests of the teller, the desires and dreams beneath those interests. Nana is telling us that they want to be noticed, that they want to make it into the pages of prestigious newspapers. This "mistake" also illuminates one of memory's central features: rather than being a passive container of facts, remembering is an active process of meaning making (Passerini 1987; Portelli 1991; James 1997; Olick and Robbins 1998).

Spontaneity thus works both as a rejection of the presence of outside agitators *and* as an affirmation of the dignity of the protesters, a dignity that runs against the dominant framing that constructs the event as a "mere wage claim." As for Mario, the cop (but for entirely different reasons), for protesters the riot was (and is) about dignity, about standing up in front of corrupt power holders.

"At that time, we wanted to think of it as an awakening, the beginning of a new political era, a historical symbol, a before and an after. We attributed a lot of symbolism to that event. . . . *but there were others, specifically one journalist, who put forward the argument that this is a pueblo that only gets angry when it doesn't get paid*," Roberto admits. Like other protesters, he is familiar with the dominant interpretation of the Santiagazo; he even acknowledges some truth in the official framing and implicitly recognizes other possible meanings besides what "we wanted to think of it at that time." But he insists on the existence of some larger—although partially unrealized—significance of the protest expressed in the burnings of what he and many others call the "symbols of corruption."

The dignifying dimension of the riot is something that many an active participant wishes to see in the events of December 16, but subsequent events (mainly the reelection of Governor Juarez) prove such an understanding uncertain. "At that time," María and René agree, "it seemed to be a positive moment in the history of Santiago. It was as if the Santiagueños were recovering their dignity, their capacity to protest. That was a positive thing . . . The Santiagazo was also a *lesson for local politicians.* The Santiagueño can put up with many things for a long time. But everything has a limit, and the Santiagueño is capable of reacting. In one way or another that [capacity] is there. 'You [politicians] can keep on adjusting, but watch out, because there has been a Santiagazo, and it can happen again.' " For them, the dignity, the moral dimension, expressed that day is a sort of potential that, as such, is open to interpretation and reinterpretation. In other words, much like the newspaper report, but again for different reasons, the history of December 16, for many protesters, "is still being written." René initially thinks the uprising is a "heroic action. I clearly remember that we used that phrase: 'A heroic action [una gesta popular].' " But seven years later, she and María think that their initial interpretations about the meanings of the riot are probably overstated: "When the people voted for those whose houses were burned [in reference to Governor Juarez], it was big disappointment. And we had to rethink our interpretation. We have idealized the event, wishing it meant something else. But what happened after that day showed us that it was not like we thought initially. We wanted to give some sense of dignity to the riot. [We thought the riot] . . . was a recovery of dignity." María adds: "[We thought it was] a revolution." Puzzled by this, I ask them, "So was or wasn't it a heroic action?" Their answer encapsulates the viewpoints of the many participants I interview: "Time will tell."

Memoria y Participación

Many participants in the riot speak about (and still try to interpret) the "lessons," "messages," or "mandates" of the uprising. The members of Memoria y Participación, the political party founded after December 16, put it clearly in a document published on the second anniversary of the event. Acknowledging, as do other protesters, competing interpretations, this document sees in the reshaping of the local political culture the main "lesson" of the upheaval: "Whether or not it was a popular rebellion, whether or not something happened in Santiago after December 16, these are open questions; the event is not yet closed, and the answers depend on our current and future actions." For them the uprising is still in the making, and they have their own version to put forward. Their understanding of the riot says that its main aim was to "purify democracy, burn down a corrupt power, and reaffirm the dignity of a people that was fed up."

Seven years after the uprising, two prominent members of MyP, Enrique Hisse and Alejandro Auat, tell me that "after the sixteenth, a struggle over the interpretation began . . . the establishment and the media won, they presented the event as a wage claim." They call this version a "shaming interpretation," a version that seeks to "erase what had happened from the memory of the Santiagueños." Against this "shaming" interpretation (or, as a local priest told me, "hopeless version"), they put forward their own "epic" rendition. Months after the riot, in one of the party's founding documents, MyP asserts that "December 16 signals a before and an after in the history of Santiago, it is a starting point for a new foundation. The burning of the three branches of government is a burning of a formal democracy that served as an instrument of oppression rather than of liberation . . . This is the clear message of December 16: nobody tried to destroy democracy but to purify it so that it is more authentic and participatory" (28 May 1994). In this document, MyP asserts that "those who say that nothing happened are wrong. December 16 significantly changes the political scenario in the province and the country: it challenges the neoliberal model that currently reigns in our America." A year and a half later, in a statement to the press, MyP still acknowledges other interpretations of the events (this time, versions that "criminalize" the protest) and insists, "Against a version that is being disseminated, we assert that after the sixteenth nothing remains the same in Santiago." The "mandate" of that day was loud and clear: "justice and participation" (4 June 1995).

In the years that follow the uprising, members of MyP, together with some unions (mainly teachers), organized two commemorations of the event: the first one in December 1994, and the second on December 1995. The first one, according to one of the leaders of MYP, "was a failure, because a sector of the party pushed to organize the festival in a soccer stadium, expecting that a lot of people would show up. If we had organized it on a street corner, it would have been a success. But the stadium was too big." Roof tiles from Government House were distributed among the musicians who played in the festival as "keepsakes" from the "epic actions of the sixteenth." The second commemoration was organized when Governor Juarez was already in office. Using bureaucratic red tape as an excuse (rallies, organizers were told, needed authorization weeks in advance), the government prohibited any public demonstration and closed off the main square, surrounding it with police guards. Members of MYP, some teachers' unions, and other small leftist parties organized a caravan around the city. "The march of the explosion," as the main newspaper called it, did not have a massive attendance as expected. Three participants were arrested for "public disorders."

A year after they first described to me the uprising as a "lesson for politicians," I ask René and María about the content of that lesson. "Well, maybe it was our wish . . . but December 16 left some lesson. Since then, they always pay on time. I know it's a small thing, but before that day, they would joke around with our salaries." Thus although the riot is not merely about wages, the lessons that government officials learned are mainly about the uprising's material claims. Recall Juan's characterization of the riot. For the man who takes the flag from the governor's office, December 16 is a "battle." This battle is about unpaid wages and rampant corruption. The "lesson" from that day is also related to wages paid on time:

JAVIER: Six year have gone by. Did you win the war?

JOSE: Winning the war means to have your job, to be paid for your job, to have a fair salary to live; and this is what this government is doing: they pay you on time, they give you a fair salary so that you can grow, study, have a dinner outside, go to the movies . . . I won't say that we won the war, but if you compare today with those days, we are in peace.

And yet the "lessons" can hardly be confined to the wage claim. When during 1998 some neighborhoods organize demonstrations claiming for potable water, the specter of the sixteenth shows up again in their slogans. "People sing, 'We will burn your house again, as we did on the sixteenth,'" I am repeatedly told. Thus the uprising has many meanings, and those meanings keep changing as local political events occur (an election, an upsurge in collective contention, etc.). In the hearts and minds of many protesters, the Santiagazo is a *project*, one that *goes beyond the pursuit of material self-interest and points at the realization of a different political culture:* "We see it as something healthy, as a sort of liberation from a deeply internalized fear. It is a breath of fresh air, a wind of hope," René states. No one puts it better than Nana, the queen of the riot, when she says, "For me, the Santiagazo is an unfinished symphony."

Coda

In the first elections after the riot, one of the targets of the protesters' fury was elected governor of Santiago for the fifth time, making even the most confident of the protesters doubtful about the real effects of the Santiagazo. Soon after taking office again in 1995, Governor Juarez appointed officer Musa Azar as the head of the agency in charge of local intelligence in Santiago del Estero, euphemistically called the Secretariat of Information (SI). Musa Azar was the chief of the Department of Police Information during the military dictatorship (1976–1983), an agency that, according to the CONADEP report, was a clandestine detention and torture center. The law of "due obedience" interrupted the judicial process against him for his participation in the detention center of the Brigada de Investigaciones del Chaco during the military genocide. It would be difficult not to see the appointment of this spy chief, and the work of political espionage carried out by the SI on union leaders, peasant organizations, politicians, and priests through a network of well-paid informants, as a consequence of the Santiagazo.[6] It takes no conspiracy theory to see the enforcement of mechanisms of social control (the key role now played by the SI, the new post that the Gendarmería Nacional set up in Santiago a year after the riot) as the product of the contentious 1993 and of its final "explosion." It is probably not one of the "lessons" protesters want local politicians to learn, but it is certainly related to the Santiagazo.

Although not massive, numerous firings in the public sector (firings that were one of the central objectives of the local adjustment law passed by the parliament on November 1993, which provoked so much rage among protesters) were carried out in the public administration of Santiago after the riot. Public employment decreased from 31,612 employees in 1993 to 26,030 in 1994 and 22,274 in 1996 (a 30 percent reduction in three years, well above that of other northwestern provinces). Again, this was certainly not one of the "lessons" that protesters wanted the local government to learn after the most important episode of collective action that the city had ever witnessed.

The Santiagazo was a collective way of contesting the spiral of decline, exclusion, and public corruption in which public employees and residents of Santiago del Estero feared being caught. As with any other episode of contention, however, it would be grossly misleading to seek to understand and explain the event by its outcomes. But the governor, his spy chief, and the adjustment as a policy priority are there to cast doubt on the memories of even the most optimistic participants in that "day of fury," and thus on their ways of making sense of collective struggle.

When writing about subaltern groups—even more so when seeking to understand their joint actions—we are always navigating between two equally pernicious traps: miserabilistic and populist interpretations (Grignon and Passeron 1991; Scheper-Hughes 1992; Wacquant 1999). Under the spell of the first, we are inclined to see protest as the self-defeating and unconducive acts of the victims of an all-powerful system. Under the influence of the second (undoubtedly more pervasive among social scientists) (see Tilly 1991), we are disposed to see every act of protest as an act of heroic resistance of a people untouched by domination.

Not every "souvenir" kept in secret or every story told about the Santiagazo is an act of resistance. But should we dismiss those keepsakes and the willingness to remember simply as worthless objects or as anecdotal efforts? Should we forget the Santiagazo simply because it didn't "change the life of the province," as the judge told me and as local politicians and officials echo? Given what we know about the Santiagazo, its aftermath, and its memories, it would be tempting to choose between the opposites described in previous chapters, choosing, let's say, between the judge's account ("The so-called Santiagazo did not exist. It didn't change the destiny of Santiago del Estero; it was peak of fever, a couple of more degrees in the heat of Santiago . . . after that, everything went back to normal") and Nana's understanding of the Santiagazo's effects: "I still think that December 16 will come back, because everything has its limits. At that time they played a lot with people's patience, with people's needs. And they are still playing now. It seems like they didn't learn the lesson. It seems like they forget. Even though there must be many [politicians] who, when stealing, are scared of being burned down."

We have no way of knowing whether Nana's (and many other protesters') best hopes or the judge's (and most local politicians') worst fears will someday, somehow, have—as Bakhtin would say—their "homecoming festival." Maybe we should, in what many (including sometimes myself) would judge an overly optimistic tone (almost a populist celebration), agree with María, one of the leaders of the teachers' union, who, when asked about the lessons of the fire, paused for a moment and said, "Time will tell."

Conclusions

Ethnography and

Recognition

It was as though, talking to me, a stranger, he had had to find a way of talking about the unmentionable past.—v. s. naipul, *A Turn in the South*

The social world gives what is rarest, recognition, consideration, in other words, quite simply, reasons for being.—pierre bourdieu, *Pascalian Meditations*

Popular uprisings can have many results ("outcomes," in the language of social movement analysts) (Giugni, McAdam, and Tilly 1998, 1999): they can force authorities to redirect resources (as happened after the Los Angeles riots in 1992), they can make a deep impact on the political system (as with the 1989 Venezuelan Caracazo), and they can lead to a reinforcement of mechanisms of control and repression (as is now happening in Argentina after the increasing wave of protests during the 1990s). Revolts can also change the life of people, or at least the way in which they understand themselves. Think about Mario, the cop, whose career was abruptly interrupted as a result of the Santiagazo; or about Nana, whose life was, in her own words, "never the same again"; or about Laura, who got her house back after (and somehow as a result of) the pueblada. Protest, we know, may have an effect on people's biographies (McAdam 1999). Biographies, in turn, shape the ways in which people make sense of protest. Nana's and Laura's actions, thoughts, and feelings during the uprisings were deeply informed by their social trajectories. Throughout this book, I have showed how, in the streets and roads of Santiago and Cutral-co, Nana and Laura drew on elements of their lives to take action and to make sense of it. I argue that we cannot fully understand what they did and how they experienced their actions if we do not delve into their life histories.

The ways in which Nana and Laura lived these popular revolts were informed not only by their singular histories but by the interactions they had with other fellow protesters and with authorities, and by the shared understandings forged jointly in the hot streets of Santiago and cold roads of Cutral-co. In other words, at the core of Nana's and Laura's contentious experiences are their own biographies and the insurgent identities fashioned during those days.

The set of dispositions that protesters bring to collective action and their shared self-understandings are crucial to grasping the ways in which they make sense of contention. Why is sense making so important? Because once we take a close look at protesters' experiences (experiences that, since conveyed in recollections, documents, and images, can better be reconstructed through ethnographic fieldwork), we see another facet of these seemingly "bread-and-butter" uprisings. In Argentina, the Santiagazo and the pueblada are by now two emblematic protests. Being the prime examples of the *estallido* (explosion) and of the *corte de ruta* (road blockade), they both stand as antiadjustment protests, as revolts against the "economic model." State retrenchment and the rise of massive unemployment are undoubtedly at the root of these (and many other) protests. But large-scale change of the kind represented by the veritable neoconservative revolution in Argentina affects neither the course nor the meaning of contention in a straightforward way. We now know that rather than expressing dissatisfactions and strain, collective action emerges from a population's political processes.[1] We should also acknowledge that the experiences of contention, the way in which protest is lived, the hopes with which it is imbued, the emotions that animate it, do not flow directly out of the structural roots of conflict. It is only in a very general (and thus superficial) sense that we can say that the Santiagazo and the pueblada were antiadjustment protests; and this assertion should be the beginning, not the end, of our investigation.

The narratives that protesters shared with me, the images I saw, and the documents I read tell a partially different story. Both protests have adjustment as their backgrounds, but structural adjustment only begins to account for protesters' lived experiences. In the streets and roads, Nana, Laura, and many others wanted to be seen and acknowledged, to be recognized and respected.[2] One of the lessons of *Contentious Lives* is that we do a great disservice to both uprisings, and to the lives of people like Laura and Nana, if in our attempt to show how globalization is "resisted" we cover all protests with the same, presumably progressive, mantle.

Because I believe that to know these protests well, to understand what they are about, still requires traditional fieldwork, "the same willingness to be uncomfortable, to drink bad booze, to be bored by one's drinking companions, and to be bitten by mosquitoes as always," as Sidney Mintz (2000) recently put it, I would like to conclude with a brief reflection on my fieldwork and on my personal and intellectual relationships with Nana and Laura.

As in many other ethnographic studies, the things I learned during the course of my research were influenced deeply by the nature of the relationships I established with those studied. To give one example: Nana, her husband Cesar, their six children, Matías, Fernanda, Julieta, Juan, Naomi and Nalé, and I became good friends in the course of my research in Santiago del Estero; out of the many conversations with them came my reconstruction of Nana's life story. After I recorded many hours of her life history, Nana's hesitation to make her story such an important part of my work grew because, as she explained to me, "I don't deserve that much attention . . . there are many other important people that made the Santiagazo . . . I've been thinking a lot these days, and I don't think it's a good idea to write the biography," she told me in an e-mail. I guess that she did not want some of the very personal things and intimate details she told me to be published in a book. It's one thing to reveal them in front of a friend—even a friend with a tape recorder—but another to read about them in a book. Much the same could be said about my relationship with Laura. I stayed at her house for four weeks, and I traveled around Cutral-co with her for another four weeks. I became her friend and the friend of her three wonderful children, Paula, Guillermo, and Miguel. Although she didn't resist my initial attempts at making her the central character of my story, she stressed that she was only a "representative of the picketers . . . only a medium through which the voices of the people could be heard." After I reassured both of them that they would have the final say in approving any written transcript, they agreed, knowing that the interpretation of their stories, however, would remain mine. They read and authorized the excerpts of their stories that I used in this book. When she handed me the originals of her notebook and diary, Laura summarized much of both her and Nana's feelings toward my work: "Take all the originals; you are the one who is working on this, not me. I offer you my trust; if you do something that betrays it, you are the one who's going to be a bad person, not me. I am positive I did the right thing."

The things I learned were also influenced by my own presence in the field. Laura, Nana, and the rest of my interviewees knew who I was, an Argentine professor living in New York trying to find out what had happened on December 16, 1993, and in June 1996. Although different in size, both cities are relatively small (200,000 residents in Santiago; 50,000 in Cutral-co/Plaza Huincul); the presence of a professor from New York is bound to be news. My presence was reported in the pages of the main local newspapers. I was interviewed three times as a "sociologist doing research on the Santiagazo" and once as a researcher studying la pueblada. I was also interviewed by local radio and TV channels. During my fieldwork, some of the protesters I talked to referred to these interviews, to things with which they agreed or disagreed. On other occasions, I contested some of their interpretations, especially when they gave credence to the rumors surrounding the "selling out" of Laura. Some might argue that I "contaminated" my object of research. In voicing my opinions about the protests and its protagonists, I rather think that I joined (inadvertently at first) the struggle over the meanings that both uprisings have for protesters and authorities (as anybody doing research on this topic would unavoidably do). This battle over the "right interpretation" has different forms in both locations, but it did begin well before I came to Santiago and Cutral-co and will go on long after I leave.

Ethnographers are not very used to being challenged by their "subjects" regarding their explanations and interpretations. When they are challenged, the reporting of the subjects' objections, sometimes incensed ones, comes in the form of after-the-fact tales from the field that, at their best (Scheper-Hughes 2000; Venkatesh 2002), serve to reflect on the position of researcher vis-à-vis her subjects and other thorny ethical and epistemological issues. At other times, we know about subjects' reactions through papers at academic conferences or verbal exchanges in journals devoted in large part to academic squabbles, a form that merely reflects and reinforces the privileged position of the scholastic view.[3] In this book, I made the objections of my interviewees part of my analysis. Not because I believe that subjects' agreements (or disagreements) with the sociologist's analysis are a measure of its validity (pace populists, it is not), but because I think that the ongoing dialogue about the aftermath of the uprisings (a dialogue I joined while I was conducting my research) is part and parcel of the construction of the event and, as such, should be included in the study of these events.

I also incorporated my informants' reactions to my own appreciations for other, more practical reasons. I am always amazed that even in the best ethnographies, we don't hear subjects, informants, or interviewees asking the researcher what her own opinions are about what she is studying. I might have violated some hidden (and to me unknown) rule of ethnography, but I was often confronted by subjects who had strong opinions about the "causes" of their actions, and a resolute interest in knowing my own opinions about those actions. "So, what do you think about the Santiagazo?" I was repeatedly asked. "I would like to know, what's your interpretation," a teacher and active participant in the Santiago uprising demanded. In the weeks we spent together, and mostly toward the end of my second visit, Laura insisted on knowing my perspective on la pueblada. When I voiced some of my tentative opinions, my friends and interviewees reacted sometimes with approval, sometimes by saying that I was wrong, and other times with puzzlement. These exchanges occurred not only during the interview process but also in other (more public) settings.

In July 2000, a few days before leaving Santiago for the last time, I gave a public lecture at the national university, where I reported my own interpretations of the episode. I personally invited all of my interviewees to the public lecture. The main local newspaper reported on it with the headline "The Santiagazo Was a Search for Respect." It was an appropriate title; it ultimately conveys one of the main arguments of this book. The Santiagazo and la pueblada were lived by many as a search for dignity, respect, and recognition. The headline also hints at one of this book's crucial general implications: as observers of protest around the world have shown, asserting pride, reclaiming dignity, and obtaining recognition from those who matter (in the case of Nana and Laura, their immediate compañeros, friends, acquaintances, and the local authorities) are constitutive dimensions of risky concerted joint action (Wood

2001a; Calhoun 1994). Collective action is likely to get nowhere unless it provides those who engage in it some prospect of attaining individual and collective respect.

Although I claim to have some knowledge about the lived experiences of protesters, it is still hard for me to convey what that public lecture meant to me. Noticing the faces of my interviewees among the public (the room was filled with more than one hundred people) made me at once happy at seeing them and nervous about their responses to my interpretations. During the ensuing debate, and in informal talks before and afterward, they were overwhelmingly concerned with one thing: the consequences, the "impact," of the Santiagazo. Was it worth the (collective) effort? Was it "useful"? If so, how? Although I don't claim to have an answer to their pressing questions, their reactions, concerns, and questions about what I said that night are now part of this book. Most people in Cutral-co and Santiago (and that night only confirmed it) have strong opinions and articulate explanations about what happened on December 16, 1993, and from June 20 to June 27, 1996. They all have stories to tell about that time, about what happened before, during, and after it. As poor a guide as those beliefs and stories might be to explain the events, they have to be taken seriously as part of the ways in which people make sense of their contentious actions.

"Everything about her," writes Pierre Bourdieu (1999, 370) about Lydia, an unemployed woman he interviews for *The Weight of the World*, "even the way she looks at you, shows her fervent desire to be listened to and, for once, to be heard, and at the same time shows her pleasure at having someone to talk to, someone to whom she can justify herself, or better yet, with whom she can feel justified and accepted. And the comparison prompted by this pressure is so intense that, bit by bit, it is she who takes over the interview, eliciting questions or suggestions that derive above all from a longing to encourage and console." Much the same could be said about my relationships with Laura and Nana. It took me a while to realize that their desire to talk was intimately related to the burden they felt they were carrying, an affliction that "is so great that when [they] decide to tell [me] about it, [they] can't keep from going on at great length, reliving each episode of [their] story with unabated passion, and often unable to hold back [their] tears" (Sandrine Garcia 1999, 338). That burden is encapsulated in the way in which Nana defines her whole life ("thirty-six years of crap") or Laura defines part of it ("the most obscure period in my life, the fourteen years of violence") and expressed in the way they both grab the opportunity afforded by the interview to carry out a deep exploration of their selves (as Laura puts it, "You are like a psychologist to me, you make me think about things I haven't thought before").

This desire to talk, to relive episodes of their lives, was also present in almost all of my interviewees. They wanted to talk about the uprisings; they wanted to share with me their experiences and thoughts. They talked willingly, and at times confessionally, about the events and their aftermaths. "With very few exceptions," writes Sudhir Kakar (1996, 91), "anthropologists have generally not described the many reasons why a community reveals itself to an outsider. Perhaps this reserve is because many anthropologists believe that the information they receive is primarily due to their personal qualities, such as a special gift for establishing rapport with strangers, fluency in the community's spoken language, evident sympathy with its ways, or other markers of an irresistible personal attractiveness which it would be immodest to talk about in public." It is not out of modesty that I do not delve into my own (if any) personal virtues as an ethnographer. "Personal qualities" aside, I do believe that to a great extent the secret of a good ethnography is the respect accorded to others and the will to learn from others' lives. It seems to me that the main reason behind subjects' decisions to open up their lives (and, as in Laura and Nana, their homes) to strangers has to do with their own expectations and hopes about our work. We should reflect on protesters' *uses* of ethnography and of the ethnographer not only for a better understanding of our place in the field (a concern that seems to be a sort of narcissistic obsession these days) but also because it impinges on the process through which we construct our object of research. It seems to me that this need to be heard is also part of a search for recognition, the ethnographic interview with a "prestigious" interlocutor being one site in which this quest can be pursued. For participants in a publicly denied riot ("in an event that people keep on saying did not exist," as Nana repeatedly told me), for picketers who spent seven days in the road "for nothing . . . after all, we didn't get much out of la pueblada," for people living in a forgotten province of a forgotten region ("the poorest province, the one that is left behind the most, where it is so hard to educate our children, to raise them healthy, where it is so hard to achieve a dignified future") or in a town always on the verge of disappearance ("in the future, this will be a town of children and old people. Those who are old enough to work will have to leave"), the ethnographic interview (far from being the hostile and intrusive scientific gaze) is "an opportunity to tell part of their story" (Scheper-Hughes 1992, 28).[4]

The dialogue established between ethnographer and subject is an occasion on which participants in the riot can re-create the joy ("It was hilarious," "like smoking a joint"), the thrill of being together ("the whole town was there, it was wonderful"); they can formulate what they expected ("At that time we wanted to see it as an awakening," "We wanted the governor to pay attention to us"); they can evaluate its impact on their own lives as well as on the life of the community ("I felt proud about it . . . and I think it is something positive"); they can make their voices heard in this "still to be written" history; and they can attempt to link their own biographies with the significance of the event and with the act of retelling,[5] as Nana does when, after complaining about the versions that deny the existence of the Santiagazo (and thereby of herself), she adds: "But what affirms me in my thirty-six years of age is that you are here, and you talk to me. And that you are leaving and going to work. I do not care what you write; you will write what you decipher about what this thing was. I am going to be very happy, whatever it is that you write; whether it was a Carnaval or not, I don't care. But I am positive I did the right thing."

The ethnographic interview may be perceived as a means of communication (Auyero and Grimson 1997), as a way for people to insert themselves into public narratives in which they are not usually allowed to have any presence, or (as we saw in the case of Santiago) as an opening to contest the official version of an event—as I realized a few days after beginning my fieldwork when the ethnographic encounter became part of the ongoing political struggle over the meanings of the riot. But the interview can be more than that. In the unusual exchange of communication that, if done with care, is offered by the ethnographic interview, actors have "an exceptional opportunity . . . to testify, to make themselves heard, to transfer their experience from the private to the public sphere" (Bourdieu 1996, 24). In the cases of Laura, Nana, and the rest, protesters have an opportunity to gain part of the respect they sought during the uprising. The interview does not generate these "in-search-of-respect" stories; it only produces conditions in which stories can emerge and develop: the space where Laura and Nana can strive to think through their lives and give an overall meaning to them, think about the many ways in which their lives were "marked"—as they both repeatedly told me—by all the "ugly things that happened." Although the interviews with both of them began as inquiries into their participation in the uprisings, Nana and Laura soon seized the opportunity to talk about the issues that most matter to them, the Santiagazo and la pueblada being two of them, but hardly the only ones. Thus began, without my intending it at first, relentless and painful reflections on the self in which I, as an ethnographer, became the vehicle, a process that in Nana's words "shook me . . . but I guess that's good, I've been thinking about these things for a long time, and it was time to let them out," or in Laura's words "It's hard to go over these things, but I feel good, really good about it." Abdelmalek Sayad (1999, 561) captures this dimension of the ethnographic encounter clearly when he says: "The presence of the 'professional' investigator provides only the looked-for opportunity to articulate the mature product of long self-study." It is important to remark, however, that the stories are not an artificial outcome of the interview interaction but an "extra-ordinary discourse . . . which was already there, merely awaiting the conditions for its actualization" (Bourdieu 1996, 24).

The ethnographic encounter can thus be an opportunity to contest an official interpretation, to make one's own viewpoint known, and an occasion to reflect on one's life. As Langelier (1989, 267) puts it: "The act of telling a story is the act of organizing experience. In telling stories we organize events and human actions into some sort of whole; we give form to the understanding of a purpose in life . . . In a most profound way, our stories tell us who we are and who we can—or cannot—be, at both surface and deep-level meaning." In this reflection, a person attempts to make sense of her life for herself and for others, including the ethnographer. In a way, then, the ethnographer, as a keeper of records (Scheper-Hughes 1992; Bourgois 1995) and as an active and methodical listener who fosters "an induced and accompanied self-analysis" (Bourdieu 1996, 24), might also play a part in an act of recognition—a recognition that individuals such as Laura and Nana actively seek through their storytelling. The moral character of the ethnographer's act of witnessing (which Scheper-Hughes retrieves from postmodernist attacks with her "good enough ethnography") finds, in this case, a protesters' need to keep venting her discontent, to keep the ("right") memory of that day alive, *and* to express her own worthiness as a protester and a person.

Why Laura, Nana, and the rest lavished on me their stories thus had less to do with my virtues or shortcomings as an ethnographer than with *their* need to tell their stories, their need to, as Portelli argues, "take arms against the threat of time, to resist time, or to harness time" (1991, 59). This recollection, furthermore, not only preserves the memory of the event but also protects "the teller from oblivion; the story builds the identity of the teller and the legacy which she or he leaves for the future" (59). In their telling, Laura, Nana, and the rest were not only fighting for the merit of their picketing and against the official memory's attempt to bury the riot but also trying to make sense of themselves as protesters who were neither manipulated nor bought off.

Much as the Carnaval was Nana's Carnaval, the Santiagazo was "her riot." The narrative of her actions during the street dancing and the street fights indicates that she "left her soul" in both the Carnaval and the riot. In retelling her story, Nana commemorates and keeps the memory of December 16—and thus her own quest for recognition and respect— alive.

When handing me her notebook, Laura told me that la pueblada was part of her past. That past, however, is part of her present self-identity. That's why she enjoys being called "la piquetera"; because, in a way, the protest still epitomizes what she aspires to in her life and that of her children. In the pickets, she says, "I earned the respect I deserve"; in signing the agreement with the governor, "I was signing against all the injustices, the humiliations, that I suffered throughout my life."

Thirst for recognition: this is what Laura's and Nana's experiences in their lives and in the uprisings are all about. Their self-understandings are now "marked" by the "purifying fire" of December 16 and by the burning tires on Route 22. They both carry their participation as a badge of honor. It was a time when they both did what needed to be done and an occasion on which, in the midst of the confusion, they did "the right thing." Retelling their stories is part of their quest for individual and collective worth; remembering that day is part of the ongoing construction of who they are and who they want to be.

Appendix

On Fieldwork, Theory,

and the Question

of Biography

Fieldwork for this book was carried out during the summers of 1999
and 2000, and during January through April 2001, and comprised archival research, in-depth interviewing, informal conversations, and photo
elicitation. Archival research included reading every issue of Santiago
del Estero's main local newspaper *(El Liberal)* for the years 1993 and
1994, and selected issues of *El Liberal* and *El Nuevo Diario* of subsequent
years, and of every issue of *La Mañana del Sur* for the years 1995 to 2000,
and selected issues of *Rio Negro*. Archival research also comprised content analysis of three major national newspapers *(La Nación, Clarín,* and
Página12) for the year before and the year after the uprisings. I read popular magazines *(Noticias* and *Gente)* that published extensive reports on
the events. In Santiago I watched a video produced by two local journalists that provides wonderful coverage of the events of December 16.
In Cutral-co I watched many locally produced videos on the uprising,
as well as footage from the local TV channel. I also read leaflets, press
communiqués, police records, and court case files to the extent that
they were available. In Santiago, I interviewed twenty residents who had
taken active part in the riot, either in the demonstrations and rallies in
the main square that preceded the burning of Government House or in
the burning and sacking of public buildings and politicians' residences.
I also interviewed six local journalists, two policemen who had been on
duty during the day of the riot, and the judge in charge of the arrested
persons. Nana's life story was recorded over a period of four weeks.
Since then I have had many conversations with her and her family. I
spent four weeks at Laura's home in General Roca (Río Negro), during

which I recorded her views of la pueblada and part of her life story. We traveled from Roca to Cutral-co, where she put me in touch with friends and former picketers. The rest of her life story was recorded in Cutral-co and on National Route 22 as we traveled around the sites of the pickets. In Cutral-co, I interviewed thirty residents, including former picketers, teachers, public employees, and subsidized unemployed. I also interviewed two former majors, one councilman, one coordinator of the local employment agency, two journalists, and the local public prosecutor. I recruited my informants though a snowball method: after each conversation or interview, I asked my respondent to suggest friends or acquaintances who might be willing to talk about the events. To ensure the representativeness of informants in Santiago, I interviewed people from different unions, with different levels of participation during the months before the event, and with diverse itineraries during the day of the uprising. In Cutral-co, I interviewed people with different levels of participation during the uprising (women and men picketers who had stayed day and night in the road blockades, residents who had participated only during the day, etc.). In both cases, some names have been changed to protect anonymity, but for the most part, people did not mind (on the contrary, they insisted on) my using their real names.

Over the course of the last two years, a set of questions kept arising during public presentations of earlier drafts of parts of this book and during the give-and-take of the review process. Does my emphasis on two biographies imply that we should be looking at individual motives in the study of contentious politics? Am I suggesting that all protesters "have to have" a troubled history in order to join collective action? *How many* "Lauras" were present in Cutral-co, and by the same token, *how many* "Nanas" do we need to have collective action of the kind expressed in the Santiagazo? What are Laura and Nana representatives of? What do their stories show that others do not? These are the critical questions that recurred in different ways as I delved more deeply into the lives of Nana and Laura. The more I learned (and spoke) about them, the more academic audiences (made up, I should add, for the most part of sociologists) wanted to know: how many of them? The more I got into specific and intimate details, the more the questions about their *representativeness* kept coming up.

On the one hand, I believe that some of the questions stem from the common concerns (and, many times, the ready-made answers) of students of protest. Because the overwhelming emphasis within the scholarship of collective contention still lies in the search for the causes or origins of collective action, it should not come as a surprise that a study that alters the focus and locus of attention would still be read and questioned with this set of preoccupations in mind. In any case, one thing should be clarified: this study is not an attempt to "bring protesters' motivations back" into the study of the origins of popular protest. Individual motives and common grievances are poor guides to explaining the emergence of collective actions.

On the other hand, if the question of "how many" is a euphemized attempt to contest the sociological legitimacy of the inquiry into the lives of two women protesters, it deserves a closer scrutiny. Neither the Santiagazo nor the pueblada was a protest in which women, as a collective actor, had an unusually important participation—of the kind we saw, for example, in the human rights movements in Argentina or Chile. Nor was gender a decisive factor as a source or catalyst of contention. Laura and Nana do not "represent" these protests; they are not the Santiagazo or the pueblada writ small—though they might embody some crucial dimensions, such as the carnivalesque or the distrust of politicians. Much of what Geertz (1973, 22) says about the detailed study of small villages could be applied to the analysis of these two women: "If localized, microscopic studies were really dependent for their greater relevance upon such a premise—that they capture the great world in the little—they wouldn't have any relevance."

Laura and Nana do, however, stand for something. In ways that are indeed present in many others protesters, but not in such luminous forms, *they incarnate the many ways in which contention and everyday life, popular struggle and biography, intertwine.* Laura and Nana represent, in ways I couldn't quite have anticipated when I began this research, some of the modes in which protesters' (young or old, men or women) experiences and memories of collective struggle are sunk in intricate seams of biographical issues. The question of how many people like Laura and Nana are out there is here replaced by the investigation of the forms in which the life histories of protesters are linked to their participation in contention.

In the rest of this appendix, I will describe the process by which I came to focus on two individuals, or, better said, on the *intersection* of two women and two protests, so as to clarify another set of queries that emerged in the course of writing and presenting earlier drafts. In the words of one insightful reviewer of the manuscript: "What kind of 'guides' are Nana and Laura? If they are Ariadnes, what kind of thread are they unfolding?"

I did not begin my fieldwork in Santiago in search of "the queen of the riot." More than three years ago, I went to Santiago with the idea of putting the "dynamics of contention" model in practice (McAdam, Tarrow, and Tilly 2001). Initially I sought to identify mechanisms and processes at the root of this riot to later examine how they operated in two other episodes (the 1996 and 1997 puebladas in Cutral-co and Plaza Huincul, and the 1999 Correntinazo in the province of Corrientes). It was by luck that I found Nana. After that the initial project slowly metamorphosed as I began, at first intuitively and then out of (sociological) curiosity, to focus more on her life. Thus I made the first move away from my interest in mechanisms and processes at the origins and course of contention. At the time, I thought Nana would assist me in understanding the experiences and memories of collective struggle; it was truly a gut reaction—which only later felt legitimate when I read that "data gathering is shaped almost casually by a lay sensibility to dramatic quality. It is not necessary or even helpful to think constantly about what scientific evidence requires; the ethnographer concentrates on getting the facts recorded in as precise detail as possible" (Katz 2002, 468). Later, as I began to dig more deeply into Nana's and Laura's lives, I decided to modify the focus of my study and concentrate on the relationship between contentious memories and individual and collective self-understandings. As I found out about Laura's personal history and her involvement in the pueblada (capturing the instant in which she changed her relationship to the protest), I started to pay more sustained attention to the continuities between everyday life and contentious episodes. Thus it was only *after* meeting Nana and Laura that I settled on the intersection of biography and protest, the collective biographies of protesting communities, and the actual emergence and course of protest as (at the same time theoretical and empirical) tasks worth pursuing as the central points of research and writing.

This should not be read as a defense of the still-popular spontaneistic ethnography, the one that tells us to "go and hang out and then tell us what you find"—ethnography as mere recording, as if facts will speak for themselves, as if the selection of sites and topics has nothing to do with attempts to answer sociological questions (see Bourdieu, Chamboderon, and Passeron 1991; Alford 1998; and Wacquant 2002). The reason why I became interested in the lives of two protesters during my fieldwork was a product of my own concern with the lack of attention to *contentious politics as lived experience* and an attempt to improve existing theories of protest (Burawoy et al. 1991). Let me further elaborate on this.

In his novel *La caverna*, Nobel Prize–winning Portuguese novelist José Saramago describes the extinction of a world, that of craftsmen, through a richly textured, fine-grained portrayal of the ways in which a family of potters live this process, a family who slowly and painfully realize that they are becoming increasingly "useless" in the face of modern technologies and changing aesthetic preferences. At the beginning of my fieldwork, I had in mind this familiarity that Saramago displays with the frames of meaning within which Cipriano and his daughter Marta go about their threatened lives as something that was needed to understand the lived experiences of contention. Paraphrasing William Whyte's classic *Street Corner Society* and Clifford Geertz's recent *Available Light*, together with the "dynamics of contention" model in mind, my initial steps in Santiago and later in Cutral-co were also guided by a conviction that students of protest should take the trouble to look closer to discover what protesters are up to, to dig into who they think and feel they are, what they think and feel they are doing, and to what end they think and feel they are doing it.

The centrality of the experiential dimension of protest is an aspect that scholars of collective action have been insisting on for quite a while now: the way in which people live and feel collective struggle is crucial to understanding what a protest or a social movement is about (Polletta 1997; Swidler 1995; Gamson 1992; Tarrow 1992). Recent interest in the emotions involved in "passionate [collective] politics" (Goodwin, Jasper, and Polletta 2001) illustrates that the attention to this constitutive dimension is usually more theorized than actually practiced in concrete empirical research. As Marc Edelman (2001, 309) puts it in his superb review of social movement scholarship, a more "genuine appreciation of the lived experience of movement participants and non-participants" is (still) badly needed. It was this theoretical and empirical gap that, together with the search for contentious mechanisms and processes, prompted my initial steps into the field. The Santiagazo and the pueblada are protests that people in Argentina and scholars of contention all over the world talk about as the prime examples of anti-adjustment struggles, and I wanted to figure out what their protagonists thought and felt about them. The project was thus in part an attempt to reconstruct, situate, and explain the protesters' points of view on these much-talked-about episodes, a task, I should add, that is still crucial in ethnographic research. As Annick Prieur (1998, 21) puts it: "I believe it is necessary and valuable to try to understand a culture in the way the participants understand it themselves, to take on their point of view—to dare to take on their point of view—regardless of how politically and morally incorrect it may be. But at the same time an account would be no more than a collection of personal testimonies if it stopped there. The challenge is to go beyond the informant's perception of the world, to try to understand why their perception is the way it is."

All this is to say that the intersection of biography and protest as a point of entry into lived experiences of protest was not there, clearly formulated, at the beginning of my research. It developed later during the fieldwork. Field research and the process by which an object of study is constructed are precisely that: processes. I will not, however, exaggerate the role of chance. Serendipity did indeed play a role, but not the one that is usually portrayed in manuals of qualitative methods or appendixes in ethnographic texts. True, finding the "queen of carnival," and coming across the moment in which Laura "decided" to stay on the barricades, were unforeseen events *but their interrogation was not.* As Bourdieu and his coauthors put it in their criticism of radical empiricism (a criticism that could be extended fully to many an ethnographic text that makes a virtue of the absence of theoretical questions): "Apprehending an unexpected fact presupposes at least the decision to devote methodical attention to the unexpected, and its heuristic value depends on the pertinence and cohesion of the system of questions that it calls into question" (Bourdieu, Chamboderon, and Passeron 1991, 14). For the case at hand, this translates into my decision to stick with Nana and Laura because they would allow me to examine a problem that has been at the top of the sociological agenda for quite a long time (Mills 1959; Elias 1991) but has rarely been attacked head-on, that is, the point at which biography and history commingle and coalesce, and particularly the ways in which these two women use (not necessarily in conscious ways) elements of their everyday lives to make sense, to experience, and to remember collective struggle. Only a theoretical operation permits us to isolate these themes, themes to which Laura and Nana, as constructed characters, are the best guides I can still think of.

Finally, it should be noted that I am hardly the first within ethnographic sociology or ethnographically informed historical research to deliberately concentrate on the construction of characters to understand the social dynamics of particular episodes or epochs. If constructed properly, characters can speak to larger issues (Atkinson 1990; Asad 1994). Martin Guerre, for example, allows Natalie Zemon Davis (1983) to examine the texture of everyday life in a village in sixteenth-century France; Mennochio, the miller of the Friuli, provides Carlo Ginzburg (1980) a window into some dimensions of sixteenth-century Italian popular culture; Rickey, the hustler, helps Loïc Wacquant (1999) to dissect the logic of racial and economic exclusion in a black ghetto in the contemporary United States, much as Willy, the Saab mechanic and repairman (Harper 1992), speaks about practical knowledge and reciprocal care in a rural New York community (for another example, see Ashforth 2000). I hope that Nana and Laura have helped the reader (as much as they helped me) to understand some dimensions of the lived experiences of two massive uprisings, some elements of the everyday life in contemporary Argentina, and their mutual imbrication.

Notes

Introduction

1 Ginsburg (1989), for example, explores the intertwinings of life cycles and commitments to collective action among grassroots abortion activists (on both sides of the divide, i.e., "right-to-life" and "pro-choice" militants); Rupp and Taylor (1987) feature the intersection of biography and activism among feminists in the American women's rights movement during the 1940s and 1950s; Rogers (1993) studies the lives of black and white civil rights leaders in New Orleans during the 1950s and 1960s, paying particular attention to the origins of their activism; Downton and Wehr (1997), in turn, examine the personal attributes and life experiences behind the long-term commitment of "persistent" peace activists. Frankel (1984) and Brodkin Sacks (1984) also hint at the organizational skills that, formerly used in creating family and community networks, women bring into their organizing efforts in the labor force. The best-known studies of the diffusion of mobilization tactics are Doug McAdam's 1988 work on the tactics and strategies learned during the Freedom Summer and later used in the student, feminist, and peace movements (see also Meyer and Whittier 1994); and Ellen DuBois's 1978 analysis of the continuity, in methods and ideologies, between the antislavery movement and the women's rights movement in the United States. For a recent approach to the relevance of biography in social movement studies, see Jasper 1997.

2 For a classic statement on resource mobilization theory, see McCarthy and Zald 1973, 1977; for the political opportunities approach, see McAdam 1982; Tarrow 1998; and also Tilly 1978. On framing (and its critics) see Snow and Benford 1988, 1992; Benford and Snow 2000; Tarrow 1992; Steinberg 1998; Poletta 1998a. For the recent "relational turn" in the sociology of collective action, focusing on the mechanisms and processes at the root of diverse episodes of contention, see McAdam, Tarrow, and Tilly 2001.

3 For a general appraisal of the virtues and shortcomings of the uses of the notion of "collective identity" in social movement literature, see Polletta and Jasper 2001.

4 The 1989 Venezuelan social upheaval, which is the example that comes immediately to mind, was very different in terms of its duration, the extent and targets of the looting (mostly stores), and the death toll (officially, 277 fatalities). See Coronil and Skurski 1991.

5 According to the Centro de Estudios para la Nueva Mayoría, road blockades became quite generalized in 1997: during that year there were 140 of them. This "new form of protest" decreased in frequency during 1998 (51 blockades) but skyrocketed during 1999 (252 blockades), 2000 (614 blockades), and 2001 (1383 blockades).

6 On the concept of repertoire of collective action as a set of means and meanings of claim making, see Tilly 1986.

7 See various issues of *Clarín*, January 2000.

8 The impact of social movements on individual lives is, according to many analysts (McAdam 1999; Polletta and Jasper 2001), one of the least-explored themes in the literature. According to McAdam (1999), "intense and sustained activism should be added to that fairly select list of behavioral experiences (e.g., college attendance, parenthood, military service) that have the potential to tranform a person's biography." Polletta and Jasper (2001), in turn, assert that participation in social movements "usually transforms activists' subsequent biographies, marking their personal identities even after the movement ends, whether or not this is an explicit goal." The same, I will argue, holds true for a onetime involvement in a contentious episode of the kind that Laura and Nana experienced.

9 For the reconstruction of the roots of the "search for respect" in practices other than popular contention, see Bourgois's 1995 account of the historical and cultural underpinnings of crack dealing. Calhoun's study of the Chinese student movement (1994) also offers a detailed analysis of the origins of the students' demands for respect and of the central place of insult in collective action dynamics.

10 Snow and Benford 1992, 137; see also Snow and Benford 1988; Gamson 1998, 1992a; for a recent critique of framing analysis see Steinberg 2000.

11 Marshall and Rossman 2000; Denzin and Lincoln 1994; Emerson 1983.

1. The Day before the Pueblada

1 In other words, they were putting forward a veritable "injustice frame" to describe Governor Sapag's actions. See Gamson 1992a, 1992b.

2 On the "stories of spontaneity" and their functions, see Polletta 1998b.

3. Being-in-the-Road

1 She is mainly referring to those interpretations put forward by most national newspapers and by other commentators (e.g., Pilar Sanchez's document [1997], which she read carefully).

2   Here I am closely following Roger Gould's approach to protesters' self-under-standings. According to him, a participatory identity is "the social identification with respect to which an individual responds in a given instance of social protest to specific normative and instrumental appeals" (Gould 1995, 13).

3   See Polletta and Jasper 2001 for an emphasis on the construction of collective identities "in and through" protest. According to them, a collective identity "describes imagined as well as concrete communities, involves an act of perception and construction as well as the discovery of preexisting bonds, interests, and boundaries. It is fluid and relational, emerging out of interactions with a number of different audiences (bystanders, allies, opponents, news media, state authorities), rather than fixed. It channels words and actions, enabling some claims and deeds and delegitimating others. It provides categories by which individuals divide up and make sense of the social world" (298).

4   Among the many transformations brought by feminism in Europe and the United States are the breaking down of what Karen Brodkin Sacks (1984) calls the "Domestic Code" and, of particular relevance to the case at hand, the politicization of private sexual experience and a construction of a politicized discourse of trauma that stresses women's victimization due to violence, the aftereffects of this victimization, and the importance of individual and collective recovery and resistance: the personal, as has been repeatedly said, became political. As Pierre Bourdieu (2001, 116) puts it: "The feminist movement has made a major contribution to a considerable enlargement of the area of what is political or can be politicized, by making it possible to discuss or challenge political objects and preoccupations excluded or ignored by the political tradition because they seem to belong to the private domain." Laura's personal troubles are indeed political in the sense that feminism, broadly understood, speaks of the term "political," but not in the sense that Laura herself gives to the term. When speaking of "politics" and "political," I am referring to indigenous categories, that is, to the definitions that actors themselves adopt: "politics," in this sense, means "party politics." For a thorough treatment of actors' points of view on politics, see Eliasoph 1998.

5   A similar process, attesting to the relevance of symbolic struggle during episodes of contention (this time between Chinese students and authorities during the Tiananmen protest), is described in Calhoun 1994.

6   Lee (2000) makes a similar argument with respect to the memories of Maoist socialism at the basis of Chinese workers' collective actions.

Introduction to Part Two

1   This is a reconstruction of the day of the riot based on the December 16, 1994, issue of the main local newspaper *El Liberal*, as well as on a book published by two young journalists from this same newspaper *(Arde Santiago)* and a compilation of articles published after the riot *(El Estallido Social en Santiago)*.

2 On the role of media in the fabrication of social phenomena, see Champagne 1999.

3 On storytelling during episodes of contention, see Polletta 1998a, 1998b.

5. The Lived 1993

1 See Informe *El Liberal* 2.

2 For a review of the corruption cases previous to December 16, see Curiotto and Rodríguez 1994.

3 In October 1993 there were elections for the local and the national parliament in the province of Santiago del Estero.

4 It is beyond the scope of this book to analyze the dynamics of the local journalistic field in the months preceding the riot. The media—especially newspapers— played a crucial role not only in unveiling corruption cases but also in pointing at suspected officials and politicians. As a protester told me: "You could read about every single corruption scandal in *El Liberal.*" During the day of the riot, some local radios also played a key role informing protesters about the residences that "the crowd" was attacking. As Mario explained: "That day, local radios told people where the crowd was . . . they broadcasted as if it [the riot] were a soccer match: 'Now the crowd is going here . . . now the crowd is going there.'"

5 "El desarrollo de la protesta que los empleados de la administración pública realizaron ayer, puso en evidencia el mosaico que conforman los distintos grupos de trabajadores con sus dirigentes, que reclamaron 'cada uno por su lado,' a pesar de sostener las mismas exigencias para sus representados. . . . las reparticiones aclararon que en cada lugar de trabajo se habían gestado las protestas; Recursos Hídricos e IPVU repitieron hasta el cansancio, que las medidas que adoptaron son exclusivamente suyas; los docentes, apenas se unieron al grueso de la manifestación de ayer frente a la Casa de Gobierno, dijeron que venían por su cuenta y por otro lado, la ATE se empecinó en asegurar que la convocatoria fue propia" (*El Liberal,* 4 September 1993).

6. The Lived Sixteenth

1 Together with its relatively small size, the layout of the city of Santiago facilitates this movement. No spatial barriers separate peripheral neighborhoods from residential neighborhoods or from the downtown area in the city of Santiago del Estero, a fact that undoubtedly relates to the ease with which hundreds of people invade and burn down more than ten public buildings and homes in one day. Twenty blocks separate the poor neighborhood "8 de Abril" (where most of the arrested on the sixteenth come from) from the Government House, with no bridges, highways, or other sorts of physical barriers in between.

Here is how an arrested participant described his actions to the police. He recalls the sacking of the house of someone who was, at the time, a national senator and is now the governor of Santiago. We do not need to take the transcript of the interrogation at face value to realize how important proximity and easy access to the targets were: "He testifies: that his address is located only three blocks from that of Senator Juarez . . . that at around 4 P.M. people began to arrive to the aforementioned senator's house. They were arriving from everywhere, walking, by car and even by carts. Given this situation, [he] decided to get closer, up to a block away from Dr. Juarez's estate and, together with his friend R. J., they were watching what happened like 'onlookers.' A little bit after that, he saw that all the people that had entered the house were taking out different objects, furniture, etc. Some were taking these with them and others were leaving them on the street. He testifies that at a certain moment he saw that a group of people left an iron table, a rug and parts of a bed on Añatuña Street. He testifies that, faced with that situation, he and R. J. decided by mutual agreement to take those objects to his house."

2   Protesters are also prevented from burning and looting their targets by the "private repression" of some homeowners, most notably the Radical Party caudillo Zavalía, who, together with a group of followers, barricades his house and shoots at protesters as they begin to surround the house. It is *after* the first shootings have stopped protesters from invading Zavalías's house that the police arrive at the scene, arresting one of the caudillo's followers on charges of possession of a weapon. Another case of private repression of the riot is that of the president of the Supreme Court who, according to *El Liberal*, "with a gun in his hand persuades people [so that they don't invade his home]." The front part of his house, however, is partially destroyed.

3   Casanegra was the former public works minister. His house was among those most damaged.

4   As Susan Phillips (1999, 20, italics mine) puts it in her study of gang graffiti in Los Angeles, "Because it is so easily produced, graffiti is often adopted by those without power, to negotiate relationships with both the society from which they are disempowered and others within their own groups. If graffiti is *a window into a culture, as has often been stated, then it is the same window that people use to look in on themselves as they actively construct the guidelines and concerns of their lives.*"

5   For the carnival as a space of forgetting, see Scheper-Hughes 1992.

6   During the previous months, *El Liberal* published various reports documenting "generalized discontent" among police agents and officers, and recurrent attempts by the chiefs to "boost" the morale of the force.

7. Nana's Life

1   Pacará is one of the poorest districts in Santiago del Estero.

2   One of Santiago's main streets.

8. Contested Memories

1   See also *Clarín*, 19 December 1999. Against this official version, opposition parties stressed structural adjustment as the main cause of the outburst. The "harshness of the savage adjustment imposed by the Finance Ministry" was responsible for the plight of the people in the provinces. As former president Alfonsín put it: "The cause is to be found in the adjustment policies which have caused almost terminal crises in the regional economies" (*Clarín*, 17 December 1993; *La Nación*, 19 December 1993). The *New York Times* (18 December 1993) captured part of these contrasting views quite clearly: "Opposition Radical Party leaders and at least one Roman Catholic bishop have called the Santiago del Estero riots a repudiation of the Menem economic reforms. . . . [the president] and his Finance Minister . . . have said instead that riots were the result of corrupt local governments and a conspiracy on the part of the political opposition to hurt the Government's image."

How did journalists report on the riot? "El Ajustazo" was the front-page headline of the largest Center-Left newspaper, making clear what was further elaborated in subsequent editions: the riot was mainly against adjustment, a cry against the "economic model." The cause of the outburst, according to *Página12*, was to be found in the three months without wages and in the omnibus law sanctioned a few days before the riot—an adjustment comprising massive layoffs of all the state employees under fixed-term contracts, retroactive suspension of salary increases as of February 1993, deregulation of public and private activities, decentralization of public services, and resolute encouragement of privatizations—in other words, the now-traditional neoliberal medicine. The protest, according to this newspaper, was a popular response "against the adjustment imposed by the national and provincial governments, the misery, the lack of essential public services—there has not been running water for the past three days—and the lack of wages for the huge public administration" (*Página12*, 17 December 1993).

The global policies imposed by the IMF and the World Bank through its allies in the Finance Ministry were causing local explosions, the newspaper said, much like those that, around the same time, were occurring in southern Mexico with the Zapatista indigenous rebellion. Indeed, various Op-Ed pieces attempted a comparison between these localized violent popular uprisings. In an article entitled *From Santiago to Chiapas*, journalist Luis Bruschtein asserted that adjustment programs were producing "their own antibodies"—the indigenous people's rebellion in Chiapas and the public employees' rebellion in Santiago. Both rebellions were illustrating the slow development of "ideologies opposing adjustment and market economy," showing that the "struggle against injustice" was far from over (Bruschtein 1994, 3). There were many differences between rebellions in the South and in the North but as another journalist from the same newspaper pointed out, in both cases, the protagonists of the upheavals had been "the victims of adjustment" (Dearriba 1994b, 4). The leading journalist of *Página12* acknowledged that the comparison was far-fetched while advancing his own diagnosis: the riot was a "spontaneous popular response to a state policy" (Verbitsky 1993, 4).

Mainstream and Center-to-the-Right newspapers were less blunt in their analyses, focusing their attention on what politicians, Catholic priests, and union leaders had to say about the causes of the riot rather than advancing their own explanations. However, for every voice that mentioned the "economic plan" at the root of the uprising, both *Clarín* and *La Nación* published disclaimers by officials from the national government stressing local—rather than national or global—causes. Although recognizing that the passing of the adjustment omnibus law and that on the day of the riot public employees had found out that their long-overdue wages were finally going to be paid with a reduction that varied between 35 percent and 50 percent were the triggers to the riot, agitators and moral outrage at local corruption figured prominently in most of these other accounts. One editorial clearly exemplifies this last position: "Many Santiagueños have doubts about who organized the disturbances in the homes of the local politicians and why. Although it was clear that the people who did it were those affected and resented by the . . . years of bad government and generalized corruption, the *precision* with which those homes were sacked was something that caught the attention of many. Never before has Argentina witnessed something like this" (*La Nación*, 18 December 1993; italics mine). "Moral fatigue" and "economic anguish" formed, according to this argument, the hotbed for agitators.

2   It is not my task to prove the truth of the judge's or others' assertions, although in this case the fear felt by many public officials at the time cannot be ruled out as a motive for their actions (in this case, liberating 144 arrested persons after only a few hours of detention). At that time, the judge predicted that the decision "will cost me my career." As I later learned, he and his family had to move from their home, because they feared becoming a target of the "enraged mob."

3   This section is based on articles published in *El Nuevo Diario*, *El Liberal*, and *La Gaceta*. I want to thank Carlos Scrimini for providing me with part of the material for this section and for his invaluable insights on the uprising and on political life in Santiago del Estero.

4   The court file of "el caso Scrimini" was moved to a federal court, no one followed up on the case, and he was never sentenced.

5   There is a plethora of essays that deal with the purported specific features of the residents of Santiago del Estero, that is, with a presumed "way of being Santiagueño." They are diversely characterized as a "basically indolent people," a people distinguished by "low self-esteem and a deeply internalized sense of failure" or by an "apparent sentiment of inferiority." Despite the obvious inadequacies of these general characterizations of a "people's way of being," akin to a "people's spirit" (for a review and critique, see Tasso 1997), they are somehow shared by many—if not all—of my interviewees, who constantly refer to "our way of being." In effect, it was really striking to listen to energetic union leaders,

activists, and intellectuals talking about the "passivity" of the Santiagueños and including themselves within this categorization.

6   See Informe *El Liberal* 1.

Conclusions: Ethnography and Recognition

1   For a classic statement on the subject, see Tilly 1997. See also Tarrow 1998.

2   Demands for collective respect as well as for justice and accountability were central in another highly significant episode of contention in the 1990s, that of Catamarca's marches of silence claiming for the clarification of María Soledad Morales's death and for the imprisonment of the murderers. See Bergman and Szurmuk 2001; Morandini 1991; Rey and Pazos 1991.

3   See, for example, Allen 1997.

4   On the different approaches to personal narratives, see Kristin Langelier's (1989) detailed study of the assumptions and interests behind five theoretical perspectives on personal narratives (as story-text, as storytelling performance, as conversational interaction, as social process, and as political praxis). It should be clear that, as Langelier herself admits, I believe these approaches not to be mutually exclusive.

5   As Sandra Stahl (quoted in Langelier 1989) points out: "Existentially, the personal experience narrator not only acts or experiences but 'thinks about' his action, evaluates it, learns from it, and tells the story—not to express his values, but to build them, to create them, to remake them each time he tells his stories."

References

Aguilar, Maria Angela, and Estela Vazquez. 2000. "De YPF a La Ruta: Un Acercamiento a Tartagal." In *Trabajo y Población en el Noroeste Argentino*, ed. Marta Panaia, Susana Aparicio, and Carlos Zurita, 327–45. Buenos Aires: Editorial La Colmena.

Alford, Robert. 1998. *The Craft of Inquiry.* New York: Oxford University Press.

Allen, Charlotte. 1997. "Spies Like Us: When Sociologists Deceive Their Subjects." *Lingua Franca* (November): 31–39.

Amin, Shahid. 1995. *Event, Metaphor, Memory: Chauri-Chaura, 1922-1992.* Berkeley: University of California Press.

Asad, Talal. 1994. "Ethnographic Representation, Statistics, and Modern Power." *Social Research* 61, no. 1: 55–88.

Ashforth, Adam. 2000. *Madumo: A Man Bewitched.* Chicago: University of Chicago Press.

Atkinson, Paul. 1990. *The Ethnographic Imagination: Textual Constructions of Reality.* London: Routledge.

Auyero, Javier. 1999. "Re-membering Peronism: An Ethnographic Account of the Relational Character of Political Memory." *Qualitative Sociology* 22, no. 4: 331–63.

———. 2001a. "Glocal Riots." *International Sociology* 16, no. 1: 33–53.

———. 2001b. "Los Estallidos en Provincia: Globalización y Conflictos Sociales." *Punto De Vista* 67: 41–48.

Auyero, Javier, and Alejandro Grimson. 1997. " 'Se Dice de Mi . . .': Notas sobre Convivencias y Confusiones entre Etnógrafos y Periodistas." *Apuntes de Investigación en Cultura y Política* 1: 81–93.

Bakhtin, Mikhail. 1984. *Rabelais and His World.* Bloomington: Indiana University Press.

Barbeito, Alberto, and Rubén LoVuolo. 1992. *La Modernización Excluyente.* Buenos Aires: Losada.

Behar, Ruth, and Deborah A. Gordon. 1995. *Women Writing Culture.* Berkeley: University of California Press.

Benford, Robert, and David Snow. 2000. "Framing Processes and Social Movements: An Overview and Assessment." *Annual Review of Sociology* 26: 611–39.

Bergman, Marcelo, and Mónica Szurmuk. 2001. "Gender, Citizenship, and Social Protest: The New Social Movements in Argentina." In *The Latin American Subaltern Studies Reader*, ed. Ileana Rodriguez. Durham: Duke University Press.

Bourdieu, Pierre. 1991. *Language and Symbolic Power.* Cambridge: Cambridge University Press.

———. 1993. *The Field of Cultural Production.* New York: Columbia University Press.

———. 1996. "Understanding." *Theory, Culture, and Society* 13, no. 2: 17–37.

———. 1997. "La ilusión biográfica." In *Razones Prácticas*, 74–83. Barcelona: Anagrama.

———. 1999. "Hanging by a Thread." In *The Weight of the World*, ed. Pierre Bourdieu et al., 370–80. Stanford: Stanford University Press.

———. 2000. *Pascalian Meditations.* Stanford: Stanford University Press.

———. 2001. *Masculine Domination.* Stanford: Stanford University Press.

Bourdieu, Pierre, et al. 1999. *The Weight of the World.* Stanford: Stanford University Press.

Bourdieu, Pierre, Jean-Claude Chamboderon, and Jean-Claude Passeron. 1991. *The Craft of Sociology: Epistemological Preliminaries.* New York: de Gruyter.

Bourgois, Philippe. 1995. *In Search of Respect.* Cambridge: Cambridge University Press.

Brass, Paul. 1996. "Introduction: Discourse of Ethnicity, Communalism, and Violence." In *Riots and Pogroms*, ed. Paul Brass, 1–55. New York: New York University Press.

Brennan, James. 1994. *The Labor Wars in Córdoba, 1955–1976. Ideology, Work, and Labor Politics in an Argentine Industrial City.* Cambridge: Harvard University Press.

Brodkin Sacks, Karen. 1984. "Computers, Ward Secretaries, and a Walkout in a Southern Hospital." In *My Troubles Are Going to Have Trouble with Me: Everyday Trials and Triumphs of Women Workers*, ed. Karen Brodkin Sacks and Dorothy Remy. New Brunswick, N.J.: Rutgers University Press.

Brubaker, Roger, and Frederick Cooper. 2000. "Beyond 'Identity.' " *Theory and Society* 29: 1–47.

Bruschtein, Luis. 1994. "De Santiago a Chiapas." *Página12*, 5 January, 3.

Bulacio, Ramón. 1994. "Una Educación Provincial Decadente." *El Estallido Social En Santiago*, 61–64.

Burawoy, Michael, Alice Burton, Ann Ferguson, Kathryn Fox, Joshua Gamson, Nadine Gartrell, Leslie Hurst, Charles Kurzman, Leslie Salzinger, Josepha Schiffman, and Shiori Ui. 1991. *Ethnography Unbound: Power and Resistance in the Modern Metropolis.* Berkeley: University of California Press.

———. 2000. *Global Ethnography, Forces, Connections, and Imaginations in a Postmodern World.* Berkeley: University of California Press.

Burke, Peter. 1978. *Popular Culture in Early Modern Europe*. London: Wildwood House.

Calhoun, Craig. 1994. *Neither Gods nor Emperors: Students and the Struggle for Democracy in China*. Berkeley: University of California Press.

Camacho, Gloria. 2001. "Relaciones de Género y Violencia." In *Estudios de Género*, ed. Gioconda Herrera, 73–98. Ecuador: Flacso.

Carreras, Julio. 1994. "Reconstruir desde las Cenizas de una Conflictuada Cultura." *El Estallido Social En Santiago*, 71–75.

Castiglione, Julio. 1994. "Prólogo." In *Arde Santiago! La Verdadera Historia del Estallido Social de Santiago del Estero que Asombró al País y al Mundo*, ed. José Curiotto and Julio Rodriguez, 1–3. Tucumán: Ediciones el Graduado.

Cerulo, Karen. 1997. "Identity Construction: New Issues, New Directions." *Annual Review of Sociology* 23: 385–409.

Champagne, Patrick. 1999. "The View from the Media." In *The Weight of the World*, ed. Pierre Bourdieu et al., 46–59. Stanford: Stanford University Press.

Christin, Rosine. 1999. "A Silent Witness." In *The Weight of the World*, ed. Pierre Bourdieu et al., 354–60. Stanford: Stanford University Press.

Coronil, Fernando, and Julie Skurski. 1991. "Dismembering and Remembering the Nation: The Semantics of Political Violence in Venezuela." *Comparative Studies in Society and History* 33, no. 2: 255–87.

Costallat, Karina. 1999. "Efectos de las Privatizaciones y la Relación Estado-Sociedad en la Instancia Provincial y Local: El Caso Cutral Co-Plaza Huincul." Buenos Aires, INAP.

Cuadros, Fernando. 1994. "Sistema de Salud Provincial en Estado de Coma." *El Estallido Social en Santiago*, 43–48.

Curiotto, José. 1994. "El Patrón Omnipotente y la Pobreza Moral." *El Estallido Social en Santiago*, 3–6.

Curiotto, José, and Julio Rodríguez. 1994. *Arde Santiago! La Verdadera Historia del Estallido Social de Santiago del Estero que Asombró al País y al Mundo*. Tucumán: Ediciones el Graduado.

da Matta, Roberto. 1991. *Carnivals, Rogues, and Heroes: An Interpretation of the Brazilian Dilemma*. Notre Dame: University of Notre Dame Press.

Dargoltz, Raúl. 1994. *El Santiagueñazo: Gestación y Crónica de una Pueblada Argentina*. Buenos Aires: El Despertador Ediciones.

Darnton, Robert. 1991. "The Great Cat Massacre of the Rue Saint-Severin." In *Rethinking Popular Culture: Contemporary Perspectives in Cultural Studies*, ed. Chandra Mukerji and Michael Schudson, 97–120. Berkeley: University of California Press.

Davis, Diane. 1999. "The Power of Distance: Re-theorizing Social Movements in Latin America." *Theory and Society* 28: 585–638.

Davis, Natalie Zemon. 1973. "The Rites of Violence: Religious Riots in Sixteenth-Century France." *Past and Present* 59 (May): 51–91.

———. 1983. *The Return of Martin Guerre*. Cambridge: Harvard University Press.

Dearriba, Alberto. 1994a. "Aquella Vieja Música de Locos." *Página12*, 15 January, 4.

———. 1994b. "Chiapas, Santiago, Su Ruta." *Página12*, 8 January, 4.

De Avelar, Sonia. 1998. "Gender Inequality and Women's Empowerment in Latin America." In *Challenging Authority: The Historical Study of Contentious Politics*, ed. Michael Hanagan, Leslie Page Moch, and Wayne te Brake. Minneapolis: University of Minnesota Press.

Denzin, Norman, and Yvonna Lincoln. 1994. *Handbook of Qualitative Research*. Thousand Oaks: Sage Publications.

Desjarlais, Robert. 1994. "Struggling Along." *American Anthropologist* 94, no. 4 (December): 886–901.

Díaz, Oscar. 1994. "La Culpa Fue Haber Callado." *El Estallido Social en Santiago*, 49–54.

Downton, James, and Paul Wehr. 1997. *The Persistent Activist: How Peace Commitment Develops and Survives*. Boulder, Colo.: Westview Press.

DuBois, Ellen Carol. 1978. *Feminism and Suffrage: The Emergence of an Independent Women's Movement in America, 1848-1869*. Ithaca, N.Y.: Cornell University Press.

Edelman, Marc. 2001. "Social Movements: Changing Paradigms and Forms of Politics." *Annual Review of Anthropology* 30: 285–317.

Elias, Norbert. 1991. *The Society of Individuals*. New York: Continuum.

Eliasoph, Nina. 1998. *Avoiding Politics: How Americans Produce Apathy in Everyday Life*. New York: Cambridge University Press.

Emerson, Robert. 1983. *Contemporary Field Research: A Collection of Readings*. Boston: Little Brown.

Entel, Alicia. 1996. *La Ciudad Bajo Sospecha: Communicación y Protesta Urbana*. Buenos Aires: Paidos.

Fano, Rafael. 1994a. "Desde 'Las Cuentas No Cierran,' al Colapso Económico." *El Estallido Social en Santiago*, 12–16.

———. 1994b. "Un Sistema Feudal Corrupto." *El Estallido Social en Santiago*, 76–78.

Farinetti, Marina. 1998. "Cuando los Clientes se Rebelan." *Apuntes de Investigación del CECYP*, no. 2/3: 84–103.

———. 1999. "¿Qué Queda del Movimiento Obrero? Las Formas del Reclamo Laboral en la Nueva Democracia Argentina." *Trabajo y Sociedad* 1 (July–September).

———. 2000. "El Estallido: La Forma de la Protesta." Unpublished manuscript. Buenos Aires.

Favaro, Orietta, and Mario Bucciarelli. 1994. "Efectos de la Privatización de YPF: La Desagregación Territorial del Espacio Neuquino." *Realidad Económica* 127: 88–99.

———. 1995. "El Nuevo Escenario Político: Elecciones y Crisis en un Espacio Provincial. El MPN: ¿Ruptura o Continuidad de una Forma de Hacer Política? *Realidad Económica* 135: 103–17.

Favaro, Orietta, Mario Bucciarelli, and Graciela Luomo. 1997. "La Conflictividad Social en Neuquén: El Movimiento Cutralquense y los Nuevos Sujetos Sociales." *Realidad Económica* 148: 13–27.

Favaro, Orietta, Mario Bucciarelli, and Maria Scuri. 1993. "El Neuquén: Límites Estructurales de una Estrategia de Distribución (1958–1980)." *Realidad Económica* 118: 123–38.

Frankel, Linda. 1984. "Southern Textile Women: Generations of Survival and Struggle." In *My Troubles Are Going to Have Trouble with Me: Everyday Trials and Triumphs of Women Workers,* ed. Karen Brodkin Sacks and Dorothy Remy, 39–60. New Brunswick, N.J.: Rutgers University Press.

Fundación Gobierno y Sociedad. 1999. *Ranking Social Provincial (Septiembre).* Buenos Aires: Fundación Gobierno y Sociedad.

Gallardo, Gustavo. 1994. "Un Costo Social Difícil de Remediar." *El Estallido Social en Santiago,* 38–42.

Gamson, William. 1988. "Political Discourse and Collective Action." In *From Structure to Action: Comparing Social Movement Research,* ed. Bert Klandermans, Hanspeter Kriesi, and Sidney Tarrow, 219–44. Greenwich, Conn.: JAI Press.

———. 1992a. "The Social Psychology of Collective Action." In *Frontiers in Social Movement Theory,* ed. Aldon Morris and Carol McClurg Mueller. New Haven: Yale University Press.

———. 1992b. *Talking Politics.* Cambridge: Cambridge University Press.

———. 1998. "Discourse, Nuclear Power, and Collective Action." In *The New American Cultural Sociology,* ed. Philip Smith. Cambridge: Cambridge University Press.

Garay, Alejandro. 1994. "El Estallido Social en La Banda." *El Estallido Social en Santiago,* 20–25.

Garcia, Sandrine. 1999. "The Stolen Work." In *The Weight of the World,* ed. Pierre Bourdieu et al., 338–53. Stanford: Stanford University Press.

García, Sergio. 1998. "Mensajes de Invierno." Neuquén, Argentina.

Geertz, Clifford. 1973. *The Interpretation of Cultures.* New York: Basic Books.

———. 2001. *Available Light: Anthropological Reflections on Philosophical Topics.* Princeton: Princeton University Press.

Gerchunoff, Pablo, and Juan Carlos Torre. 1996. "Las Políticas de Liberalización Económica en la Administración De Menem." *Desarrollo Económico* 36, no. 143: 733–68.

Ginsburg, Faye. 1989. *Contested Lives: The Abortion Debate in an American Community.* Berkeley: University of California Press.

Ginzburg, Carlo. 1980. *The Cheese and the Worms: The Cosmos of a Sixteenth-Century Miller.* Baltimore: Johns Hopkins University Press.

Giugni, Marco, Doug McAdam, and Charles Tilly, eds. 1998. *From Contention to Democracy.* Lanham: Rowman and Littlefield.

———. 1999. *How Social Movements Matter.* Minneapolis: University of Minnesota Press.

Goodwin, Jeff, James Jasper, and Francesca Polletta. 2001. *Passionate Politics: Emotions and Social Movements.* Chicago: University of Chicago Press.

Gould, Roger. 1995. *Insurgent Identities: Class, Community, and Protest in Paris from 1848 to the Commune.* Chicago: University of Chicago Press.

Grignon, Claude, and Jean-Claude Passeron. 1991. *Lo Culto y lo Popular.* Buenos Aires: Nueva Visión.

Gusfield, Joseph. 1994. "The Reflexivity of Social Movements: Collective Behavior and Mass Society Theory Revisited." In *New Social Movements: From Ideology to Identity,* ed. Hank Johnston, Joseph Gusfield, and Enrique Laraña, 58–78. Philadelphia: Temple University Press.

Harper, Douglas. 1992. *Working Knowledge: Skill and Community in a Small Shop.* Berkeley: University of California Press.

Helvacioglu, Banu. 2000. "Globalization in the Neighborhood: From the Nation-State to the Bilkent Center." *International Sociology* 15, no. 2: 329–45.

Holquist, Michael. 1990. *Dialogism: Bakhtin and His World.* London: Routledge.

Honneth, Axel. 1995. *The Struggle for Recognition: The Moral Grammar of Social Conflicts.* Cambridge: Polity Press.

Informe El Liberal 1. 2000. "Informe Reservado." Santiago del Estero, Argentina.

Informe El Liberal 2. 2000. "Los Cimientos del Poder." Santiago del Estero, Argentina.

Iñigo Carrera, Nicolas. 1999. "Fisonomía de las Huelgas Generales de la Década de 1990." *PIMSA 1999,* 155–73.

James, Daniel. 1997. "Tales Told Out on the Borderlands: Doña Maria's Story, Oral History, and Issues of Gender." In *The Gendered Worlds of Latin American Women Workers: From Household and Factory to the Union Hall and Ballot Box,* ed. John French and Daniel James, 31–53. Durham, N.C.: Duke University Press.

———. 2000. *Doña María's Story: Life History, Memory, and Political Identity.* Durham: Duke University Press.

Jasper, James. 1997. *The Art of Moral Protest.* Chicago: University of Chicago Press.

Jozami, Marcelo. 1994. "Cansado de Tanta Corrupción." *El Estallido Social en Santiago,* 26–32.

Kakar, Sudhir. 1996. *The Colors of Violence: Cultural Identities, Religion, and Conflict.* Chicago: University of Chicago Press.

Katz, Jack. 1999. *How Emotions Work.* Chicago: University of Chicago Press.

———. 2002. "From How to Why: On Luminous Description and Causal Inference in Ethnography (Part II)." *Ethnography* 3, no. 1: 63–90.

Klachko, Paula. 1999. "Cutral Co y Plaza Huincul: El Primer Corte De Ruta." *PIMSA 1999,* 121–54.

Korzeniewicz, Roberto Patricio, and William C. Smith. 2000. "Poverty, Inequality, and Growth in Latin America: Searching for the High Road." *Latin America Research Review* 35, no. 3: 7–54.

Langelier, Kristin. 1989. "Personal Narratives: Perspectives on Theory and Research." *Text and Performance Quarterly* 9, no. 4: 243–76.

Laufer, Ruben, and Claudio Spiguel. 1999. "Las 'Puebladas' Argentinas a partir del 'Santiagueñazo' de 1993: Tradición Histórica y Nuevas Formas de Lucha." In *Lucha Popular, Democracia, Neoliberalismo: Protesta Popular en América Latina en los Años del Ajuste,* ed. Margarita Lopez Maya, 15–44. Venezuela: Nueva Sociedad.

Laurell, Asa Cristina. 2000. "Structural Adjustment and the Globalization of Social Policy in Latin America." *International Sociology* 15, no. 2: 309-28.

Lee, Ching Kwan. 2000. "The 'Revenge of History': Collective Memories and Labor Protests in North-Eastern China." *Ethnography* 1, no. 2: 217-37.

Lopez Maya, Margarita, ed. 1999. *Lucha Popular, Democracia, Neoliberalismo: Protesta Popular en América Latina en los Años del Ajuste.* Venezuela: Nueva Sociedad.

Luna, Gabriela. 1994. "Un Largo Camino de Inacción, Injusticia y Corrupción." *El Estallido Social en Santiago,* 55-60.

Mansbridge, Jane, and Aldon Morris, eds. 2001. *Oppositional Consciousness: The Subjective Roots of Protest.* Chicago: University of Chicago Press.

Marshall, Catherine, and Gretchen Rossman. 2000. *Designing Qualitative Research.* Thousand Oaks: Sage.

McAdam, Doug. 1982. *Political Process and the Development of Black Insurgency, 1930-1970.* Chicago: University of Chicago Press.

———. 1988. *Freedom Summer.* New York: Oxford University Press.

———. 1999. "The Biographical Impact of Activism." In *How Social Movements Matter,* ed. Marco Giugni, Doug McAdam, and Charles Tilly, 119-49. Minneapolis: University of Minnesota Press.

McAdam, Doug, Sidney Tarrow, and Charles Tilly. 2001. *Dynamics of Contention.* Cambridge: Cambridge University Press.

McCarthy, John, and Mayer Zald. 1973. *The Trend of Social Movements in America.* Morristown, N.J.: General Learning Press.

———. Resource Mobilization and Social Movements. *American Journal of Sociology* 82: 1212-41.

Meyer, David, and Nancy Whittier. 1994. "Social Movement Spillover." *Social Problems* 41, no. 2: 277-98.

Miller, Byron, and Deborah Martin. 1998. "Missing Geography: Social Movements on the Head of a Pin?" Paper presented at the Association of American Geographers.

Mills, C. Wright. 1959. *The Sociological Imagination.* London: Oxford.

Mintz, Sidney. 2000. "Sows' Ears and Silver Linings." *Current Anthropology* 41, no. 2: 169-89.

Montenegro, Rodolfo. 1994. "La Destrucción Moral del Ser Humano." *El Estallido Social en Santiago,* 17-19.

Morandini, Norma. 1991. *Catamarca.* Buenos Aires: Planeta.

Naipaul, V. S. 1989. *A Turn in the South.* New York: Vintage Books.

Neveu, Eric. 2000. *Sociología de los Movimientos Sociales.* Ecuador: Abya-Ayala.

Olick, Jeffrey. 1999a. "Collective Memory: The Two Cultures." *Sociological Theory* 17, no. 3: 333-48.

———. 1999b. "Genre Memories and Memory Genres: A Dialogical Analysis of May 8, 1945, Commemorations in the Federal Republic of Germany." *American Sociological Review* 64 (June): 381-402.

Olick, Jeffrey, and Joyce Robbins. 1998. "Social Memory Studies: From 'Collective

Memory' to the Historical Sociology of Mnemonic Practices." *Annual Review of Sociology* 24: 105–40.

Oxhorn, Philip. 1998. "The Social Foundations of Latin America's Recurrent Populism: Problems of Popular Sector Class Formation and Collective Action." *Journal of Historical Sociology* 11, no. 2: 212–46.

Passerini, Luisa. 1987. *Fascism in Popular Memory: The Cultural Experience of the Turin Working Class.* Cambridge: Cambridge University Press.

Phillips, Susan. 1999. *Wallbangin': Graffiti and Gangs in L.A.* Chicago: University of Chicago Press.

Pile, Steve, and Michael Keith. 1997. *Geographies of Resistance.* London: Routledge.

Polletta, Francesca. 1997. "Culture and Its Discontents: Recent Theorizing on Culture and Protest." *Sociological Inquiry* 67: 431–50.

———. 1998a. "Contending Stories: Narrative in Social Movements." *Qualitative Sociology* 21, no. 4: 419–46.

———. 1998b. " 'It Was like a Fever . . .' Narrative and Identity in Social Protest." *Social Problems* 45, no. 2: 137–59.

Polletta, Francesca, and James Jasper. 2001. "Collective Identity and Social Movements." *Annual Review of Sociology* 27: 283–305.

Portelli, Alessandro. 1991. *The Death of Luigi Trastulli and Other Stories: Form and Meaning in Oral History.* Albany: State University of New York Press.

Pozzi, Pablo. 2000. "Popular Upheaval and Capitalist Transformation in Argentina." *Latin American Perspectives* 27, no. 114: 63–87.

Prieur, Annick. 1998. *Mema's House, Mexico City: On Transvestites, Queens, and Machos.* Chicago: University of Chicago Press.

Programa de las Naciones Unidas para el Desarrollo (PNUD). 1996. *Informe Argentino sobre Desarrollo Humano.* Buenos Aires.

Ragin, Charles, and Howard Becker. 1992. *What Is a Case?* Chicago: University of Chicago Press.

Ray, Raka. 1999. *Fields of Protest.* Minneapolis: University of Minnesota Press.

Rey, Alejandra, and Luis Pazos. 1991. *No Llores por Mí, Catamarca: La Intriga Política de un Crimen.* Buenos Aires: Sudamericana.

Robertson, Roland. 1995. "Glocalization: Time-Space and Homogeneity and Heterogeneity." In *Global Modernities,* ed. M. Featherstone et al. London: Sage.

Rodriguez, Alfredo, and Lucy Winchester. 1996. "Cities, Democracy, and Governance in Latin America." *International Social Science Journal* 14 (March): 73–83.

Rodriguez, Julio. 1994. "Clase Dirigente Carente de Autoridad Moral." *El Estallido Social en Santiago,* 33–37.

Rofman, Alejandro. 2000. "Destrucción de las Economías Provinciales." *Le Monde Diplomatique,* August, 6–7.

Rogers, Kim Lacy. 1993. *Righteous Lives.* New York: New York University Press.

Roy, Beth. 1994. *Some Trouble with Cows.* Berkeley: University of California Press.

Rubins, Roxana, and Horacio Cao. 2000. "Las Satrapías de Siempre." *Le Monde Diplomatique,* August, 8–9.

Rudé, George. 1964. *The Crowd in History.* New York: John Wiley and Sons.

Rule, James. 1988. *Theories of Civil Violence.* Berkeley: University of California Press.

Rupp, Leila, and Verta Taylor. 1987. *Survival in the Doldrums: The American Women's Rights Movement, 1945 to 1960s.* New York: Oxford.

Saade, Alesio. 1986. *Cutral Co: Tiempos De Viento, Arena y Sed.* Bahia Blanca: Imprenta Encestando.

Saint-Upéry, Marc. 2001. "El Movimiento Indígena Ecuatoriano y la Política del Reconocimiento." *Iconos* 10: 57–67.

Sanchez, Pilar. 1997. *El Cutralcazo: La Pueblada de Cutral Co y Plaza Huincul.* Buenos Aires: Cuadernos de Editorial Agora.

Saramago, José. 2000. *La Caverna.* Buenos Aires: Alfaguara.

Sawers, Larry. 1996. *The Other Argentina.* Boulder, Colo.: Westview.

Sayad, Abdelmalek. 1999. "The Curse." In *The Weight of the World,* ed. Pierre Bourdieu et al., 561–79. Stanford: Stanford University Press.

Scheper-Hughes, Nancy. 1992. *Death without Weeping: The Violence of Everyday Life in Brazil.* Berkeley: University of California Press.

———. 2000. "Ire in Ireland." *Ethnography* 1, no. 1: 117–40.

Schuster, Federico. 1999. "La Protesta Social en la Argentina Democrática: Balance y Perspectivas de una Forma de Acción Política." Unpublished manuscript.

Scott, James. 1977. "Patronage or Exploitation?" In *Patrons and Clients in Mediterranean Societies,* ed. Ernest Gellner and John Waterbury. London: Duckworth.

———. 1985. *Weapons of the Weak: Everyday Forms of Peasant Resistance.* New Haven: Yale University Press.

———. 1990. *Domination and the Arts of Resistance.* New Haven: Yale University Press.

Scribano, Adrian. 1999. "Argentina 'Cortada': Cortes de Ruta y Visibilidad Social en el Contexto del Ajuste." In *Lucha Popular, Democracia, Neoliberalismo: Protesta Popular en América Latina en los Años del Ajuste,* ed. Margarita Lopez Maya, 45–72. Venezuela: Nueva Sociedad.

Snow, David, Daniel M. Cress, Liam Downey, and Andrew W. Jones. 1998. "Disrupting the 'Quotidian': Reconceptualizing the Relationship between Breakdown and the Emergence of Collective Action." *Mobilization* 3, no. 1: 1–22.

Snow, David E., and Robert Benford. 1988. "Ideology, Frame Resonance, and Participant Mobilization." In *From Structure to Action: Comparing Social Movement Research,* ed. Bert Klandermans, Hanspeter Kriesi, and Sidney Tarrow, 197–217. Greenwich, Conn.: JAI Press.

———. 1992. "Master Frames and Cycles of Protest." In *Frontiers in Social Movement Theory,* ed. Aldon Morris and Carol McClurg, 133–55. New Haven: Yale University Press.

Somers, Margaret. 1995. "What's Political or Cultural about Political Culture and the Public Sphere?" *Sociological Theory* 13, no. 2: 113–44.

Somers, Margaret, and Gloria Gibson. 1994. "Reclaiming the Epistemological

'Other': Narrative and the Social Constitution of Identity." In *Social Theory and the Politics of Identity*, ed. Craig Calhoun, 37–99. Oxford: Blackwell.

Soria, Oscar. 1994. "Las Peleas del Poder: Un Drama Teatral de la Escena Política." *El Estallido Social en Santiago*, 65–70.

Stallybrass, Peter, and Allon White. 1986. *The Politics and Poetics of Transgression*. Ithaca, N.Y.: Cornell University Press.

Steinberg, Marc. 1995. "The Road of the Crowd." In *Repertoires and Cycles of Collective Action*, ed. Mark Traugott, 57–88. Durham, N.C.: Duke University Press.

———. 1998. "The Riding of the Black Lad and Other Working-Class Ritualistic Actions: Toward a Spatialized and Gendered Analysis of Nineteenth-Century Repertoires." In *Challenging Authority: The Historical Study of Contentious Politics*, ed. Michael Hanagan, Leslie Page Moch, and Wayne te Brake. Minneapolis: University of Minnesota Press.

———. 1999. *Fighting Words: Working-Class Formation, Collective Action, and Discourse in Early Nineteenth-Century England*. Ithaca, N.Y.: Cornell University Press.

———. 2000. "The Talk and Back Talk of Collective Action: A Dialogic Analysis of Repertoires of Discourse among Nineteenth-Century English Cotton Spinners." *American Journal of Sociology* 105, no. 3: 736–80.

Swidler, Ann. 1995. "Cultural Power and Social Movements." In *Social Movements and Culture*, ed. Hank Johnston and Bert Klandermans, 25–40. Minneapolis: University of Minnesota Press.

Swyngedouw, Eric. 1997. "Neither Global nor Local: 'Glocalization' and the Politics of Scale." In *Spaces of Globalization: Reasserting the Power of the Local*, ed. Kevin Cox, 137–66. New York: Guilford Press.

Tarrow, Sidney. 1992. "Mentalities, Political Cultures, and Collective Action Frames: Constructing Meaning through Action." In *Frontiers in Social Movement Research*, ed. Aldon Morris and Carol McClurg, 174–202. New Haven: Yale University Press.

———. 1996. "The People's Two Rhythms: Charles Tilly and the Study of Contentious Politics." *Comparative Studies in Society and History* 38, no. 3: 586–600.

———. 1998. *Power in Movement: Social Movements and Contentious Politics*. New York: Cambridge University Press.

Tasso, Alberto. 1997. "¿Cómo Somos y Por Qué?" *Quipu de Cultura* 8: 5–6.

———. 1999a. "Juárez Epica y Ocaso de una Pasión Provinciana." Unpublished manuscript.

———. 1999b. "Sistema Patronal: Dominación y Poder en el Noroeste Argentino." Unpublished manuscript.

Taylor, Charles. 1989. "Embodied Agency." In *Merleau-Ponty: Critical Essays*, ed. Henry Pietersma, 47–70. Washington: Center for Advanced Research in Phenomenology.

Tenti, Emilio. 2000. "Exclusión Social y Acción Colectiva en la Argentina de Hoy." *Punto de Vista* 67: 22–28.

Tharoor, Shashi. 2001. *Riot: A Love Story.* New York: Arcade.

Thatcher Ulrich, Laurel. 1991. *A Midwife's Tale: The Life of Martha Ballard, Based on Her Diary, 1785-1812.* New York: Knopf.

Thompson, E. P. 1993. *Customs in Common.* New York: New Press.

Tilly, Charles. 1978. *From Mobilization to Revolution.* Reading, Mass.: Addison Wesley.

———. 1986. *The Contentious French.* Cambridge: Harvard University Press.

———. 1991. "Domination, Resistance, Compliance . . . Discourse." *Sociological Forum* 6, no. 3: 593-602.

———. 1996. "Conclusion: Contention and the Urban Poor in Eighteenth- and Nineteenth-Century Latin America." In *Riots in the Cities,* ed. Silvia Arrom and Servando Ortoll, 225-42. Wilmington, Del.: Scholarly Resources.

———. 1997. *Roads from Past to Future.* Lanham, Md.: Rowman and Littlefield.

———. 1998a. "Political Identities." In *Challenging Authority: The Historical Study of Contentious Politics,* ed. Michael Hanagan, Leslie Page Moch, and Wayne te Brake. Minneapolis: University of Minnesota Press.

———. 1998b. "The Trouble with Stories." In *Teaching for the 21st Century: The Handbook for Understanding and Rebuilding the Social World of Higher Education,* ed. Ronald Aminzade and Bernice Pescosolido. Thousand Oaks: Pine Forge Press.

———. 2002. *Stories, Identities, and Political Change.* Lanham, Md.: Rowman and Littlefield.

———. Forthcoming. "Large-Scale Violence as Contentious Politics." In *Handbook of Research on Violence,* ed. Wilhelm Heitmeyer and John Hagan. Boulder, Colo.: Westview.

Useem, Bert. 1998. "Breakdown Theories of Collective Action." *Annual Review of Sociology* 24: 215-38.

Venkatesh, Sudhir. 2002. " 'Doin' the Hustle': Constructing the Ethnographer in the American Ghetto." *Ethnography* 3, no. 1: 91-111.

Verbitsky, Horacio. 1993. "La Música Maravillosa." *Página12,* 19 December, 8-9.

Wacquant, Loïc. 1995. "The Pugilistic Point of View: How Boxers Think and Feel about Their Trade." *Theory and Society* 24: 489-535.

———. 1999. "Inside 'The Zone': The Social Art of the Hustler in the American Ghetto." In *The Weight of the World,* ed. Pierre Bourdieu, 140-67. Stanford: Stanford University Press.

———. 2002. "Scrutinizing the Street: Poverty, Morality, and the Pitfalls of Urban Ethnography." *American Journal of Sociology* 107, no. 6: 1468-1532.

Walton, John. 1989. "Debt, Protest, and the State in Latin America." In *Power and Popular Protest: Latin American Social Movements,* ed. Susan Eckstein, 299-328. Berkeley: University of California Press.

———. 1998. "Urban Conflict and Social Movements in Poor Countries: Theory and Evidence of Collective Action." *International Journal of Urban and Regional Research* 22, no. 3: 460-81.

Walton, John, and Charles Ragin. 1990. "Global and National Sources of Political

Protest: Third World Responses to the Debt Crisis." *American Sociological Review* 55 (December): 876–90.

Walton, John, and David Seddon. 1994. *Free Markets and Food Riots: The Politics of Global Adjustment.* Oxford: Blackwell.

Walton, John, and Jon Shefner. 1994. "Latin America: Popular Protest and the State." In *Free Markets and Food Riots,* ed. John Walton and David Seddon, 97–134. Oxford: Blackwell.

Whyte, William Foote. 1943. *Street Corner Society: The Social Structure of an Italian Slum.* Chicago: University of Chicago Press.

Wolf, Diane, ed. 1996. *Feminist Dilemmas in Fieldwork.* Boulder, Colo.: Westview Press.

Wood, Elisabeth. 2001a. "The Emotional Benefits of Insurgency in El Salvador." In *Passionate Politics: Emotions and Social Movements,* ed. Jeff Goodwin, James Jasper, and Francesca Polletta, 267–81. Chicago: University of Chicago Press.

———. 2001b. "Pride in Rebellion: Insurrectionary Collective Action in El Salvador." Unpublished manuscript.

Zolberg, Aristide. 1972. "Moments of Madness." *Politics and Society* (winter): 183–207.

Zurita, Carlos. 1999a. "Estratificación Social y Trabajo: Imágenes y Magnitudes en Santiago del Estero." *Trabajo y Sociedad* 1 (July–September): 1–22.

———. 1999b. "Estructura del Empleo y Formas de Trabajo en una Ciudad Tradicional de la Argentina." Unpublished manuscript.

———. 1999c. *El Trabajo en una Sociedad Tradicional: Estudios sobre Santiago del Estero.* Santiago del Estero, Argentina: CICYT-UNSE.

Index

Javier Auyero is an assistant professor in the
Department of Sociology at the State University
of New York at Stony Brook. He is the author of
*Poor People's Politics: Peronist Survival Networks
and the Legacy of Evita* (Duke, 2000).

Library of Congress Cataloging-in-Publication Data
Auyero, Javier.
Contentious lives : two Argentine women, two protests,
and the quest for recognition / Javier Auyero.
p. cm. — (Latin America otherwise)
Includes bibliographical references and index.
ISBN 0-8223-3128-4 (cloth : alk. paper)
ISBN 0-8223-3115-2 (pbk. : alk. paper)
1. Women political activists—Argentina—Case studies.
2. Protest movements—Argentina—Case studies.
3. Experience—Social aspects. 4. Collective behavior.
I. Title. II. Series.
HQ1236.5.A7 A92 2003   303.48'4'0982—dc21   2002152971